THE MERCHANT OF VENICE

OTHER TITLES IN THE GREENHAVEN PRESS LITERARY COMPANION SERIES:

BRITISH AUTHORS

Jane Austen
Joseph Conrad
Charles Dickens
J.R.R. Tolkien

BRITISH LITERATURE

Animal Farm
Beowulf
Brave New World
The Canterbury Tales
Frankenstein
Great Expectations
Hamlet
Heart of Darkness
Jane Eyre
Julius Caesar
Lord of the Flies
Macbeth
Othello
Pride and Prejudice
Romeo and Juliet
Shakespeare: The Comedies
Shakespeare: The Histories
Shakespeare: The Sonnets
Shakespeare: The Tragedies
A Tale of Two Cities
Tess of the d'Urbervilles
Wuthering Heights

THE GREENHAVEN PRESS
Literary Companion
TO BRITISH LITERATURE

READINGS ON

THE MERCHANT OF VENICE

Clarice Swisher, *Book Editor*

David L. Bender, *Publisher*
Bruno Leone, *Executive Editor*
Bonnie Szumski, *Series Editor*

Greenhaven Press, Inc., San Diego, CA

E 2002047

Every effort has been made to trace the owners of copyrighted material. The articles in this volume may have been edited for content, length, and/or reading level. The titles have been changed to enhance the editorial purpose. Those interested in locating the original source will find the complete citation on the first page of each article.

Library of Congress Cataloging-in-Publication Data

Readings on The Merchant of Venice /
  Clarice Swisher, book editor.
      p.   cm. — (The Greenhaven Press literary
  companion to British literature)
    Includes bibliographical references and index.
    ISBN 0-7377-0178-1 (pbk. : alk. paper). —
  ISBN 0-7377-0179-X (lib. : alk. paper)
    1. Shakespeare, William, 1564–1616. Merchant of
  Venice. 2. Venice (Italy)—In literature. 3. Jews in
  literature. 4. Comedy. I. Swisher, Clarice, 1933–   .
  II. Series.
  PR2825.R43   2000
  822.3'3—dc21   99-29478
                                                          CIP

Cover photo: Stock Montage, Inc.

Copyright © 2000 by Greenhaven Press, Inc.
PO Box 289009
San Diego, CA 92198-9009
Printed in the U.S.A.

"If to do were as easy as to know what were good to do, chapels had been churches, and poor men's cottages princes' palaces."

—*Portia,*
Merchant of Venice, *I, ii, 13–15*

CONTENTS

Foreword   10

Introduction   12

William Shakespeare: A Biography   13

Characters and Plot   30

Chapter 1: Background

1. The Historical Context of *The Merchant of Venice*
by Dennis Kay   37
The Merchant of Venice reflects the historical and personal events and controversies of Shakespeare's day. A scandal involving a Portuguese Jew accused of being a traitor had caused considerable anti-Semitism in England; Londoners were talking of foreign trade and usury; and Shakespeare was building his personal fortune.

2. The Venetian Setting Enhances the Play's Meaning
by A.D. Nuttall   44
In Shakespeare's day Venice was reputedly a city in which the wealthy and daring acquired great fortunes and lived in style and luxury. Subtly and ironically this atmosphere colors the interpretation of the play's contrasting themes, such as love and money, Jew and Christian, morality and profit, and mercy and justice.

Chapter 2: Major Themes

1. *The Merchant of Venice:* A Critique of Puritanism
by Paul N. Siegel   53
The play's themes of hypocricsy, selfish disregard for others, and moral rigidity, exemplified by Shylock, are evident historically in Elizabethan attitudes toward the Puritans, in medieval legendary images of the Jews, and in modern American society as well.

2. *The Merchant of Venice* Portrays a World of Love and Music
by Mark Van Doren   60
Themes of love, money, and generosity expressed in musical and poetic language create a happy and comic atmosphere from which virtuous characters oust Shylock, who in

sharp contrast is miserly, full of hate and bitterness, and who speaks in a rasping voice using ugly diction.

3. **Religion in** *The Merchant of Venice*
   by Peter Milward   69

   The Merchant of Venice is replete with references to both the Old and New Testaments, suggesting themes and giving meaning particularly to Shylock's lines, but also to Portia's and the lines of many other characters as well. Beneath the literal level of the play, Shakespeare reveals Elizabethan criticism of Puritans; what is seen as Jewish can be interpreted as Puritan.

Chapter 3: Characterization

1. **Characters in** *The Merchant of Venice*
   by William Hazlitt   78

   Shylock operates in Venice with determination and mounts a spirited defense in the trial scene. Portia succeeds admirably at the trial, but neither she nor her maid Nerissa have the charm and wisdom of women in other Shakespearean plays. Launcelot provides humor, and Gratiano is the jester.

2. **Shylock and the Venetian Christians**
   by Arthur Quiller-Couch and John Dover Wilson   85

   Though he is cruel, Shylock evokes some sympathy while Antonio's Christian friends evoke none. Shylock's bitterness is justified when his beloved daughter betrays him, but Bassanio and the other friends have no reason for their thoughtless, heartless, and self-centered behavior.

3. **Shylock: A Villain with Humanity**
   by John Russell Brown   92

   Shylock is a cruel villain intent on revenge rather than repayment; nonetheless, Shakespeare gives him other dimensions to humanize him. He is an old man, robbed and betrayed by his daughter; he is a fool shouting wildly in the streets; and he is an unapologetic usurer.

4. **Portia Fails the Test for Inner Gold**
   by Harold C. Goddard   99

   Portia is glamorous, rich, and successful, but Shakespeare portrays another side of her in the trial scene. She offers to the court her thoughts on mercy, valuable to the giver and receiver alike when it is freely given, yet she fails both her first and second chances to show mercy to Shylock.

5. **Antonio: The Neurotic Gambler** *by Ralph Berry*   110

   All of the major characters in *The Merchant of Venice* risk something for money and love, but Antonio's agreement with Shylock is irrational. That Antonio risks his body in the bond and resigns himself to losing his life suggests the modern psychological interpretation of a compulsive gambler.

Chapter 4: Structure and Language

1. **Two Contrasting Worlds in** *The Merchant of Venice* **by** *Norman N. Holland*   119
The plots of *The Merchant of Venice* are played out in two settings. In Venice, Shakespeare creates a harsh masculine world where inhabitants compete, exact hard justice, and endure scarcity and anxiety. In contrast Belmont is a world where beauty, myth, music, abundance, and love prevail.

2. **The Play as a Fairy Tale**
by Harley Granville-Barker   129
Blending two vastly different fairy tales into a unified play requires special attention to time, place, emphasis, characterization, and theme. Shakespeare effectively bridges time and distance, blends musical language with direct prose, and manipulates plot elements to balance the stories, develop characters, and link themes.

3. *The Merchant of Venice* **Is a Comedy**
by Elmer Edgar Stoll   138
That Shylock is a comic villain establishes *The Merchant of Venice* as a comedy. Shylock's nature is established when the good characters condemn him and praise Bassanio and Antonio; when his daughter and servant identify his villainous qualities before he appears onstage; and when he reveals his hate and ill will. He is a miser, a moneylender, and a Jew, whom Elizabethans were ready to ridicule.

4. **Poetry and Prose in** *The Merchant of Venice*
by F.E. Halliday   146
The Merchant of Venice contains some of the most beautiful poetry in all of Shakespeare's plays, examples of which appear in the opening lines, the casket scenes, and the scene in Belmont in act five. Moreover, Shylock's prose and the dramatic court scene mark two new developments in Shakespeare's playwriting skills.

5. **The Language of Argument in** *The Merchant of Venice* **by** *G.R. Hibbard*   154
The primary mode of expression in *The Merchant of Venice* is the language of argument and persuasion whether the characters are speaking in prose or verse. The two characters whose speech is most distinctive are Antonio, who speaks only poetry, and Shylock, whose language is characterized by several different features.

Chapter 5: Evaluation

1. *The Merchant of Venice:* **An Imperfect Step Toward Later Comedies** *by D.A. Traversi* 164

   Though the elements in *The Merchant of Venice* are not clearly unified, the play marks a development from Shakespeare's earlier comedies and anticipates his later mature ones. In spite of imperfections, the play is an interesting retelling of old stories, contains fascinating characters, and employs musical poetic language.

2. *The Merchant of Venice* **Lacks Dramatic Unity** *by Gareth Lloyd Evans* 172

   The Merchant of Venice is a theatrically effective play, but it lacks dramatic unity. Shakespeare has created a fairy-tale world, but introduces in Shylock a character with realistic human emotions and motives, making him and his world irreconcilable with the Belmont fantasy world.

3. *The Merchant of Venice* **Is Clear, Simple, and Successful** *by E.M.W. Tillyard* 180

   The public has long enjoyed and praised *The Merchant of Venice*, perhaps because it works simply and moves smoothly. Audiences seem to overlook a couple of minor plot flaws and accept characters who change roles or assume allegorical qualities. With all its glamour and simplicity, the play has substance and meaning.

Chronology 187

For Further Research 192

Index 196

FOREWORD

*"'Tis the good reader that
makes the good book."*

Ralph Waldo Emerson

The story's bare facts are simple: The captain, an old and scarred seafarer, walks with a peg leg made of whale ivory. He relentlessly drives his crew to hunt the world's oceans for the great white whale that crippled him. After a long search, the ship encounters the whale and a fierce battle ensues. Finally the captain drives his harpoon into the whale, but the harpoon line catches the captain about the neck and drags him to his death.

A simple story, a straightforward plot—yet, since the 1851 publication of Herman Melville's *Moby-Dick*, readers and critics have found many meanings in the struggle between Captain Ahab and the whale. To some, the novel is a cautionary tale that depicts how Ahab's obsession with revenge leads to his insanity and death. Others believe that the whale represents the unknowable secrets of the universe and that Ahab is a tragic hero who dares to challenge fate by attempting to discover this knowledge. Perhaps Melville intended Ahab as a criticism of Americans' tendency to become involved in well-intentioned but irrational causes. Or did Melville model Ahab after himself, letting his fictional character express his anger at what he perceived as a cruel and distant god?

Although literary critics disagree over the meaning of *Moby-Dick*, readers do not need to choose one particular interpretation in order to gain an understanding of Melville's

10

novel. Instead, by examining various analyses, they can gain numerous insights into the issues that lie under the surface of the basic plot. Studying the writings of literary critics can also aid readers in making their own assessments of *Moby-Dick* and other literary works and in developing analytical thinking skills.

The Greenhaven Literary Companion Series was created with these goals in mind. Designed for young adults, this unique anthology series provides an engaging and comprehensive introduction to literary analysis and criticism. The essays included in the Literary Companion Series are chosen for their accessibility to a young adult audience and are expertly edited in consideration of both the reading and comprehension levels of this audience. In addition, each essay is introduced by a concise summation that presents the contributing writer's main themes and insights. Every anthology in the Literary Companion Series contains a varied selection of critical essays that cover a wide time span and express diverse views. Wherever possible, primary sources are represented through excerpts from authors' notebooks, letters, and journals and through contemporary criticism.

Each title in the Literary Companion Series pays careful consideration to the historical context of the particular author or literary work. In-depth biographies and detailed chronologies reveal important aspects of authors' lives and emphasize the historical events and social milieu that influenced their writings. To facilitate further research, every anthology includes primary and secondary source bibliographies of articles and/or books selected for their suitability for young adults. These engaging features make the Greenhaven Literary Companion series ideal for introducing students to literary analysis in the classroom or as a library resource for young adults researching the world's great authors and literature.

Exceptional in its focus on young adults, the Greenhaven Literary Companion Series strives to present literary criticism in a compelling and accessible format. Every title in the series is intended to spark readers' interest in leading American and world authors, to help them broaden their understanding of literature, and to encourage them to formulate their own analyses of the literary works that they read. It is the editors' hope that young adult readers will find these anthologies to be true companions in their study of literature.

INTRODUCTION

The Merchant of Venice offers the audience and the reader glamour, suspense, and wit. The romantic world of Belmont has a rich princess, competing suitors, and a prince charming. In the Venetian world of business lives the eccentric, hate-filled Shylock, who exacts revenge against Christians. Readers follow the suspense of two plots, waiting to see if Bassanio will choose the casket that wins him his beloved Portia and watching to see if Shylock really will exact a pound of flesh from the body of Antonio.

Critics of *The Merchant of Venice* have been unable to agree on the success of the plot or the interpretation of characters, and it is considered one of Shakespeare's problem plays. For example, Shakespeare's characters are ambiguous. Shylock elicits the audience's sympathy on one hand and their satisfaction for justice on the other. Portia seems the ideal woman—rich, beautiful, sensitive, and generous—yet she displays a heartless and crude nature in the last two acts. Bassanio is at once charming and irresponsible while Antonio is both noble and foolish.

Finally, *The Merchant of Venice* offers the opportunity to consider relevant moral and psychological issues and to think of the play's individuals and events as being representative of a broader society. For instance, act four raises the question of how law should be applied—by the letter or by the circumstances—and how punishment should be meted out—as equal to the crime or with mercy.

This play continues to charm audiences and readers with its characters and stories. No one will ever know if Shakespeare was too busy or too preoccupied to tidy up his play or if he deliberately invited his audience to enter into the interpretation; either way, *The Merchant of Venice* gives actors a creative opportunity to define roles and gives readers and audiences a special opportunity to give the play meaning.

WILLIAM SHAKESPEARE: A BIOGRAPHY

By today's standards, factual information about William Shakespeare is meager indeed; no diaries, journals, or letters survive to help biographers ascertain the author's personality or his opinions and feelings. Diligent scholars have, however, located institutional records to identify Shakespeare's place of birth and upbringing and the essential events in his family life. They have unearthed records identifying some of his employment history and economic holdings. To supplement the record, scholars have turned to the text of his works and knowledge of Elizabethan history and beliefs to understand Shakespeare the man. Not surprisingly, interpretations differ. As critic Harry Levin observes: "We are less acquainted with what went into his work than what came out of it."

BIRTH AND FAMILY

William Shakespeare was born in Stratford (today called Stratford-upon-Avon) in Warwickshire, a county in the heart of England, on April 23 or 24, 1564. Scholars have assumed this date is correct by counting two or three days before his baptism in Holy Trinity, the Stratford Church of England, which occurred on April 26.

Shakespeare's mother, Mary Arden, came from an old county family. His father, John Shakespeare, was a glove maker; a trader in wool, timber, and barley; and, for a time, a prominent community leader and officeholder. The elder Shakespeare began public service as the town ale taster in 1557 and subsequently performed the offices of burgess, constable, town treasurer, alderman, and bailiff, or mayor. In the early 1580s, however, John Shakespeare's financial troubles led to the loss of both his wealth and his governing positions.

William was the third of eight children born to Mary and John Shakespeare. Two daughters—Joan, christened in September 1558, and Margaret, christened in December 1662—

died young. Four siblings, born after William, reached adult-
hood: Gilbert, christened in October 1566; a second Joan,
christened in 1569; Richard, christened in March 1573 or
1574; and Edmund, christened in 1580. Another daughter,
Anne, died when she was eight.

EDUCATION

Though no school records exist, Shakespeare likely attended
a typical English school. In such schools, young children usually spent their first year in an elementary school studying
arithmetic and catechism (a book summarizing the basic
principles of Christianity in question-and-answer form) and
learning to read and write in English. After age seven, Shakespeare probably attended the grammar school known as
King's New School, where he received rigorous training in
Latin taught by Oxford graduates who often had advanced de-
grees.

Students were expected to be in their seats by 6:00 A.M. in
the summer and 7:00 A.M. in the winter. The school day began
and ended with Bible readings, psalm singing, and prayers.
Students were drilled in Latin grammar, logic, rhetoric, composition, public speaking, and literature—all in Latin. The
curriculum included the Roman dramatists Seneca, Terence,
and Plautus; Renaissance religious texts; the Roman poets
Horace, Virgil, and Ovid; the complete works of Dutch Renaissance scholar Erasmus; and the works of Roman orators,
philosophers, and historians.

Shakespeare, who drew from Ovid's *Metamorphoses* for his
own plays and poems, likely remembered this classic from
his grammar school days. Years later, playwright Ben Jonson
disparagingly called Shakespeare's learning "small Latin and
less Greek," but this opinion is disputed by biographer Dennis Kay, who says in *Shakespeare: His Life, Work, and Era*, "To
argue, as some do, that a man of Shakespeare's background
could not have been sufficiently learned to write the works attributed to him, is to fly in the face of the evidence."

Shakespeare's education extended well beyond the Stratford grammar school. Elizabethan law required regular attendance in the Protestant Church of England, so Shakespeare would have grown up listening to readings from the
Bible and the *Book of Common Prayer*, the liturgical book of
the Church of England. Scholars have counted in Shakespeare's plays allusions to forty books of the Bible and many
references to the commandments, quotations from psalms,

and lines from the prayer book. In *Shakespeare the Man*, biographer A.L. Rowse calls Shakespeare a man educated in "the university of life." His plays display detailed knowledge of the entertainment, social mores, and culture of his native Warwickshire. Scholar and critic George R. Price says in *Reading Shakespeare's Plays* that we may

> be sure that the knowledge of hawking, hunting, and archery, of horses, dogs, and wild things, of peddlers, shepherds, and farm folk—this store of information in his plays and poems was not acquired only from books, but indicates a normal freedom to roam the countryside and enjoy himself.

Though he lived far from London, Shakespeare had at least a few opportunities to experience some of its cultural riches while a boy in Stratford. When John Shakespeare was bailiff, probably in 1569, troupes of players began to perform plays in the Guild Hall in Stratford and continued to stage plays every year from the time William was five years old. Though there are no records of John Shakespeare's attendance, as a bailiff he would surely have brought his family to the entertainments. In 1575, Shakespeare had another taste of London life when Queen Elizabeth I visited the earl of Leicester at his castle at Kenilworth, a few miles from Stratford. Called a progress, the queen's entourage included courtiers on horseback, coaches, hundreds of servants, and numerous carts hauling supplies. County crowds gathered to watch the procession go by and perhaps hear a word from the queen. During the queen's stay—which lasted nearly a month—crowds surrounded the castle to watch the pageants, water shows, and fireworks displays prepared in the queen's honor. Shakespeare alludes to entertainments like these in *A Midsummer Night's Dream* and *Twelfth Night*, perhaps recalling the spectacles he saw as a boy.

EARLY MANHOOD

Though no record confirms this, Shakespeare left school at about age sixteen. When he was eighteen years old, he married Anne Hathaway, who was eight years older than he. Biographers have made much of the information that banns (public announcements of the proposed marriage) were called only once, on December 1, 1582, rather than the usual three times; the inference is that church officials hurried the marriage because Anne was already pregnant. However, because Elizabethan custom considered betrothal a binding agreement and in some instances the same as marriage, her pregnancy was less unusual than modern customs might consider it.

After the marriage, the couple lived with Shakespeare's family on Henley Street in Stratford. On May 26, 1583, their first child, Susanna, was baptized; twenty months later the young couple had twins, baptized Hamnet and Judith on February 2, 1585. Aside from the facts of his marriage and children, little is known about the way he spent his days. Kay speculates:

> He may have traveled, worked as a schoolmaster, a soldier, or a lawyer, trained as an actor, embraced (or left) the Roman Church, poached deer, or indulged in bouts of heavy drinking. Whatever he did, he found some way of passing the time between leaving school in the late 1570s and springing into action—and celebrity—on the professional stage in London at some time in the late 1580s.

According to one of the myths surrounding Shakespeare's life, he was caught poaching deer in a park belonging to Sir Thomas Lucy of Cherlecote, near Stratford. Historian Nicholas Rowe speculates that Shakespeare might have had to leave his business and family and take refuge in London to avoid prosecution.

FIRST YEARS IN LONDON

The years 1585 to 1592 are called the "lost years" because no records of any kind document Shakespeare's movements or activities during the period. He probably went to London sometime between 1585 and 1587, possibly joining up with a company of traveling actors or striking out alone on foot. By one route, a man could walk to London in four days if he made twenty-five miles a day, and he could have lodged at inns along the way for a penny a night. In *Shakespeare: A Compact Documentary Life*, Samuel Schoenbaum describes the city Shakespeare would have found on his arrival:

> The great city of contrasts spawned stately mansions and slum tenements, gardens and midden-heaped lanes. With the Court close to hand, it was the vital nerve-center for the professions, trade, and commerce, and the arts; London nourished the English Renaissance. Only in the metropolis could a playwright of genius forge a career for himself.

Violent and spectacular entertainments were popular among Londoners of all classes: acrobatic shows and tumbling stunts, bear- and bull-baiting. According to historian Roland Mushat Frye, "The theatres were in daily competition with these bloody sports. It is small wonder that the stage plays tended so much to violent action."

Attending plays, however, was the most popular form of

entertainment for all classes. Plays were first performed in courtyards, but by the time Shakespeare arrived, London had several theaters. The first, built in 1576 by James Burbage, was called simply the Theatre, and the Fortune, the Swan, the Curtain, and the Rose followed. The theaters were constructed with an open stage surrounded by uncovered space where a standing crowd viewed the performance. Three levels of covered seats surrounded the open space. Each theater had an all-male resident company of actors performing plays and competing with all of the other theaters for popular approval. Female parts were played by boys usually recruited from the boys' choirs in the cathedrals. (Not until 1660 did a woman act onstage.) During the twelve days of Christmas, the companies performed plays in Queen Elizabeth's court to entertain royal guests; throughout the year, traveling troupes drawn from the companies also performed plays in towns and cities outside London.

A common tale that surrounds Shakespeare is that he began his career by holding patrons' horses outside the theater; another says that he began as a prompter's attendant. He may have done both jobs for a short time and then advanced to acting before becoming the company's writer. Kay acknowledges that "we are no nearer knowing how and when Shakespeare began writing plays, nor do we know how he acquired the skills and experience to fit him for his profession." Price suggests that Shakespeare's choice of an acting career must have grieved the heart of his parents because society looked on actors as riffraff at worst, and men of questionable reputation at best. Though attending plays was popular London entertainment, many moralists complained that the jokes were too bawdy and that young men neglected their church duties in favor of playgoing.

THE EMERGENCE OF A PLAYWRIGHT

Shakespeare, an outsider in London, a country man lacking the sophistication and easy manners of Cambridge and Oxford University men, studied the ways of a gentleman, found a mentor, and read widely. Shakespeare looked to Cambridge-educated playwright Christopher Marlowe, who was the same age but who preceded Shakespeare in skillfully combining drama with poetry. Shakespeare studied three successful plays staged in the late 1580s: Thomas Kyd's *Spanish Tragedy* and Marlowe's *Tamburlaine* and *The Jew of Malta.* He emulated romantic elements and imitated the poetic techniques of the works of two British poets: Sir Philip Sidney's sonnets and *The Arcadia,* a prose romance, and Edmund Spenser's *The Faerie Queene,* a poem about glory and the queen. Moreover, Shakespeare, who loved his country and its history, read the *Chronicles,* published in 1577 and reissued in 1587 by Raphael Holinshed, a historian who came to London early in Elizabeth's reign. Holinshed borrowed from an earlier historian, Edward Halle, whose *Chronicles* also recounted the events of England's history, especially the past royal families. Since there were no copyright laws in effect in the sixteenth century, writers borrowed from and paraphrased the works of other writers. Shakespeare depended on Holinshed's *Chronicles* most heavily as the source for the history plays, but he also drew on Halle and other sources.

Records show that Shakespeare had already made his mark as a playwright by 1592. *The Tragedy of Titus Andronicus,* Shakespeare's first tragedy, was the first play to appear in 1594 in printed form, but without the author's name. Shakespeare reflects England's political debate of the 1590s concerning the wars with France in his three-part play *Henry VI.* In *The Comedy of Errors,* Shakespeare structures the plot according to a popular school text, Plautus's *Menaechmi.* And *Richard III,* a play with one star player, the callous villain King Richard, anticipates *MacBeth.* The popularity of Shakespeare's earliest plays elicited a comment in a journal left by Robert Greene, a popular Cambridge-educated playwright. In his *Groatsworth of Wit,* Greene, complaining that the professional actors had forsaken university men like him, specifically attacked Shakespeare:

> Yes trust them not: for there is an upstart Crow, beautified with our feathers, that with his *Tygers hart wrapt in a Players hyde,*[1] supposes he is as well able to bombast out a blanke verse as the best of you: and beeing an absolute *Johannes fac totum*[2], is in his owne conceit the onely Shake-scene in a countrey.

After Greene's death in 1592, his literary executor, Henry Chettle, issued a printed apology, saying "I am as sorry as if the original fault had been my fault. . . . Besides, divers of worship have reported his [Shakespeare's] uprightness of dealing, which argues his honesty, and his facetious grace in writing, that approves his art."

About the time that Greene's comment appeared, plague spread through London, lasting through 1593, and the lord

---

1. a play on Shakespeare's line from *3 Henry VI,* "O tiger's heart wrapt in a woman's hide!" 2. a "jack do-everything"; a jack of all trades

mayor ordered the theaters closed. Without theater work, Shakespeare made his first appeal to the reading public. He had wanted to be a poet, which he considered a noble occupation; acting and writing plays, he thought, were merely means to support a family. On April 18, 1593, the printer Richard Field obtained license to publish Shakespeare's poem *Venus and Adonis*, which focuses on the lustful passion of the goddess of love, and on May 9, 1594, license to publish another poem, *The Rape of Lucrece*, about the moral dilemma of a chaste Roman wife who commits suicide to escape the shame of having been raped by Tarquin. Shakespeare proofread the copy and monitored the publication of both poems. The typesetter, who selected letters from the type case and placed them as he read the handwritten copy to be reproduced in print, was the only individual ensuring accuracy of the type; if he misread the manuscript, errors appeared in the publication.

Shakespeare also wrote a series of 154 sonnets, which celebrate a beautiful young man and express powerful passion for a mysterious dark lady at whose hands the poet suffers greatly. Since neither the young man nor the dark lady is named, critics have gone to great lengths to verify their identity. Most critics conclude that the twenty sonnets dedicated to the young man and the many others that celebrate him in glowing terms refer to the earl of Southampton, who had become Shakespeare's patron. No less critical energy has been devoted to determining whether the sonnets are autobiographical. Most critics concur that they are not, but biographer A.L. Rowse, who thinks they are, agrees that the young man is the earl of Southampton and identifies the dark lady as Emilia Bassano, the daughter of an Italian musician in the queen's court.

THE TURNING POINT IN SHAKESPEARE'S CAREER

In 1594 Shakespeare turned away from sonnet writing and established himself with an acting company since, with the end of the plague, the theaters reopened and the earl of Southampton's patronage ended. By the summer of 1594, a group of actors formerly with other companies had formed a company under the patronage of Henry Lord Hunsdon, lord chamberlain to the queen, calling themselves Lord Chamberlain's Men. They played at various theaters—the Theatre, the Curtain, and the Swan. Among the company's permanent members were Henry Condell, John Heminge, Shakespeare, Richard Burbage (son of the Theatre's builder, James Burbage), William Sly, and Will Kempe. Burbage, the famous

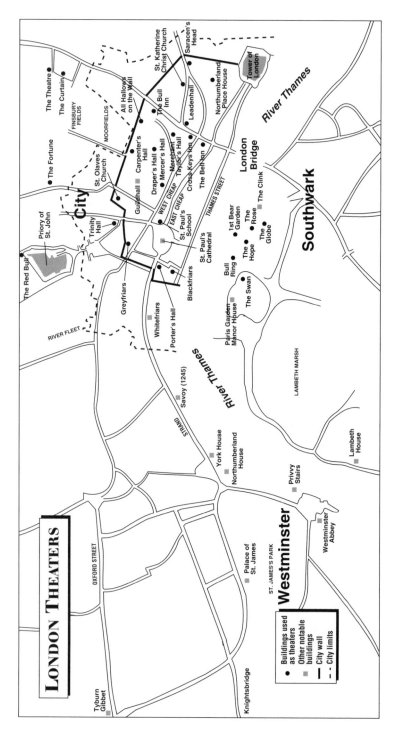

tragedian, and Kempe, the famous comedian, played leading roles in plays Shakespeare wrote specifically for their talents. From then on, Shakespeare was completely involved in the theater: He wrote for the company, acted in the plays, shared in the profits, and eventually became an owner. While in London, he worked hard and played little; he lived during those years as a lodger in quiet rooms near the playhouses, where he could write without interruption.

Shakespeare's major early successes came between 1593 and 1598. *Love's Labour's Lost,* probably the only play without a borrowed plot, portrays current social and political life. It was published in 1598, the first with his name identified as the author. Critics have called it and *The Two Gentlemen from Verona* lyrical because they contain passages of beautiful description and passionate feelings. Shakespeare's style in these early comedies shows evidence of the influence of playwright John Lyly, whose adaptions from Greek mythology are written in euphuistic style, an artificial style rich in repartee and word play, musically turned lyrics, and elaborate imagery. With *A Midsummer Night's Dream,* Shakespeare had already gone beyond Lyly in creating a more inventive plot and more interesting characters from the fairy world. *The Taming of the Shrew* and *The Tragedy of Romeo and Juliet* exemplify other characteristics of his early plays—intricate plots and long explanatory speeches written in verse.

Shakespeare also wrote history plays about England's past kings: *Richard II; Henry IV, Part 1* and *Part 2; Henry V;* and *King John.* After the early *Richard III,* Shakespeare realized that the War of the Roses had originated in the reign of Richard II, and wrote the later play about an earlier king. The two parts of *Henry IV* portray Henry's undoing and the preparation of his son Hal to become Henry V. *King John,* described by scholars as puzzling and uneven, depicts the political crises of an early-thirteenth-century king whose reign was poorly suited for a play

The two-part play *Henry IV* was particularly popular with the audiences, who loved the humor of the fat knight Falstaff. Falstaff's unrestrained indulgence in sensual pleasures, his love of telling big lies, and his own laziness are set against great humor and consistent wit. Biographer Sidney Lee says, "Shakespeare's purely comic power culminated in Falstaff; he may be claimed as the most humorous figure in literature." After Falstaff disappeared as a character in the history plays, Queen Elizabeth requested that Shakespeare write another in which Falstaff falls in love. Shakespeare complied with *The Merry Wives of Windsor*, but in this play Falstaff is the butt, not the creator, of humor. During this period, Shakespeare also wrote the comedies *Much Ado About Nothing* and *The Merchant of Venice*, both of which have two stories, or threads, of interest.

Shakespeare received praise from many sources for his early works. Among the most notable were comments by Francis Meres, a learned Cambridge graduate, who, in *Palladis Tamia: Wit's Treasury*, called Shakespeare the greatest man of letters. Meres writes,

> So the sweet witty soul of Ovid lives in mellifluous and honey-tongued Shakespeare, witness his *Venus and Adonis*, his *Lucrece*, his sugared *Sonnets* among his private friends, etc.
>
> As Plautus and Seneca are accounted the best for Comedy and Tragedy among the Latins: so Shakespeare among the English is the most excellent in both kinds for the stage. . . .
>
> As Epius Stolo said, that the Muses would speak with Plautus's tongue if they would speak Latin: so I say that the Muses would speak with Shakespeare's fine filed phrase, if they would speak English.

Ben Jonson, who criticized Shakespeare's learning, also praised him, calling him the "Soul of the age! / The applause, delight, and wonder of our stage, . . . not of an age, but for all time." Shakespeare was called witty and gentle, qualities reflected by antiquarian and gossip John Aubrey, who writes, "He was a handsome, well-shap't man: very good company, and of a very readie and pleasant smoothe Witt."

IMPORTANT PERSONAL EVENTS

Despite his growing fame, Stratford was still the center of Shakespeare's personal life. In 1596 and 1597, Shakespeare was occupied with three significant family matters. First, in August 1596, Shakespeare returned to Stratford when Hamnet died. With the death of his eleven-year-old son, Shakespeare lost hope of perpetuating the family in his name since Anne Shakespeare was forty and could not be expected to have another child. Shakespeare expressed his grief in the play he was writing at the time, *King John*:

> Grief filles the room up of my absent child,
> Lies in his bed, walks up and down with me,
> Puts on his pretty looks, repeats his words,
> Remembers me of all his gracious parts,
> Stuffs out his vacant garments with his form.

Second, even though he had no son to carry on the family

name, Shakespeare pressed to obtain the title and coat of arms of a gentleman, a status evidently important to him. So that he could be considered born the son of a gentleman, Shakespeare applied and paid cash for a grant in the name of his father. On October 20, 1596, Garter King of Arms William Dethick issued a coat of arms with a falcon and a silver spear and declared Shakespeare a gentleman by birth. The family evidently felt themselves entitled to the honor, for they chose as their motto the phrase *Non sanz droict* ("Not without right"). Finally, in May 1597, Shakespeare purchased New Place, a large home in the center of Stratford with two barns and two orchards and gardens. Before he was thirty-five years old, Shakespeare had achieved the status of gentleman, property owner, and playwright, but he had lost his only male heir.

In 1597 James Burbage, who had built the Theatre in 1576, died, and the Lord Chamberlain's Men lost their lease. At approximately the same time, Puritans increased their opposition to what they perceived as the immorality of the city theaters. To circumvent Puritan criticism, the Lord Chamberlain's Men found backing to dismantle the Theatre, move the boards across the Thames from London's city center, and rebuild the theater, which they renamed the Globe. By this time, Shakespeare had acquired enough wealth to buy an eighth of the shares in the new theater.

The Globe outshone its competitors. It held two thousand spectators and was equipped with a bigger stage, a cellerage for graves and ghosts, a curtained space for intimate and surprise scenes, and a balcony. The audience was closer to the players, and the players had more flexibility to move quickly from scene to scene. *Henry V*, in which Shakespeare played the part of the chorus, anticipates the Globe. In the prologue, he refers to the new theater with excitement:

> A kingdom for a stage, princes to act
> And monarchs to behold the swelling scene! . . .
> Can this cockpit[5] hold
> The vasty fields of France? Or may we cram
> Within this wooden O[4] the very casques[5]
> That did affright the air at Agincourt[6]?

In the epilogue, Shakespeare displays his characteristically humble attitude toward himself, writing,

> Thus far, with rough and all-unable pen,
> Our bending author hath pursued the story,

---

3. and 4. playhouse 5. helmets 6. the French village where Henry V defeated a larger French army.

In little room confining mighty men,
Mangling by starts the full course of their glory.

Though he himself may have been self-assured, he speaks as a humble gentleman throughout his works, self-deprecatingly calling himself "a worthless boat," "inferior far" to Marlowe. Others found this attitude charming, and Shakespeare gained a reputation for congeniality.

OUTPOURING OF COMEDIES AND TRAGEDIES

After 1598 Shakespeare's comedies and tragedies appeared quickly one after another. He turned from English history to Roman history and used *Lives*, by Greek philosopher and biographer Plutarch, as a source for plots. *The Tragedy of Julius Caesar*, dated 1599, explores Brutus's character and motives. In addition, Shakespeare wrote three comedies to suit Will Kempe's talents. Besides *The Merry Wives of Windsor*, Kempe starred in *As You Like It* and *Twelfth Night*, whose title comes from its performance before the queen during the Twelfth Night of 1599–1600.

After 1600 Shakespeare wrote his greatest tragedies, distinguished from the earlier works by more subtle language and deeper spirit. *Hamlet* and *Othello* came first. Shakespearean scholar and critic G.B. Harrison says that "*Hamlet* is in every way the most interesting play ever written"; for nearly four hundred years, it has challenged actors and scholars to interpret Hamlet's character. *Othello*, a unified and focused play, portrays evil in the character of Iago as he exploits Othello's jealousy and Desdemona's innocence to destroy them and their love.

The opening of the Globe marked a new phase in Shakespeare's reputation and art. Firmly established as the leading dramatist in London, Shakespeare's art became more refined and subtle. Price says, "Art has replaced artifice. The style has become so fully expressive of the thought that audiences and readers are unconscious of the poet's devices." Shakespeare, who was interested in the workings of the human psyche, objectively displayed his characters' minds in the actions and speeches he wrote for them. The soliloquies of Brutus, Hamlet, and Iago, for example, lay bare their intentions and their very souls.

Among his friends and fellow playwrights, Shakespeare had a reputation for writing with little revision. Aubrey reports playwright Ben Jonson's opinion of Shakespeare's method of writing: "He was wont to say that he never blotted out a line in his life. Sayd Ben Johnson, I wish he had blotted out a thousand." In the annual Shakespeare Lecture of the British Academy in 1972, M.M. Mahood acknowledges faults in the texts. Mahood says, "Shakespeare's plays abound in loose ends, false starts, confusions, and anomalies of every kind." Many of the faults occur in the comedies; for example, in *The Taming of the Shrew*, the characters of Sly and the Hostess disappear from the play.

Though Shakespeare continued to write, the period from 1598 to 1604 brought significant personal events. In September 1601 his father died in Stratford. The following May, Shakespeare bought 107 acres of farmland in Old Stratford for £320 and in September he purchased a cottage on Walkers Street. On March 24, 1603, Queen Elizabeth, who had actively supported Lord Chamberlain's Men, died. James I succeeded her, took over the company, renamed it the King's Men, and supported the players even more avidly than the queen had, making them an official part of the court, doubling their salaries, and increasing their annual court appearances from three per year to thirteen. In addition, he gave them license to perform in any town or university. These changes required Shakespeare to pay greater attention to the approval of two audiences, the court and the Globe. Shakespeare's increase in income allowed him to invest £440 in tithes in parishes in Stratford and surrounding towns, investments that brought additional income of £60 a year.

THE KING'S MEN

From 1603 to 1608, as a member of the King's Men, Shakespeare's plays changed again. He wrote two transitional comedies in which he experimented with techniques to work out dramatic problems. *All's Well That Ends Well*, an uneven play seldom performed, involves a young woman who tricks a man into becoming her husband. *Measure for Measure*, called a problem play because the plot poorly fits the theme, concerns a woman who compromises her chastity to save her brother.

After 1604 Shakespeare's tragedies probed deeply into the minds of their heroes. *The Tragedy of King Lear* was first performed in King James's court during the Christmas holidays of 1606. Critics regard *Lear* as Shakespeare's greatest play. The play has a double plot: Lear suffers at the hands of his daughters; Gloucester suffers at the hands of his son. Both die, but each has one child who remains loyal. The play's greatness lies in the psychological depth of Lear's character and the stark reality of both human nature and nature's elements.

Shakespeare wrote *Macbeth* in 1606 as a tribute to James I on the occasion of a state visit from the king of Denmark. The play is set in Scotland, James's home before he became king of England. The good character Banquo is a member of the Scottish Stuart family, an ancestor of James. Shakespeare also honored the king, who was interested in witchcraft, by incorporating the three witches into the play. Though he did not find King James I an honorable man, Shakespeare fulfilled his duty to the king upon whose patronage he depended. Like *Lear, Macbeth* reaches below the rational level into the subconscious, where primitive experiences lie in recesses of the mind; the tragic Macbeth and Lady Macbeth, having plotted the murder of King Duncan to put Macbeth on the throne, see their plot undone and suffer mental anguish before they, too, die.

After the four great tragedies, Shakespeare returned to Plutarch's *Lives* as a source for three more. *The Tragedy of Antony and Cleopatra* picks up the story of Roman history where *Julius Caesar* left off. *The Tragedy of Coriolanus* is a political play in which Shakespeare exposes the weakness of all manner of politicians. *Timon of Athens*, an unfinished play, tells about an ancient Greek mentioned briefly in Plutarch's *Lives*.

During this period, when Shakespeare wrote one or more plays a year and kept a busy schedule of productions at court and at the Globe, a few facts are known about his personal life. His daughter Susanna married a well-known medical doctor from Stratford named John Hall on June 5, 1607. In September 1608, his mother, Mary Arden Shakespeare, died, and in October 1608, Shakespeare was named godfather to the son of Stratford alderman Henry Walker, named William in honor of Shakespeare.

THE FINAL PERIOD

After the outpouring of tragedies, Shakespeare used the changes in theater ownership and attendance to create a new kind of dramatic art. Blackfriars, a private theater owned by Richard Burbage, had been leased to a boys' company. Burbage, Shakespeare, and other actors bought back the lease and began performances there for upper-class audiences, more like those at the royal court. Blackfriars audiences liked new plays, while the public audiences at the

Globe preferred old favorites. This situation suited Shakespeare, whose new plays for Blackfriars were neither comedies nor tragedies. Some critics have called them romances; others, tragicomedies. Rowse says: "For all their happy endings, these plays have an atmosphere full of suggestion and symbol, suffused with tears."

Shakespeare wrote four plays in this new form. *Pericles* is a transitional play, portions of which appear to have been written by a second playwright. After experimenting with *Pericles*, Shakespeare wrote *Cymbeline*, probably in 1610, a melodrama about an innocent girl who flees mistreatment and encounters a host of crises before she is reunited with her repentant husband. *The Winter's Tale*, written in 1610 or 1611, is a moving tale of wrongs committed by one generation and reconciled by the next.

The Tempest, a play written for James I to celebrate a court wedding, is Shakespeare's farewell to the theater. This fairy tale about a magician and his beautiful daughter ends with the reconciliation of two generations. G.B. Harrison praises *The Tempest*, saying,

> Shakespeare has finally achieved complete mastery over words in the blank-verse form. This power is shown throughout the play, but particularly in some of Prospero's great speeches, . . . or in his farewell to his art. There is in these speeches a kind of organ note not hitherto heard. Shakespeare's thought was as deep as in his tragedies, but now he was able to express each thought with perfect meaning and its own proper harmony.

Prospero, the magician of *The Tempest*, recounts his tricks in words that some critics think apply aptly to Shakespeare. After cataloging the marvels he has conjured up over the years, from raging storms to corpses rising from the grave to a dimmed sun, he announces, "This rough magic / I here abjure. . . . I'll break my staff, / Bury it certain fathoms in the earth, / And . . . I'll drown my book." Shakespeare's only play after this farewell was *Henry VIII*, a series of historical episodes full of pageantry, music, and ceremony. During the June 29, 1613, performance of *Henry VIII*, a spark from a cannon set the thatch roof of the Globe alight and burned the building to the ground. Though the Globe was rebuilt in 1614, there is reason to believe that the players' books and many of Shakespeare's original manuscripts were lost in the fire.

From 1612 on, Shakespeare divided his time between Stratford and London and once went to Parliament to lobby for better roads between the two cities. In 1612 his brother Gilbert died, followed by his brother Richard the next year. Shakespeare spent 1614 and 1615 in Stratford enjoying his retirement and his daughters, but information about his wife, Anne, seems to be nonexistent. The parish register of Holy Trinity shows that on February 10, 1616, Shakespeare's younger daughter, Judith, was married to Thomas Quiney, the son of Shakespeare's old friend Richard Quiney. On March 25, 1616, while he was in fine health, Shakespeare made a will. He left a dowry and additional money to Judith and all lands and houses to his older daughter, Susanna, and her heirs. He left his wife to the care of his daughters and willed her the next-best bed, perhaps reasoning that Susanna and her husband needed the bigger, better one. To his sister, he left money for clothes and the home on Henley Street. He gave small amounts of money to friends and money for rings to fellow actors of the King's Men. And he left money for the poor in Stratford. A month later, after a trip to London, he suddenly became ill and died on April 23, 1616, at age fifty-two. As he lay dying, the chapel bell knelled for the passing of his soul, for the man for whom love was the center of the universe and the central subject of his many works.

THE FIRST FOLIO

During his lifetime, Shakespeare never made any effort to publish his works, other than the two long poems. His plays belonged to the members of the theater company, who sold individual plays for publication when readers requested them in the early 1600s. In 1623—the year Anne Hathaway Shakespeare died—two actors from the King's Men, Henry Condell and John Heminge, collected Shakespeare's plays and published them in what is known as the First Folio; they have been in print ever since. In their introduction, Condell and Heminge appealed to readers "from the most able, to him that can but spell. Read him, therefore, and again, and again. And if then you do not like him, surely you are in some manifest danger not to understand him."

Some skeptics, doubting Shakespeare's genius and education, have speculated that someone else wrote his plays. Doubts appeared as early as 1694 and recurred in 1785, when Francis Bacon was identified as a probable author; James Spedding, Bacon's editor and biographer, however, dismisses the notion. He says, "I doubt whether there are five lines together to be found in Bacon which could be mistaken for Shakespeare, or five lines in Shakespeare which could be mistaken for Bacon." In 1921 Thomas Looney theorized in

Shakespeare Identified that Edward de Vere, the seventeenth earl of Oxford, was the true Shakespeare, basing his research on the correspondences between de Vere's travels, education, and social class and details in the plays. Most reputable critics believe that such doubts are put forth by the uninformed. As Price says, "No first-rate scholar has ever accepted the evidence offered by the Baconians or others who argue that Shakespeare did not write the dramas that his fellow-actors, Heminge and Condell, published as his."

CHARACTERS AND PLOT

MAIN CHARACTERS

Shylock: a rich Jew, a hardheaded businessman
Antonio: a merchant of Venice, a respected and loved citizen
Bassanio: Antonio's friend, one of Portia's suitors
Portia: a rich heiress from Belmont, sought after by several
  suitors
Nerissa: Portia's waiting maid
Jessica: daughter of Shylock
Lorenzo: in love with Jessica
Gratiano: friend to Antonio and Bassanio, in love with Nerissa
Salanio: friend to Antonio and Bassanio
Salarino: friend to Antonio and Bassanio
Salerio: friend to Antonio and Bassanio
Launcelot Gobbo: a clown, servant to Shylock

PLOT

The Merchant of Venice combines two stories. In one story a
cruel Jew, Shylock, agrees to lend money to a Christian, Antonio, on condition that the debtor forfeit a pound of flesh if
the money is not repaid by a certain date. The case comes to
trial and Shylock is outwitted. In the other story, Portia awaits
the suitor who will correctly guess which of three caskets
contains her portrait, a method of selecting a husband de-
creed by her father before he died. Shakespeare alternates
scenes from each story and resolves them together in the final act.

The play opens on a street in Venice, where Bassanio tells
Antonio that he desires Portia and wishes to be one of her
suitors, but he needs money to travel to Belmont, where Portia lives, and to present himself suitably. Antonio agrees to
help him, but his cash is invested in a fleet of ships; however,
he assures Bassanio that his reputation and good name will
qualify him to borrow money. Bassanio discusses a loan with

Shylock, who assesses Antonio's holdings in ships and his available cash. Antonio arrives, and in an aside Shylock expresses his hatred for Antonio because he is a Christian and because he lends money without charging interest, a practice that undercuts his own chances for usury. Shylock reminds Antonio that in the Rialto, the gathering place for merchants, Antonio publicly called him a "cutthroat dog," spat upon his coat, and ridiculed him personally and professionally. Antonio says he may spit on him again for his unfair interest charges. After insults are traded, Shylock agrees to lend three thousand ducats for three months, but if the loan is not repaid at the specified time, Shylock will extract a pound of flesh from whatever part of Antonio's body he chooses; Antonio, convinced his ships will return a month before the loan comes due, bringing him adequate cash, agrees to the conditions. Shylock sends for the money.

In Belmont, Portia expresses her weariness as a parade of suitors try for her hand. She bemoans the will left by her dead father that she marry the man who chooses the right casket of three, leaving her neither the choice of a lover she prefers nor the chance to refuse one she dislikes. Nerissa, Portia's maid, names the present suitors, and Portia describes them, finding fault with each—the Neapolitan prince, the country Palatine, the French lord, the young baron of England, the Scottish lord, and the young German. Four suitors leave, and the prince of Morocco arrives, proclaiming his virtues to Portia and begging for the opportunity to win her. After dinner, he contemplates each casket carefully. The first one is gold, inscribed with the words, "Who chooseth me shall gain what many men desire." The second one, of silver, carries the promise, "Who chooseth me shall get as much as he deserves." The third is made of lead and carries the warning, "Who chooseth me must give and hazard all he hath." Gold is the Moroccan's choice, and inside he finds a scroll with a verse that opens, "All that glistens is not gold." Failing to win Portia's hand, he leaves as agreed.

In Venice, Launcelot Gobbo the clown, who muddles his attempts to use big words, debates whether to stay with his master Shylock, whom he calls a devil, or to leave him. The clown plays tricks on his half-blind father as Bassanio and his friends arrive. Bassanio has learned that his friend Gratiano will accompany him to Belmont. At Shylock's house, Launcelot, having decided to leave Shylock, says goodbye to the Jew's daughter, Jessica, who gives him a secret letter to deliver to Lorenzo, telling him she would become a Christian and marry him. Bassanio has invited Shylock to a dinner at which Bassanio's friends will entertain with a masque; suspicious of Bassanio's motive, Shylock leaves his house with orders to Jessica to lock the windows and not look upon the entertainers. As soon as her father has gone, however, Jessica disguises herself as a boy, gathers jewels and ducats from her father's house, finds Lorenzo and the rest of the masked entertainers, and leads the parade as the torchbearer. After the feast, Antonio reports that Bassanio and Gratiano have sailed, and Salarino and Salanio report that Shylock is raging over Antonio's generosity to Bassanio and over Jessica's running off with Lorenzo.

In Belmont the arrogant, proud prince of Aragon has arrived to play the casket game for Portia's hand, vowing never to woo another to marry should he fail. Like the Moroccan, he studies the inscriptions but chooses the silver casket. Inside he finds a portrait of a blinking idiot and the message "There be fools alive, I wis/ Silvered o're, and so was this." A servant enters to announce that a young handsome Venetian has arrived bearing gifts and comporting himself humbly and courteously. Portia longs to see one who comes with such fine manners.

On a street in Venice, Salanio asks Salarino for news from the Rialto. There the talk is of their friend Antonio, whose ship carrying rich cargo was wrecked in the English Channel, a loss for which both friends express regret. Shylock arrives and rages about his rebellious daughter and about his loan to a "bankrupt," who ought to look to his bond when he is tempted to act smug in the marketplace or to call Shylock a usurer. When Salarino suggests that Shylock would never take human flesh, which is good for nothing, Shylock's anger erupts. He can bait fish with Antonio's flesh to take his revenge for the times Antonio has disgraced him, prevented him from making money, scorned him as a Jew, and turned his enemies against him. Just as a servant calls Salanio and Salarino to Antonio's house, Shylock's friend Tubal, a Jew, arrives to report that he has not found Jessica, but that another of Antonio's ships has foundered coming from Tripolis. Shylock rails against losing the money that Jessica took, but delights at Antonio's bad luck; he vows to pursue the agreement, and asks Tubal to hire an officer to arrest Antonio.

In a room in Portia's house, Bassanio, Gratiano, Portia, and Nerissa gather for the third casket game with Bassanio the player. Portia, who has fallen in love with Bassanio, begs him to stay with her a month or two at least before he risks failure. Bassanio declares his love for Portia and opts to see the caskets immediately, as waiting is torment. Portia orders music and a song while Bassanio contemplates each casket and its inscription. Prompted by the brightness of the gold and silver caskets, he delivers a long speech on the deception of bright appearances, after which he chooses the lead casket in which he finds Portia's picture and a verse that ends with the lines, "Turn you where your lady is / And claim her with a loving kiss." Portia expresses her pleasure, declares her fair mansion his, and gives him a ring, with the warning that parting from it, losing it, or giving it away means the ruin of his love. Bassanio vows not to part from it until death. Nerissa and Gratiano wish the couple joy and announce that while waiting they have fallen in love and wish to marry. Bassanio and Portia declare that they will all be honored at a feast. Salerio, who has brought Lorenzo and Jessica with him, arrives with a letter from Antonio describing the loss of his ships at sea. Salerio informs them that Shylock has demanded the duke not deny him the justice of the bond and that twenty merchants have tried to persuade Shylock to relent, but have failed. Jessica confirms her father's intention. Portia offers to pay Shylock many times the three thousand ducats and tells Bassanio and Gratiano to go to Venice to Antonio, but only after she and Bassanio have been to the church to wed. Nerissa and Portia will remain in Belmont until their return.

On a street in Venice the jailer has arrested Antonio, who pleads with Shylock to hear him, but Shylock refuses to listen and continues to insist on his pound of flesh. Salarino hopes for the duke's intervention.

After Bassanio has left for Venice, Portia, Lorenzo, Jessica, and Nerissa write a letter to Portia's cousin Doctor Bellario in Padua asking him to defend Antonio in his trial. Balthasar, Portia's servant, delivers the letter. Portia and Nerissa disguise themselves as boys and leave for Venice. After they leave, Launcelot Gobbo arrives to warn Jessica that she is in danger from her father. Lorenzo and Jessica, who have been instructed to care for the mansion, invite Launcelot to dinner.

Antonio's trial opens in Venice with the duke expressing his sadness to Antonio and his expectations to Shylock that he will show mercy and withdraw his demands. Shylock has sworn to have his due and refuses to forfeit his bond, even to the point of threatening the duke's city charter should he try to force him. Shylock says he has no other reason than his passionate hatred and loathing for Antonio. Antonio is resigned and urges no further pleading with his resolute enemy. Just when the duke is ready to dismiss the court unless Doctor Bellario arrives, Salerio enters with a letter from the doctor sent by a messenger, who is Nerissa in disguise. In the letter the doctor explains that he is sick but has sent in his place a young doctor from Rome named Balthasar, a bright, capable judge who has been briefed on the case. Portia, disguised as Balthasar, is called in and begins the questioning, which she interrupts to argue that mercy is a virtue superseding justice and that Shylock, should he choose mercy, would be more powerful than if he had merely obtained justice. Shylock chooses the law. Portia reads the bond and declares that the defendant must pay the forfeit and that Shylock may lawfully claim a pound of flesh.

Portia orders Antonio to bare his chest. Antonio bids farewell to Bassanio urging him not to grieve because he falls for his friend's sake. Portia tells Shylock that he must cut the flesh from Antonio's breast—"The law allows it, and the court awards it"—but warns him that the bond does not allow him to take so much as a drop of blood, and that if he does so, by law Venice will confiscate his lands and goods. Shylock asks if that is the law, and when assured by Portia that it is, he asks for the ducats. Portia tells the Jew that he wants justice and must cut off the flesh, but shed no blood, and if he misses the weight of a pound by a hair's worth, either more or less, he must die. Defeated, Shylock asks to withdraw his bond, keep his wealth, and leave. But Portia has one more condition. The laws of Venice state that an alien who attempts to take the life of a citizen must give half his goods to the citizen and the other half to the state and that his life lies at the mercy of the duke. Portia orders Shylock to get down and beg mercy of the duke, who pardons him before he kneels. Antonio requests that half of his portion be left to Shylock for his living and that when Shylock dies all of his possessions be deeded to Lorenzo and Jessica. Portia calls for the deed of gifts for Shylock to sign, but he requests to sign it at home since he is ill, a favor which Portia grants.

The duke invites Portia to dinner, an invitation she refuses, and urges Antonio to make her a payment, which Portia says she has already received in the form of satisfaction in outwitting Shylock. At Bassanio's request that she take some remembrance, Portia requests gloves from Antonio and the ring from Bassanio, who explains that it is a keepsake from his wife. She derides him for offering a gift and then refusing to give it, and she leaves. Antonio persuades Bassanio to let her have the ring, which Gratiano takes to Portia on her way. On the street where Portia and Nerissa seek directions to Shylock's house for the signing, Gratiano catches them, and Portia accepts Bassanio's ring, and Nerissa determines to get the ring she gave to Gratiano. The two women agree that they will have fun teasing their husbands when they arrive in Belmont.

Lorenzo and Jessica are enjoying the moonlit evening on the avenue leading to Portia's mansion when Stephano comes to announce the arrival of Portia and Nerissa. Lorenzo orders the musicians to play in the night air to welcome the women, sweet music Portia and Nerissa take note of as they near the house. They have arrived with just enough time to swear all the servants to silence concerning their absence before Bassanio, Antonio, and Gratiano arrive. Portia welcomes Antonio, and Nerissa quarrels with Gratiano for having given her ring to the judge's clerk. Hearing them, Portia proclaims that her husband would never have given away her gift when Gratiano reveals that Bassanio has given his ring to the judge. In defense Bassanio argues that Portia would have begged him to give the doctor the ring for saving Antonio's life. Portia and Nerissa vow not to go to bed with their husbands until the rings are returned and vow to go to bed with the doctor and his clerk, who have them. Antonio steps into the quarrel and urges the women to recognize that the rings went to the ones who saved his life. Bassanio asks to be pardoned and vows never again to break an oath with Portia, and Antonio offers to forfeit his life to assure that Bassanio will be true. Portia accepts the arrangement and gives the ring to seal the agreement. Bassanio recognizes it, and Portia reveals their disguises and secrets, and Nerissa returns Gratiano's ring. For Antonio she has a letter telling him that three of his ships have come safely into harbor with rich cargo intact. Nerissa delivers the deed to Lorenzo and Jessica willing all Shylock's possessions to them on his death. Morning has almost arrived and the entire party enters the house.

CHAPTER 1

Background

The Historical Context of *The Merchant of Venice*

Dennis Kay

Dennis Kay relates *The Merchant of Venice* to Shakespeare's developing career and to the broader context of Elizabethan events and social concerns. Kay identifies topical issues reflected in the play, such as mercantilism, conflicting attitudes toward usury, the role of women, and possible references to Shakespeare's personal career. Dennis Kay is the editor of *Sir Philip Sidney: An Anthology of Modern Criticism* and author of *William Shakespeare: His Life and Times* and *William Shakespeare: Sonnets and Poems*.

When in the summer of 1598, the Lord Chamberlain's Men[1] sought to block the unauthorized publication of a successful comedy, the entry in the Stationers' Register referred to "a booke of the Marchaunte of Venyce or otherwise called the Jewe of Venyce." The alternative title suggests that, as in the Henry IV plays, the theatrical prominence of one of the characters[2] had enabled that figure to take on a life independent of—and perhaps in opposition to—the play which spawned it. And that independence, that tendency of Shylock to be viewed separately from the original circumstances of his creation, has created problems, especially in this century. While it has proved possible to provide a feminist interpretation of *The Taming of the Shrew*, what many regard as the manifest anti-Semitism of *The Merchant* has not been so easily argued away.

SHAKESPEARE BRINGS TOGETHER THEMES AND TECHNIQUES

In performance, as in performances of [Christopher] Marlowe's remarkable *The Jew of Malta*, considerable sympathy

1. the company of actors Shakespeare wrote for and acted in 2. a reference to the popular, comic Falstaff

Excerpted from *Shakespeare: His Life, Work, and Era*, by Dennis Kay. Copyright © 1992 by Dennis Kay. Reprinted by permission of William Morrow and Company, Inc.

is aroused for the Jewish figures—though only after they have been shown to conform to crude and hostile stereotypes. In each of the plays, by the end the real focus of attack is the hypocrisy and complacency of the professed Christians. Indeed, the degradation and defeat of the Jew is a spectacle that shows the onstage audience in a distinctly unfavorable light in a way that recalls the endings of the two earlier romantic comedies *Love's Labour's Lost* and *A Midsummer Night's Dream.*

The play brings together material from his earliest comedies—stories from Italian novellas, topics from humanist debate such as the relationship between Justice and Mercy—with techniques and themes from the romantic comedies and the histories. Its juxtaposition of worlds, its collocation of systems of values, as well as its creation of the huge and memorable part of Shylock for Kemp[3], creator of Falstaff and Dogberry [in *Much Ado About Nothing*], to play, locate the script firmly enough in this phase[4] of Shakespeare's writing career. The role played by money is very considerable. Money is woven into the texture of the romance-story of ships and storms, and it is the stuff of which the wooing in the play is made. We are made fully aware of Portia's status as an object, a prize, a commodity. The retreat from the world of business to that of love and retirement in the two earlier comedies has been reversed. If *Henry IV* had examined the place of honor, of chivalry, in the harsh world of politics, *The Merchant* places a series of ideals—love, truth, justice—in the potentially hostile environment of the marketplace.

REFERENCES TO THE LOPEZ AFFAIR

The play mingles the immediate and the faraway, the fairytale with the commercial. Its connection with the world around it is easily demonstrated. It draws upon, for instance, the popular hostility to Jews that had been whipped up in 1594 by the earl of Essex and his supporters in prosecuting a Portuguese Jew called Lopez for treason. Lopez was a physician who had been in the service of the earl of Leicester before being taken on by the queen herself. He became involved in political conspiracy, especially after the arrival

---

3. William Kemp was a great comic actor for whom Shakespeare created roles. 4. between the Early Period and Balanced Period, around 1595–1596

in London in 1592 of Don Antonio, a claimant to the Portuguese throne. But Essex sought to use him in his own intrigues, as a means of cultivating a source of intelligence about Spain and Portugal not available to his gray-bearded colleagues on the Privy Council. Lopez went along with this, but made sure the queen was informed of any new developments before Essex was. This gave rise to bad feeling between the men, and eventually Essex denounced him as a traitor, plotting to poison both Don Antonio and the queen. At first Essex was laughed to scorn and went off to sulk in his chamber. But he came back with new accusations, with more substantial evidence, and stirred up popular anxiety about possible plots and assassinations. In February Lopez was tried and found guilty of plotting the queen's death, and several accomplices were also convicted.

In May Marlowe's *Jew of Malta*, revived for performance at the Rose, appeared in a printed edition. And in June Lopez and his associates were executed, protesting their innocence to the last. The convicted men were taken on a long last journey: by water across the Thames from Westminster to Southwark—we know that Marlowe's play and *Titus Andronicus* were playing that week at Newington Butts, not far away—and then on hurdles over London Bridge and through the crowds up Leadenhall Street and out along what is now Oxford Street to the gibbet at Tyburn. Lopez caused mirth in the crowd at Tyburn by crying out that he loved the queen as much as he loved Jesus Christ. He was then hanged, drawn, and quartered.

The wretched Lopez became a focus for the anxieties of a population encouraged to be afraid of traitors, of cunning fifth columnists in their midst who would stop at nothing to achieve their diabolical ends. And the continuing success of Marlowe's play in revivals after 1594 kept the image—in a distorted, mythologized form—fresh in the minds of citizens.

OTHER HISTORICAL REFLECTIONS

But while Shakespeare may have recalled the Lopez case, and while he obviously drew upon Marlowe's play, the earlier piece was not the occasion or spur for the composition of *The Merchant.* There are several other points of intersection with people and events of the 1590s. The queen's musicians, for instance, included no fewer than eight members of the Bassani family, and there were in Elizabethan London numerous contacts with Venice and the Venetians. It is now usually accepted that *The Merchant* alludes to events much later than 1594. The most obvious instance is the allusion to Essex's capture of two great Spanish galleons off Cadiz in June 1596. One of the ships, the *San Andres*, renamed the *Andrew*, came to stand in the popular mind as the archetypal treasure ship. Its name is used in this way by Salarino in the opening scene of the play:

> I should not see the sandy hourglass run
> But I should think of shallows and of flats,
> And see my wealthy Andrew docked in sand,
> Vailing her high top lower than her ribs
> To kiss her burial. . . .

Even from its early days, British imperialism always had a powerful mercantile element. In proposals for new ventures, whether for expeditions to far-off lands or for more domestic enterprises such as enclosures, investors are promised both honor and profit. The world of the *Merchant*

PORTIA'S LITERAL INTERPRETATION OF THE LAW

In this excerpt from the trial scene in act 4, Portia, disguised as the judge Balthasar, leads Shylock to believe he is winning his case, but in her strict reading of the law, she insists that a pound of flesh excludes even a drop of blood and by measure cannot be more or less than a pound by even a hair. Erring on either point severely threatens Shylock's property and life.

> POR. A pound of that same merchant's flesh is thine.
> The court awards it, and the law doth give it.
> SHY. Most rightful judge!
> POR. And you must cut this flesh from off his breast.
> The law allows it, and the court awards it.
> SHY. Most learned judge! A sentence! Come, prepare!
> POR. Tarry a little. There is something else.
> This bond doth give three here no jot of blood.
> The words expressly are "a pound of flesh."
> Take then thy bond, take thou thy pound of flesh,
> But in the cutting it if thou dost shed
> One drop of Christian blood, thy lands and goods
> Are, by the laws of Venice, confiscate
> Unto the state of Venice.
> GRA. O upright judge! Mark, Jew. O learnèd judge!

corresponds in many ways to that of Elizabethan London, and the competing social and economic forces are shown in their complex interrelationships; and we saw earlier that usury was something with which Shakespeare himself was familiar enough. He was happy to go to court to recover debts, as we shall see. His father had been involved in legal action, and had perhaps lost his fortune, as a result of the confused ways in which Elizabethans tried to reconcile their need to borrow money with their scripture-based conviction that it was an undesirable activity. The play mirrors the contradictions and equivocations in Elizabethan practice, and the presentation of Shylock indicates the deep unease and hostility aroused by the emerging economic system.

This set of problems of tone is connected with the play's variety of styles and diversity of genres. Formally, the play eventually submits to the dictates of the comic form, but it strains at the leash considerably. And some features, notably Shylock himself, almost succeed in taking over the piece and

---

SHY. Is that the law?
POR.   Thyself shalt see the act,
For, as thou urgest justice, be assured
Thou shalt have justice, more than thou desirest.
        GRA. O learnèd judge! Mark, Jew, a learnèd judge!
        SHY. I take this offer, then. Pay the bond thrice
And let the Christian go.
        BASS.   Here is the money.
        POR. Soft![1]
The Jew shall have all justice. Soft! No haste.
He shall have nothing but the penalty.
        GRA. O Jew! An upright judge, a learnèd judge!
        POR. Therefore prepare thee to cut off the flesh.
Shed thou no blood, nor cut thou less nor more
But just a pound of flesh. If thou cut'st more
Or less than a just[2] pound, be it but so much
As makes it light or heavy in the substance,
Or the division of the twentieth part
Of one poor scruple[3]—nay, if the scale do turn
But in the estimation of a hair—
Thou diest and all thy goods are confiscate.

1. Soft: pause a little. 2. just: exact. 3. scruple: minute portion (actually, 20 grains).

The Merchant of Venice, act 4, scene 1, 299–332.

leading it in quite different directions. The problems the audience faces in recognizing the sort of performance being staged for it, and adjusting its expectations accordingly, are related to the moral and interpretative problems that the play addresses. So we can perhaps see *The Merchant*, along with *Much Ado* [*About Nothing*], as Shakespeare's first "problem plays."

The play deals with the problematic relationship between justice and equity, or between the letter and the spirit of the law. This was a topic with which Elizabethans, a most litigious people, were very concerned, as the fifth books of Philip Sidney's romance *Arcadia* and of Edmund Spenser's epic *The Faerie Queene* illustrate. To complicate matters, Shakespeare fills *The Merchant* with biblical language, and it might be thought at first glance that he is staging a conflict between Old Testament literalism championed by Shylock and the new dispensation of Christ as championed by Portia. In an odd and surprising way, the roles are reversed in the trial scene. It is Shylock who keeps to the spirit of the bond, while Portia quibbles about the text of the agreement in a most literal-minded fashion. And, at a broader level, the behavior of the Christians as the play proceeds is—to put it at its mildest—such as to open up a gulf between ideal and practice.

POSSIBLE PERSONAL ISSUES REFLECTED IN THE PLAY

The Merchant is a disturbing play, and it may also reflect anxiety and unease on the part of its author. For although he was building a play from elements he had used before—novella story, gender-reversal, fairytale, and so on—some of them are given a new twist here. An example is the treatment of Portia. Her role may well have been a troubling one for Elizabethans. They had got used to the idea of a female monarch, and in principle were in favor of female education. But Portia takes on the job of a professional at the very moment when the legal profession was establishing, codifying, regulating itself. The situation anticipates the way Helena in *All's Well That Ends Well* joins that other "male" profession, medicine. And it may be that the bawdy exchanges in which Portia is involved in Act V are more than just a comic relief from the tensions of the trial scene, more than a playful use of the same quibbling intelligence that had resolved the crisis. Perhaps Shakespeare shared the nervousness of many of his contemporaries when faced with a woman doing a man's job, and so creates for her a vein of coarseness, of verbal licentiousness, wholly out of keeping with what we have seen before but typifying the male Elizabethan's edgy response to the power of an active and learned woman.

For whatever reason, the play seems to have had a relatively short period of popularity; there are no records of productions between 1605 and the 1740s. After that, it was a different story. Only *Hamlet* has been as frequently performed over the centuries. In the Romantic period *The Merchant* was Shylock's play; like the parts of Hamlet and Richard III, that of Shylock became a central role in the repertoire of the great celebrity actors, with productions habitually built around his melancholy tale. But that is another matter. The Elizabethan *Merchant* was a play of delicate and subtle ensemble writing, where balance, juxtaposition, and shades of comparison combined to create a theatrical experience of marked ambiguity. And these ambiguities seem to have been both deliberate and unconscious. For not only was Shakespeare creating a play of ideas, a challenging problematical work of mixed genre; he was also at some level restaging the situation of parts of his own life and career at the time. Some of the uncertainties are Shakespeare's own.

By the time of *The Merchant* Shakespeare was in a sense suspended between Stratford and London, between the city and the country, between the court and the city, between the rising generation of politicians and their elderly predecessors. He was restoring his family's fortunes both materially and less tangibly with the coat of arms. And it was perhaps just beginning to dawn on him after the death of [his son] Hamnet that his hopes of defeating time, of speaking to posterity, could be focused as much on his occupation as a scriptwriter as upon his reassembling of estates in Stratford.

The Venetian Setting Enhances the Play's Meaning

A.D. Nuttall

A.D. Nuttall, comparing the glamor of Venice to the glamor of Hollywood and Paris of more recent times, describes Venice as a city splendid in riches, luxury, and daring. Nuttall argues that subtly and ironically Shakespeare uses this atmosphere to emphasize contrasting themes: love and money, Jew and Christian, morality and profit, and mercy and justice. A.D. Nuttall, who teaches English at the University of Sussex, was the 1979 winner of the South East Arts Literature Prize. He is the author of *Overheard by God: Fiction and Prayer in Herbert, Milton, Dante, and St. John.*

Venice, to the Elizabethans, was in some ways what Hollywood was to the rest of the world in the 1930s, or perhaps it would be better to say a mixture of Hollywood and Paris: *the* glamorous, daring, brilliant, wicked city. Even today as the senile, jewel-encrusted Bride of the Adriatic sinks malodorously beneath the waters of the Lagoon, one can glimpse, in the real city, what the effect must once have been. The rest of the world is black, white and grey and here alone, among gilded lions, rosy brick and white marble stained with green, is the Coloured City. The most neutral description of Venice begins to sound like overwriting. Many things, to be sure, have changed. The city of sexual licence has become oddly puritanical; notices in the *vaporetto* stops[1] alert the visitor to the possible indecorousness of his or her costume. Meanwhile the frescoed walls still blaze with the great

1. ferry boat and steamer stops along the canals

Venetian scenes of social splendour, ruffs, brocade, fruit, wine and amazing people. . . .

Venice was the single, most spectacular example of the power of wealth to beget wealth, and its miraculous setting in the sea is emblematic of that power. Venice is the landless landlord over all.

The crucial part of this finds expression in Shakespeare's *The Merchant of Venice*. It is in a way futile to search for the sources of Shakespeare's knowledge of Venice. . . . London was full of vigorous talk and Venice was an excellent subject of conversation. For all we know Shakespeare may have visited Venice himself in 'the missing years'. The word 'merchant' alerts us first. In his plays set in England merchants hardly figure. We may revive the original impact of the title if we substitute 'the Capitalist' for 'the Merchant', but such 'equivalents' are never truly equivalent. Then, the imagery of money, the chink of coins pervades this play as it does no other. Moreover, this golden imagery is in places pointed very sardonically;[2] it is applied with an almost brutal directness to the central romantic love story of the play. . . .

THE VALUE OF MONEY IS UNCONSCIOUSLY ASSUMED

The Merchant of Venice offers a disquieting simplicity. Bassanio tells of his love in these words:

> In Belmont is a lady richly left,
> And she is fair and fairer than that word,
> Of wondrous virtues.

(I. i. 161–2)

First he tells us of the money and then, in simple, joyous juxtaposition, of her beauty and virtue. Bassanio is not an out-and-out fortune-hunter who is after Portia for her money. He really loves her and her wealth is simply a component of her general attractiveness. There is a certain repellent ingenuousness about Bassanio. He can trust his own well-constituted nature. It would never allow him to fall in love with a poor woman; for, after all, poor women are not attractive. After such a start a strange light is cast on the rest of his speech:

> her sunny locks
> Hang on her temples like a golden fleece,
> Which makes her seat of Belmont Colchos' strond,
> And many Jasons come in quest of her.[3]

(I. i. 169–72)

---

2. scornfully; mockingly 3. Jason sailed to the shore of Colchos in the *Argo* to fetch away the Golden Fleece.

The Golden Fleece in another context would have been a paradox of love language. Here it is uncomfortably close to the centre of Bassanio's interest.

Shakespeare deliberately involves Bassanio's love from the outset in a faintly humiliating financial atmosphere. But he plants no overt stylistic signals of what he is about so that the effect is faint indeed. . . . Bassanio's first move in his courtship is less than heroic. It is to touch his friend Antonio for a loan so that he can improve his sartorial image.

It is curious how wit can consist in the very avoidance of an expected complexity. One may compare the conversational practice known in the slang of forty years ago as 'kidding on the level'; the speaker makes a remark which sounds ironic but the real joke lies in the fact that every word is literally intended: 'Hello darling, you know I hate your guts.' Shakespeare with his strangely bland coupling in this play of the language of love and the language of money is in a manner kidding on the level. Even Portia, who is generous in her love, speaks of her own money as one of her attractions in a strangely unconscious manner when she says to Bassanio,

> You see me, Lord Bassanio, where I stand,
> Such as I am. Though for myself alone
> I would not be ambitious in my wish
> To wish myself much better, yet for you
> I would be trebled twenty times myself,
> A thousand times more fair, ten thousand times more rich,
> That only to stand high in your account[4]
> I might in virtues, beauties, livings[5], friends,
> Exceed account. But the full sum of me
> Is sum of something which, to term in gross,
> Is an unlesson'd girl.
>
> (III. ii. 149–60)

Notice how wealth is twice placed at the summit of an ascending rhetorical scale involving character and beauty. The accountant's language, 'to term in gross', is uncomfortably close to what is actually going on. An imprudent director—I could not call him perverse—might well have Bassanio surprised by these words in the very act of appraising with his eye the value of the room's hangings.

But Portia is not really unconscious. She understands Bassanio with that peculiar, pitiless clarity of love which char-

4. estimation 5. possessions

acterizes all the great Shakespearean heroines, these women who so utterly transcend their contemptible lovers. After she has said that she will pay off Antonio's debt for Bassanio, she says to her betrothed,

Since you are dear bought, I will love you dear.

(III. ii. 315)

The play on 'dear' is not wholly comfortable and, at the same time, the love is real and unstinting.

It is perhaps not surprising that this speech should help to make one of the principal 'echoes' of the play:

'Tis dearly bought, 'tis mine, and I will have it.

(IV. i. 100)

This time it is not one of the nice people who speaks. It is Shylock and he is talking about a pound of flesh cut from the breast of Antonio.

SHAKESPEARE IRONICALLY BLENDS MONEY, MORALITY, AND LOVE

The Merchant of Venice is about the Old Law and the New; about the low Jewish justice of an eye for an eye and a tooth for a tooth and the way this justice is transcended by Christian charity and mercy. The climactic trial scene is archetypal. The black-clad Jew haggling for the flesh of the fair-skinned Christian, the supervening figure of Justice who is also Love, all this is the stuff of legend. It recalls the medieval *Processus Belial*, as has often been observed, in which the Virgin Mary defends Man against the Devil who lays legal claim to his soul. Behind this analogue lies the doctrine of the atonement itself, in which God paid the legal price for man with his son who was also himself. In the fact of such powerful patterning all ethical ambiguities, we shall be told, must surely fall silent. The Jew is wicked, unhappy, usurious, greedy, vengeful. The Christians are happy, generous, forgiving. This, it might be said, is the plain meaning of the play, and it takes a determined 'Transparent' critic to darken it. In fact it is not difficult to do so. For as soon as we enter the fiction and treat the figures of the drama as possible human beings in a possible, great mercantile city, everything feels slightly different.

It is true, of course, that certain archetypes operate powerfully in the play. But it is not true that they are the only thing there, that the mind should be arrested at their level of generality, that there is nothing behind them. It is Shakespeare's way to take an archetype or a stereotype and then work, so to speak, against it, without ever overthrowing it. Shakespeare himself darkens the pristine clarity of these ethical oppositions and he does so, in the first instance, with allusions to money. To this he adds the figure of Antonio, about whom shadows gather from the beginning. If Bassanio's love for Portia sounds uneasily shallow and mercenary, Antonio's love for Bassanio is disquietingly intense. The stereotypical impression of Christian society in *The Merchant of Venice* is of a world of felicity, conviviality, parties, easy commerce of like spirits, harmony. In all this Antonio is from the first incongruous. He is melancholic. Later, when he is in great peril, he sees himself as in some way polluted and wishes to die:

> I am a tainted[6] wether[7] of the flock,
> Meetest for death; the weakest kind of fruit
> Drops earliest to the ground, and so let me.
>
> (IV. i. 114–16)

In the first scene of the play Antonio is left alone with Bassanio and says, with an air of one coming to the point,

> Well; tell me now what lady is the same
> To whom you swore a secret pilgrimage,
> That you to-day promis'd to tell me of?
>
> (I. i. 119–21)

Bassanio does not answer, but dwells at length on his lack of cash. Antonio with extreme generosity places at his friend's disposal,

> My purse, my person, my extremest means.
>
> (I. i. 138)

The reference to 'person' and 'extremest means' evidently looks forward to the horror so narrowly averted in Act IV. . . .

Antonio loves Bassanio with a love so intense as to throw Bassanio's more decorous love for Portia into unhappy relief. Some may feel that this secondary inference is merely monstrous and inherently improbable. But in a manner the thought of Antonio in love occurred to Solanio within the play before it occurred to any spectator or reader outside it, for at I. i. 46 he suddenly says to Antonio,

> Why, then, you are in love.

Antonio answers, 'Fie, fie!' Solanio treats this as a negative but, strictly speaking, it is not. The New Arden editor J. Russell Brown notes with admirable precision that it is 'an ex-

6. diseased. 7. castrated ram

clamation of reproach rather than a clear negative'. Of course Solanio does not suggest that Antonio is in love with Bassanio. He merely plants the idea that Antonio's melancholy is connected with love and then the play itself, with overwhelming singleness of purpose, directs us to a single love object. Antonio's love is exercised against the bias of financial interest. Setting aside the more obvious impediments, one could not imagine Antonio speaking of Bassanio in the unconsciously self-interested way Bassanio spoke of Portia. Bassanio sees Portia as the centre of his future happiness and wealth. Antonio looks very differently at Bassanio; he sees the beloved extinction of both wealth and happiness.

A seed is thus planted at the back of our minds and the progress of the drama brings it to an obscure flowering. In II. viii Solanio describes the parting of Bassanio and Antonio, in which Antonio was unable to hold back his tears, and comments, 'I think he only loves the world for him' (II. viii. 50). While the dapper Bassanio seeks joy and a fortune in Belmont, Antonio, for mere love, faces mutilation and death in the city. When all seems to be over Antonio says to Bassanio,

> Commend me to your honourable wife;
> Tell her the process of Antonio's end;
> Say how I lov'd you; speak me fair in death;
> And, when the tale is told, bid her be judge
> Whether Bassanio had not once a love.
>
> (IV. i. 268–72)

The story of the caskets ceases to be an inert, decorative centrepiece and becomes charged with latent irony. Bassanio, dressed up to the nines with someone else's money, is mockingly rewarded with the gift proper to plain virtue. The leaden casket bore as its legend,

> Who chooseth me must give and hazard all he hath.
>
> (II. vii. 16)

W.H. Auden in one of the most brilliant critical remarks of the century observed that this requirement is met by two people in the play, neither of whom is Bassanio. It is met by Antonio and Shylock. That is where the real *agon*[8] lies. . . .

ECONOMIC REALITIES IN VENICE

In the course of the play we are told certain things about the state of Venice. The Christians have among them 'many a

---

8. a conflict, especially between the protagonist and antagonist in a drama

purchased slave' (IV. i. 90). Jews are employed when ready capital is needed. They are considered as aliens (as emerges when Shylock forfeits his goods and places his life at the Doge's, mercy, on the ground that he sought the life of a *Venetian* citizen). All this Auden brings out in his admirable essay. Shakespeare is clearly aware of the covert manner in which Christian merchants make money breed, which is by the ancient doctrine a kind of usury ('usury' originally referred to any form of interest and was later—very revealingly—restricted to *excessive* interest). Shakespeare is likewise aware of the lower, 'coarser' kinds of interest for which Shylock and his kind are needed. He shows with great clarity the almost exclusively mercantile character of the Venetian economy:

> the trade and profit of the city
> Consisteth of all nations.

> (III. iii. 30–1)

Here it is Antonio who speaks. . . .

A recent historian of Venice in the sixteenth century, Brian Pullan, notes, 'Jews were deemed to be there for the purpose of saving Christians from committing the sin of usurious lending', and again, 'The Venetians had consistently combined the attitude of ritual contempt for the Jews with a shrewd and balanced appreciation of their economic utility.' He quotes the diarist, Marino Sanuto, 'Jews are even more necessary than bakers to a city, and especially to this one, for the sake of the general welfare.' It is quite obvious that Shakespeare, Sanuto, Pullan are all discussing a single, real object. . . .

Thus as the Christians need the Jews, so the Jews need the Christians to practise usury on. The symbiosis is more perfectly symmetrical than we may have thought. Shylock, however, breaks with his religion, in particular with *Deuteronomy* 24:6, when he agrees to take Antonio's *life* as a pledge. The passage in *Deuteronomy* uses the metaphor of a millstone: 'No man shall take the nether or the upper millstone to pledge: for he taketh a man's life to pledge'; the metaphor suggests that 'life' is here equivalent to 'means of living'. We may compare *Ecclesiasticus* 34:22, 'He that taketh away his neighbour's living, slayeth him.' Shylock makes precisely this equation at IV. i. 371–2:

> you take my life
> When you do take the means, whereby I live.

This pattern of scriptural reference would tend to reinforce an impression, already subliminally present in the play, that the Christians, in taking away Shylock's capital, are doing to him what he wished to do to Antonio. The act of mercy has an inner likeness to the act of revenge. Shakespeare completes the ironic pattern by making Antonio say to Portia, 'Sweet lady, you have given me life and living' V. i. 286). It is typical of Shakespeare's genius that in his great comedy of economic reality he finds the single point where language most powerfully asserts the interdependence of economics and humanity, in the etymological affinity between a person's *life* and a person's *living*. This is in its turn analogous to the economic and ethical meanings of *worth* and *value.* . . .

THE ECONOMIC REALITY OF VENICE DEFINES MORALITY

That Shakespeare's picture of Venice is not one of minute, documentary accuracy is obvious. The law shown in this play, for example, is fairy-tale law, not real law. But Shakespeare's art in this play remains—not only in the obvious triumphs of probable human motivation at the level of individual character, but also at the less accessible level of influences and conditions—cognitive, with a breath-taking intelligence. He saw the economic peculiarity of Venice and then made the second, greater leap of perceiving how an economic fabric may condition the very nature of moral action: mercy and charity lose their primal simplicity; in the new order personal loyalty, bereft of traditional feudal support, is both sharpened and made more dubious. . . .

We are in danger of forgetting the real generosity, however produced, of the Christians, the real ferocity, however explained, of Shylock. They did forgive Shylock. Shylock would have torn open the breast of Antonio. These are things which no theatrical experience of the play will ever let you forget. As William Empson says, we must view the Bassanio-Portia relationship with 'a generous scepticism which can believe at once that people are and are not guilty.' So Shakespeare will not let us rest even here. The subversive counterthesis is itself too easy. We may now begin to see that he is perhaps the least sentimental dramatist who ever lived. We begin to understand what is meant by holding the mirror up to nature.

CHAPTER 2

Major Themes

READINGS ON
THE MERCHANT OF VENICE

The Merchant of Venice: A Critique of Puritanism

Paul N. Siegel

Paul N. Siegel maintains that *The Merchant of Venice* remains relevant to readers at the end of the twentieth century. He contends that Shylock is hypocritical, selfish, and morally rigid, reflecting Elizabethan attitudes toward Puritanism and American attitudes of racism. Shylock's defeat is a triumph of health and life. According to Siegel, Shylock embodies the images of the medieval stereotype of Jews, the rigid religious Puritan, and the racial bigot. Paul N. Siegel, who taught at Long Island University in New York, is the author of *Shakespearean Tragedy and the English Compromise* and *His Infinite Variety: Major Shakespearean Criticism Since Johnson.*

What can Shylock mean for us in the twentieth century, with the inexpugnable memory of Auschwitz[1] in our minds?.... While it is true that Shylock was for the Elizabethans the Jew of medieval legend, he was not merely that; he also had contemporary significance. It is through an understanding of Shylock's meaning for the Elizabethans that I believe we can come to an understanding of his meaning for our own time.

Shylock, as we shall see, must have strongly reminded the Elizabethans of the Puritans in their midst, for these early Puritans were a minority of outsiders who were sharply attacked and derided. They were, of course, the fathers of our own Pilgrim fathers. Shylock is not only the ancestor, then, of the American Jews whose grandparents came to this country from European ghettos but, in a sense, of the Amer-

1. World War II concentration camp, site of mass extermination of Jews, who were demonized by the Nazis

icans who proudly trace their family line to the Mayflower passengers. . . .

THE CONNECTION BETWEEN JEWISH MONEY LENDER AND PURITAN USURER

The connection between the villainous Jewish moneylender of folk tradition, whom Shakespeare made a richly colorful figure, the member of an alien, exotic race, and the Elizabethan Puritan usurer is not pointed up by any direct allusion in the play. However, a contemporary audience, alive to the issues of its own time, does not need the pointers that posterity does. . . .

There are many expressions of Elizabethan opinion that indicate that Puritanism was a similar generally current concern and that Judaism, Puritanism and usury were so connected in the popular mind that many of Shylock's traits would have reminded Shakespeare's audience of the Puritan usurers of its own time. In the romantic world of *The Merchant of Venice* the audience could catch piquant resemblances to the world with which it was familiar.

Usury was a burning social issue of the day. Always excoriated, the moneylender was a man of increasing importance during this period of nascent capitalism, squeezing landowners impoverished by fixed rents at a time of rising prices and squeezing craftsmen no longer producing for a local market but for a complex commercial organization and in need of credit to maintain production. The moneylender appeared an arrant individualist, who for his own selfish purposes disrupted the traditional relationships of a hierarchical society founded upon the laws of man's nature.

The association of usury and Puritanism appears as early as 1572 in [politician and writer] Thomas Wilson's *Discourse Upon Usury.* The contemporary usurer, Wilson repeats several times, is worse than the Jewish moneylender, who no longer existed in England since Judaism was outlawed. The Jewish moneylender, Wilson observes, had at least followed his own creed and did not pretend to be a member of the Christian commonwealth. And the typical contemporary usurer is the Puritan. . . .

PURITAN HYPOCRISY AND SHYLOCK'S HYPOCRISY

The common accusation made by the satirists and dramatists against the Puritans was that they were hypocrites. Thus [writer Thomas] Nashe includes under hypocrisy "all

Machiavilisme, puritanisme, and outward gloasing with a mans enemie." Critics who have sought to soften Shakespeare's picture of Shylock have failed to notice his consummate hypocrisy; they accept his statement that his proposal of a pound of flesh as surety is a "merry sport" (I. iii. 146) and find that he only desires payment after his thirst for revenge has been aroused by the elopement of Jessica. But Shylock is not a man for "merry sport."

As soon as Antonio enters, Shylock expresses in soliloquy his profound hatred for him as a Christian who brings down the rate of interest by lending gratis in "low simplicity" (the audience would have understood it to be in Christian charity)....

Until Shylock announces his desire for revenge in a burst of rage, he continues to be hypocritical. In spite of his previously declared religious scruples at dining with Christians, he accepts Bassanio's invitation to join him in the fellowship of the banquet-table, but he goes "in hate, to feed upon/ The prodigal Christian" (II. v. 14–15). So too does he recommend Launcelot Gobbo to Bassanio, not out of friendliness to either, but with the design of ridding himself of a heavy-eating, inefficient servant and fastening him as an added expense upon Bassanio.

Puritan hypocrisy was generally portrayed as taking the form of a pretence of being better than other men, and the Puritan was presented as stiff-necked rather than obsequious, but he could be made on occasion to be self-abasing if it served his need....

SHYLOCK AS A PURITAN STEREOTYPE

Shylock's pharisaism,[2] like that of the Puritans, takes the form of contempt for merrymaking and revelry. "What, are there masques?" he exclaims in the very accents of the Puritan.

> Hear you me, Jessica:
> Lock up my doors; and when you hear the drum
> And the vile squealing of the wry-necked[3] fife,
> Clamber not you up to the casements[4] then,
> Nor thrust your head into the public street
> To gaze on Christian fools with varnish'd[5] faces,
> But stop my house's ears, I mean my casements:
> Let not the sound of shallow foppery enter
> My sober house.
>
> (II. v. 28–36)

2. characteristic of the Pharisees, who were known for their hypocritical observance of the letter of the religious and moral law without regard for the spirit; sanctimoniousness 3. making the player twist his neck 4. windows that open on hinges 5. wearing painted masks

His narrow, ungenerous mind, meanly restricted to money-making, renders him incapable of unbending to laughter; it is the antithesis of the well-rounded personality of the Renaissance gentleman Bassanio.

Like the morally rigid Puritans, Shylock is intolerant of others and attributes to them his own spiritual defects. Immediately after Launcelot has pointed up for us the contrast between Bassanio's munificence and Shylock's miserliness, Shylock tells Launcelot that Bassanio will not allow him to eat and sleep all day long as he did. . . .

Shylock's malevolence is presented as diabolically inhuman. Medieval literature had given the story of man's redemption in the symbolic form of his being freed by the "ransom" of Christ from a bond to the Devil, an unrelenting creditor with the characteristics of a usurer. The Jew had also been portrayed as a devil serving Satan. By having Shylock referred to as a devil again and again, Shakespeare continued this tradition. But Puritans as well as Jews were called devils in Shakespeare's time. Certain that they were on the side of the angels, Anglicans regarded all those not of their party as being of the devil's party and made "the Devil is a Puritan" a cant phrase. The pious exterior of the Puritan, it was charged, concealed the spirit of the Devil. Those who owed money to a Puritan usurer found that they had the devil to pay. . . .

The Elizabethan satire of Puritanism does not, of course, present the whole truth about it, just as the medieval stereotype that Shakespeare borrowed does not tell the truth about Jews of the time. No doubt both Elizabethan Puritans and medieval Jews did exhibit traits that were the result of their social and economic positions, but these traits were caricatured by hostile observers. . . . The achievements through history of both Puritans and Jews could not have been predicted from the stereotypes available to Shakespeare.

SHYLOCK EXEMPLIFIES A UNIVERSAL MISERLY SPIRIT

But if neither stereotype has validity today, why does Shylock still hold our attention? I suggest that, accurately understood, he is both comic and frightening because he portrays the worst side of the new capitalist individualism born in Shakespeare's time. He is the spirit of that economic self-seeking which is indifferent to the welfare of others, stultifying those whom it possesses and oppressing the rest of humanity. Jewishness, Puritanism, usury are only incidental; this spirit is what is universal in him. One does not need to be hostile toward Jews to laugh at his comic rigidity and shudder at his ferocious hatred of all those who oppose his purposes. . . .

As Tubal alternately tells him of Antonio's losses and of Jessica's spending, and as he responds first with exultation and then with dismay, Shylock is like a marionette being jerked this way and that. The scene has been prepared for by a description of him running through the streets calling for his jewels, his daughter and his ducats; each is only a lost possession whose competing claim with the others for his grief drives him to comic distraction. In his frenzy he resembles a mechanism controlled by two push-buttons, whirling crazily when both buttons are pressed at once. All of the previous suffering of his race is as nothing compared with his present suffering over monetary losses; he wishes his daughter dead if he might recover his jewels: "The curse never fell upon our nation till now, I never felt it till now—two thousand ducats in that, and other precious, precious jewels. I would my daughter were dead at my foot, and the jewels in her ear" (III. i. 89–93). With Jessica safely away, Shylock's bizarre, inhuman behavior becomes comical.

This element of the comical remains as the time for settling accounts approaches, although the element of the sinister now predominates. Shylock displays that "professional callousness" which is "a mode of pride." "Gaoler, look to him," he exclaims. "Tell me not of mercy,/ This is the fool that lent out money gratis" (III. iii. 1–3). Those like Antonio, who are not governed by his business code, he looks upon as fools. He himself can think no other way. "I'll have my bond," (III. iii. 4) he vows, in comic repetition. The bond, the sacred business contract, is all. When Portia suggests that a doctor stand by to prevent Antonio from bleeding to death in discharging his debt, Shylock replies, "I cannot find it, 'tis not in the bond" (IV. i. 262). If compassion is not written into the contract, then one is not under any obligation to feel it or act by it.

SHYLOCK SYMBOLIZES RACISM

Ironically, Shylock, the typical Jew for the anti-Semites, is like the hate-filled racist. Inflexibly insisting on committing his senseless cruelty, he states:

You'll ask me, why I rather choose to have
A weight of carrion flesh, than to receive
Three thousand ducats. I'll not answer that,
But say it is my humour;[6] is it answered?
What if my house be troubled with a rat,
And I be pleased to give ten thousand ducats
To have it ban'd.[7] What, are you answered yet? . . .
So I can give no reason, nor I will not,
More than a lodg'd[8] hate, and a certain loathing
I bear Antonio.

(IV. i. 40–61)

To Bassanio's "Do all men kill the things they do not love?"
he retorts, "Hates any man the thing he would not kill?" (IV.
i. 66–67). These words, in their avowal of an irrational hatred that will be satisfied only by killing, in their comparison
of men with rats to be similarly exterminated, breathe forth
the spirit of the gas chambers [at Auschwitz]. If he does not
understand now the reasons for his hatred, he had earlier
revealed the underlying spring that impels him to action:

I hate him for he is a Christian
But more, for that in low simplicity
He lends out money gratis, and brings down
The rate of usance[9] here with us in Venice.

(I. iii. 43–47)

Antonio, an outsider, has intruded upon Shylock's business,
does not play according to the rules of the business game
and is making things difficult for him. Shylock's feeling is
the sort that a middle-class anti-Semite today might voice
concerning a Jewish business competitor.

Although Shylock has the psychology of the racist, he has
the external features of the medieval stereotype of the Jew—a
stereotype which, by the way, resembles the contemporary
racist stereotype of the Negro: each is presented as bogey-
man, beast and buffoon; the image of the Negro with the ra-
zor is the counterpart of the image of the Jew with the knife.
The cannibalistic images, associated with Shylock throughout the play, are suggestive of the medieval legend, continuing through the Renaissance, that Jews delighted in secretly
feasting on the flesh of murdered Christians. That Shylock,
despite his possessing characteristics of the Jew of medieval
legend, is not *merely* a fairy-tale monster is due to Shakespeare's having breathed life into the stereotype by giving
him the spirit of the contemporary *home economicus.*

6. whim 7. poisoned 8. deep-seated 9. usury; excessive interest

Shylock's defeat at the hands of Portia is the joyous triumph of the harmonious society over the disturbing force which threatens it, the triumph of the healthy, balanced person over mechanical codes (the law of Venice is on Shylock's side), the triumph of life over death. The successive escapes of the irrepressible Launcelot Gobbo, who is representative of the life-force, and of the charming, witty Jessica from the gloomy household of the humorless Shylock prefigure this triumph. *The Merchant of Venice* is indeed what [critic] Susanne Langer calls comedy: "an image of human vitality holding its own in the world." It is not a problem play.

The Merchant of Venice Portrays a World of Love and Music

Mark Van Doren

Poet and critic Mark Van Doren argues that Shakespeare weaves themes of love, money, generosity, and music together to create a happy and essentially comic atmosphere in *The Merchant of Venice.* Though Shylock, with his rasping voice, ugly speech, and cruel intent, threatens this atmosphere, the other players isolate him and throw him out. Moreover, Van Doren argues that Shylock evokes no pity, a necessary element to consider him a tragic figure. Mark Van Doren, who taught at Columbia University in New York, is the author of *Collected Poems,* a book of short stories, and critical studies of Henry David Thoreau, John Dryden, E.A. Robinson, and Nathaniel Hawthorne.

When Bassanio declares, early in the comedy of which he is so casually the hero, "To you, Antonio, I owe the most, in money and in love" (I, i, 130–1), he characterizes the world he lives in and the only world he knows. It is once more, and fully now, the gentlemen's world whose tentative capital for Shakespeare had been Verona. The capital moves to Venice; the atmosphere enriches itself until no element is lacking; and a story is found, or rather a complex of stories is assembled, which will be adequate to the golden air breathed on fair days and through soft nights by creatures whose only function is to sound in their lives the dear depths of human grace. In such a world, or at any rate in such inhabitants of it, there is no incompatibility between money and love. Shylock cannot reconcile the two; but Shylock is not of this world, as the quality of his voice, so harshly discordant with the dominant voices of the play, will inform any attentive ear.

In Belmont is a lady richly left, and Bassanio does not hesitate to say that Portia's wealth is necessary to his happiness. But it is necessary only as a condition; that she is fair and good—how much of either he has still to learn—is more than necessary, it is important. She will tell him when he has won her by the right choice of caskets that she wishes herself, for his sake, still richer than she is—not merely in money but in "virtues, beauties, livings, friends" (III, ii, 158). All of which, sincerely as it is spoken, does not obscure or deny the background for this life of an enormous and happy wealth. The play opens with a conversation between gentlemen whose voices sigh and smile with thoughts of riches. Salarino cannot believe but that Antonio's mind is tossing on the gilded ocean:

> There, where your argosies[1] with portly[2] sail,
> Like signiors and rich burghers[3] on the flood,
> Or, as it were, the pageants[4] of the sea,
> Do overpeer[5] the petty traffickers
> That curtsy to them, do them reverence,
> As they fly by them with their woven wings.[6]
>
> (I, i, 9–14)

He appears to be wrong, but his eloquence has supplied a correct symbol for these folk of whom he is one: for these arrogant yet gentle creatures whose fine clothes stream on the air of Venice and whose golden, glancing talk tosses, curtsies, and plays a constant music among their still uncorrupted thoughts.

The Play's Sadness Touched by Grace

Antonio is abstracted and sad for no reason that he knows. Shakespeare's source named a reason, but it has been suppressed in the interest of a mood the play must have. Melancholy in this world must not have in it any over-ripeness as in the case of Jaques, any wildness as in the case of Hamlet, any savagery as in the case of Timon.[7] It must remain a grace, perhaps the distinctive grace of this life which is still young enough for satiety to mean not sourness, not spiritual disease, but a beautiful sadness of that sort which it is the highest pleasure not to explore. Much is said of satiety. Por-

---

1. An argosy is a great merchantship. 2. swelling 3. citizens, businessmen 4. spectacles, such as are shown on floats in a parade 5. look down on 6. sails 7. Jaques in *As You Like It*, Hamlet in *Hamlet*, and Timon in *Timon of Athens*

tia and Nerissa begin their scene (I, ii) with talk of weariness and surfeit. But it is charming talk, unclouded by any such "unmannerly sadness" as Portia soon criticizes in her suitor the County Palatine, who suggests "a death's-head with a bone in his mouth." The sadness of her class is a mannerly sadness. Antonio knows with Gratiano that all things

Are with more spirit chased than enjoy'd.

(II, vi, 13)

But he has not known it long enough to become other than what Bassanio calls him:

The dearest friend to me, the kindest man,
The best-condition'd and unwearied spirit
In doing courtesies.

(III, ii, 295–7)

He wearies himself with his want-wit sadness, and thinks he wearies others; but he is not too tired for courtesies, and Bassanio's concern for him when news comes to Belmont of Shylock's insistence on the bond is deep, unspoiled, and serious. Antonio can say

I am a tainted[8] wether of the flock,
Meetest for death,

(IV, i, 114–5)

without causing embarrassment in his hearers or incurring the charge of self-love. He is in short one of Shakespeare's gentlemen: one who wears darker clothes than his friends but knows perfectly how to wear them.

LOVE AND GENEROSITY

Love is the natural language of these men and women: love, and its elder brother generosity. Not generosity to Shylock, for he is of another species, and cannot receive what he will not give. But generosity to all friends, and an unmeasured love. The word love lies like a morsel of down in the nest of nearly every speech, and the noblest gestures are made in its name. Portia's surrender to Bassanio of

This house, these servants, and this same myself

(III, ii, 172)

is absolute. And so is the gift of Antonio's life to Bassanio, for there are more kinds of love here than one.

I think he only loves the world for him,

(II, viii, 50)

8. diseased

says Salanio, and Antonio counts on Bassanio's silent understanding of the truth. "If your love do not persuade you to come," he writes to him at Belmont, "let not my letter" (III, ii, 323–5). Nor is there any rivalry between Antonio and Portia. It is enough for her that he is her husband's friend:

> that this Antonio,
> Being the bosom lover of my lord,
> Must needs be like my lord.
>
> (III, iv, 16–8)

And it is enough for him that she is his friend's beloved:

> Commend me to your honourable wife.
> Tell her the process of Antonio's end;
> Say how I lov'd you, speak me fair in death,
> And, when the tale is told, bid her be judge
> Whether Bassanio had not once a love.
>
> (IV, i, 273–7)

Neither man knows that Portia is listening to this, but the fact that she is, and that "The Merchant of Venice" is after all a comedy, does not invalidate the mood.

The language of love is among other things intellectual. So we are not surprised to encounter abstractions in the graceful discourse of our lords and ladies. They are what make it, indeed, as graceful as it is, with its expert alternation of short and long words, its accomplished and elaborate ease such as Shylock's tongue never knows. It is natural for Portia to credit Antonio with

> a like proportion
> Of lineaments, of manners, and of spirit
>
> (III, iv, 14–5)

to that of Bassanio, "her governor her king." It is as natural for her to speak of mercy as a "quality" and an "attribute" as it is for her to reveal upon occasion that nippiness of wit which keeps the conversation of all such people sound and sweet.

> Fie, what a question's that,
> if thou wert near a lewd interpreter![9]
>
> (III, iv, 79–80)

> I'll have that doctor for my bedfellow.
>
> (V, i, 233)

The intellect and the wit, and the familiarity with abstractions, have much to do with the effect of music which is so strong and pure throughout "The Merchant of Venice." Not

---

9. one who sees a lewd meaning in her words

only do the words of the lovers maintain an unbroken, high, golden chime; but actual music is frequently in our ears.

> Let music sound while he doth make his choice;
> Then, if he lose, he makes a swan-like end,[10]
> Fading in music.
>
> (III, ii, 43–5)

So Portia commands as Bassanio broods before the caskets. And there is no clearer sign that the world is itself again when Shylock goes than the burst of melody, both verbal and performed, with which the fifth act soars upon recovered wings. The sweet wind, the sweet moonlight, the sweet soul of Jessica melt into one singing whole with the sweet touches, the sweet harmony, the sweet power of music.

> I am never merry when I hear sweet music
>
> (V, i, 69)

sighs Jessica with mannerly sadness. But that is as it should be in the world of Belmont and Venice; and there is of course Portia's wit to civilize the scene.

> He knows me as the blind man knows the cuckoo,
> By the bad voice.
>
> (V, i, 112–3)

Nor are these people unaware that ultimate music is unheard. "We cannot hear," says Lorenzo, the harmony that is in immortal souls. Much as they love music, they love the melodies of silence more.

> Soft stillness and the night
> Become the touches of sweet harmony,
>
> (V, i, 56–7)

says Lorenzo now, for somewhat the same reason that Bassanio had once found the plainness of a leaden casket moving him more than eloquence (III, ii, 106), and still earlier had fallen in love with Portia, because of the "fair speechless messages" he received from her eyes. Music no less than love is absolute in the world of Venice and Belmont.

[Playwright] Nicholas Rowe in 1709 was of the opinion that Shylock's contribution to the play made it a tragedy. "There appears in it such a deadly spirit of revenge, such a savage fierceness and fellness, and such a bloody designation of cruelty and mischief, as cannot agree either with the style or characters of comedy." As time has gone on this has come more and more to seem true. Yet it is but a seeming

---

10. Swans were supposed to sing only once, just before death.

truth. Shylock is so alien to the atmosphere of the whole, so hostile and in his hostility so forceful, that he threatens to rend the web of magic happiness woven for the others to inhabit. But the web holds, and he is cast out. If the world of the play has not all along been beautiful enough to suggest its own natural safety from such a foe, it becomes so in a fifth act whose felicity of sound permits no memory of ducats and bonds and long knives whetted on the heel. Comedy or not, "The Merchant of Venice" by such means rescues its tone. If this is not comedy, there is no other in the play. The possibilities in Gratiano's loquacity are never developed, and the Gobbos are poor clowns.

SHYLOCK RUNS CONTRARY TO THE PLAY'S TONE AND MUSIC

The voice of Shylock comes rasping into the play like a file; the edge of it not only cuts but tears, not only slices but saws. He is always repeating phrases, half to himself, as misers do—hoarding them if they are good, unwilling to give them wings so that they may spend themselves generously in the free air of mutual talk.

> Three thousand ducats; well. . . .
> For three months; well. . . .
> Antonio shall become bound; well.
>
> (I, iii, 1–6)

They are short phrases; niggardly, ugly, curt. They are a little hoarse from their hoarding, a little rusty with disuse. And the range of their sound is from the strident to the rough, from the scratchy to the growled.

> The patch[11] is kind enough, but a huge feeder;
> Snail-slow in profit, and he sleeps by day
> More than the wild-cat. Drones hive not with me.
>
> (II, v, 46–8)

The names of animals are natural to his tongue, which knows for the most part only concrete things, and crackles with reminders of brute matter. Salarino, musing of shipwrecks in the opening scene, bethinks him straight of dangerous rocks,

> Which, touching but my gentle vessel's side,
> Would scatter all her spices on the stream,
> Enrobe the roaring waters with my silks.
>
> (I, i, 32–4)

Shylock in the third scene rewrites Salarino's passage in his own idiom:

11. fool

> But ships are but boards, sailors but men; there be land-rats
> and water-rats, water-thieves and land-thieves, I mean pi-
> rates, and then there is the peril of waters, winds, and rocks.
>
> (I, iii, 21-5)

Land-rats, and water-rats: the very sound of the words announces their malice, confesses the satisfaction with which
their speaker has cursed them as they left his lips. He will go
on in the play to remind us of the cur, the goat, the pig, the
cat, the ass, the monkey, and the mule.

> *Tubal.* One of them showed me a ring that he had of your
> daughter for a monkey.
>
> *Shylock.* Out upon her! Thou torturest me, Tubal. It was my
> turquoise; I had it of Leah when I was a bachelor. I would not
> have given it for a wilderness of monkeys.
>
> (III, i, 123-8)

An animal itself is howling, and the emphasis upon "wilderness" is shrill beyond the license of human rhetoric. We may
feel pity for the man who remembers Leah, but the spectacle of such pain is not pleasant, the wound is animal, self-
inflicted, and self-licked. "I never heard," says Salanio,

> a passion so confus'd,
> So strange, outrageous, and so variable.
>
> (II, viii, 12-3)

This was when Shylock ran out into the streets and declared
the loss of his ducats with his daughter; but he is always
strange to the play and outrageous, though in most crises he
can cover his agitation with the curt voice of craft, with the
insistent sound of a cold hatred.

> I'll have my bond; I will not hear thee speak.
> I'll have my bond; and therefore speak no more. . . .
> I'll have no speaking; I will have my bond.
>
> (III, iii, 12-17)

Nor is he disposed to justify his conduct by a show of reason. If he knows the language of reason he does not use it; if
he knows his motives he will not name them.

> So can I give no reason, nor I will not,
> More than a lodg'd hate and a certain loathing
> I bear Antonio.
>
> (IV, i, 59-61)

It is by no means odd that such a man should detest music. The favored citizens of this world love it so much that
they live only for the concord of sweet sounds, and Lorenzo
can dismiss any other kind of man as fit for treasons, stratagems, and spoils (V, i, 85). Shylock is another kind of man.

Music hurts his ears as it does Malvolio's,[12] and he is as contemptuous of merry-making, which he calls "shallow foppery." A masque in the street brings no comfort of melody; he notes only "the vile squealing of the wry-neck'd fife" (II, v, 30), and holds his ears. So must we hold ours against so hideous a phrase; and withhold, perhaps, our assent from the implication that any musical instrument can be a deformed thing. Or a perverting thing, for there are men, says Shylock in another place, who

> when the bagpipe sings i' the nose,
> Cannot contain their urine.
>
> (IV, i, 49–50)

That is the sort of interest he has in music, in the ridiculous noises which dull and soft-eyed fools with varnished faces can only pretend to believe ennobling. And that is why, since also he is without the concord in his thoughts which love composes, the repetitions of his speech are so lacking in resonance, so sullen in their accent and so blighting in their tone.

> Ho, no, no, no, no!
>
> (I, iii, 15)

> Why, there, there, there, there! A diamond gone, cost me two thousand ducats in Frankfort![13] The curse never fell upon our nation till now. I never felt it till now. Two thousand ducats in that; and other precious, precious jewels. I would my daughter were dead at my foot, and the jewels in her ear! Would she were hears'd[14] at my foot, and the ducats in her coffin! . . . I thank God, I thank God. Is't true, is't true? . . . I thank thee, good Tubal; good news, good news! Ha, ha! . . . Thou stick'st a dagger in me. I shall never see my gold again. Fourscore ducats at a sitting! Fourscore ducats! . . . I am very glad of it. I'll plague him; I'll torture him. I am glad of it. . . . Nay, that's true, that's very true. Go, Tubal, fee me an officer[15]; bespeak[16] him a fortnight before . . . Go, go, Tubal, and meet me at our synagogue; go, good Tubal; at our synagogue, Tubal.
>
> (III, i, 87–136)

That repetitions like these occur in prose is not what distinguishes them. The prose of Falstaff[17] will contain as many with an entirely different result, with the effect indeed of a great man spending his breath freely. What distinguishes the style of Shylock is in the end, no doubt, one of its author's se-

---

12. Malvolio in *Twelfth Night* 13. famous for its fairs, at which fine jewelry was sold 14. on her bier 15. hire an officer of the law, one who made arrests for debts 16. order; reserve 17. in *Henry IV* Parts 1 and 2 and *The Merry Wives of Windsor*

crets. But we can hear the difference between him and the brethren of Antonio. And in the quality of that difference we should have no difficulty in recognizing Shylock as the alien element in a world of love and friendship, of nightingales and moonlight sleeping sweetly on a bank.

Where Shakespeare's sympathies lay it has long since been useless to inquire. His gentlemen within the code are as harsh to Shylock as Shylock is to them; however much love they have, they cannot love him. Nor has Shakespeare made the least inch of him lovely. He would seem in fact to have attempted a monster, one whose question whether a Jew hath eyes, hands, organs, dimensions, senses, affections, and passions would reveal its rhetorical form, the answer being no. Yet Shylock is not a monster. He is a man thrust into a world bound not to endure him. In such a world he necessarily looks and sounds ugly. In another universe his voice might have its properties and its uses. Here it can issue as nothing but a snarl, an animal cry sounding outrageously among the flute and recorder voices of persons whose very names, unlike his own, are flowing musical phrases. The contrast between harmony and hate, love and discord, is here complete, and Shakespeare for the time being is content to resolve it in comedy. Even in his tragedies it cannot be more complete.

Religion in *The Merchant of Venice*

Peter Milward

Peter Milward identifies *The Merchant of Venice* as a religious play both because characters liberally quote the Old and New Testaments and because the central theme, of strict adherence to the law versus mercy, is biblical. According to Milward, Elizabethan audiences would have found the play topical not because conflict between Jews and Christians was familiar, but rather because Shylock would have reminded them of the Puritans. Puritan religious practices, including literal interpretation of the Bible and strict adherence to sobriety and thrift, offended many Elizabethans. Peter Milward is a Catholic priest and has taught literature at Sophia University in Tokyo. He is the author of *Living and Learning in Japan, Christian Themes in English Literature*, and *Shakespeare's Tales Retold.*

It is generally recognized that *The Merchant of Venice*, with its deep undercurrent of religious meaning and allusion, is one of Shakespeare's more religious plays. [Critic] Richmond Noble, in his study of *Shakespeare's Biblical Knowledge*, goes so far as to assert that

> From the point of view of Scriptural quotations it is the most important of all the plays, for in it Shakespeare affords evidence of having studied the Bible closely in his delineation of Shylock.

It is not merely a question, however, of counting the number of quotations, or of noting how many of them come from the mouth of Shylock. What is of more importance is to study the use Shakespeare makes of these quotations—not forgetting other kinds of religious allusion—not only for the delineation of Shylock as a Jew, but also in relation to the central theme of the play, involving the other characters as well.

Excerpted from *The Mediaeval Dimension in Shakespeare's Plays*, by Peter Milward. Copyright © 1990 by Peter Milward. Reprinted by permission of the Edwin Mellen Press.

To begin with, there is no doubt that Shylock's language is distinctly Scriptural.... In addition to Shylock, it is Portia who stands out from among the other characters of the play for the number of her references to the Bible. But in her case, it is significant that they all cluster together in one speech, her famous hymn to mercy in the trial-scene (iv. 1). Noble rightly draws attention to the echoes of *Ecclesiasticus* (xxxv. 19, xxviii. 2–5), the *Psalms* (ciii, cxxxvi, and cxliii. 2), and the Lord's prayer (Matt. vi). He might also have added the echo of Prov. xx. 28:

> Mercy and truth preserve the king; and his throne is upholden by mercy.

THE THEME OF LAW VERSUS MERCY

Implicit in all these references, there is a fundamental thematic contrast on which the whole play may be said to hinge. On the one hand, Shylock explicitly stands for "law" and "judgment" (iv.i). He rigidly adheres to his "bond" (iii.3), in strict accordance with the Mosaic principle of "an eye for an eye, and a tooth for a tooth." Such an attitude corresponds with his habitual references to merely external details of the Bible, the letter which kills, in contrast to the spirit which gives life. (II Cor. iii. 6) On the other hand, Portia stands for "sacrifice" (iii. 2)—not in the sense in which sacrifice is so often contrasted with mercy in both the Old and New Testament (cf. Hos, vi. 6; Matt. ix. 13), but in that of self-sacrifice, according to the ideal of Christ himself. (cf. Matt. xx. 28) Hence in the trial-scene, while admitting the claims of justice, she makes her celebrated appeal for mercy in words which not only echo various passages of the Bible, but touch on the very heart of God's message to his people.

This contrast between the old and new, the letter and the spirit, is chiefly emphasized in the clash between Shylock and Portia at the trial of Antonio. But it is re-echoed again and again in Shylock's relations with other characters of the play. Already at the opening of the trial, it is implied in the exchange between the Duke and Shylock:

> "How shalt thou hope for mercy, rendering none?"
> "What judgment shall I dread, doing no wrong?"

This Pharisaic[1] attitude of Shylock is even more clearly expressed in his criticism of Antonio: "How like a fawning

---

1. The Pharisees were members of an ancient Jewish sect that emphasized strict interpretation and observance of Mosaic law with a self-righteous attitude.

publican he looks!" (i. 3)—with its overtones of Christ's parable of the Pharisee and the Publican[2] (Luke xviii. 9–14). A similar contrast is suggested in his criticism of Bassanio as "the prodigal Christian" (ii. 5), where he as it were identifies himself with the elder brother in the parable (Luke xv), who was traditionally interpreted as standing for the Jewish people. He even draws explicit attention to "the difference of old Shylock and Bassanio" in the same scene.

THE THEME OF OLD AND NEW EVIDENT IN SUB-PLOT

The echoes of this fundamental contrast in the main plot also penetrate the structure of the sub-plot. The amusing scene in which the comic character of Lancelot Gobbo first appears, with his debate between conscience and the fiend, is on this very point. He is portrayed as running away from his "old master the Jew" to his "new master the Christian"––from Shylock to Bassanio, described in universal terms (ii. 4). His departure, in turn, prepares the way for the further elopement of Shylock's daughter, Jessica, with Lorenzo the Christian. This, too, is presented in terms not merely of romance, but also of religion. For in eloping with Lorenzo, Jessica herself becomes a Christian and declares herself, in Pauline language, "saved" by her husband (iii. 5; cf. I Cor. vii. 14). Her absconding with her father's ducats, so scandalous on a naturalistic interpretation of the play, is perhaps merely a variation on the theme of the "spoils of the Egyptians", in a Christian sense. Thus Lancelot and Jessica each serve to illustrate the change from the old to the new dispensation: Lancelot, as servant first to the devil, then to the grace of God (cf. Rom. vii. 6 and viii. 21); Jessica, as the "daughter of Jerusalem" under the Old Law, then as the bride of Christ under the New.

All this is more or less on the surface of Shakespeare's text, and is readily accepted by Shakespearean scholars. But beneath the surface of the text, there are many hidden references to the religious situation in Shakespeare's England, which can only be recognized by comparing the language of the play with the religious writings of the time. Such a comparison has already been made, up to a point, in connection with the character of Shylock. It was [critic] E. E. Stoll who first drew the attention of scholars to a significant parallel

2. The Pharisee bragged and was proud; the Publican was humble.

between him and the Puritans of Shakespeare's time. "Of what", he asked, "would the figure of Shylock remind the audience?" Not so much of the Jews, who were few and far between in the England of Elizabeth; but rather "of the precisians[3] and Pharisees in the midst"—namely, the Puritans. His interesting suggestion was more fully developed by [critic] P. N. Siegel, in an important article on "Shylock and the Puritan Usurers", with an abundance of illustrations from contemporary discussions of usury (such as [statesman] Thomas Wilson's *Discourse upon Usury*, 1572), and from the anti-Puritan writings of the dramatists, [John] Marston, [Ben] Jonson and [Thomas] Middleton. Strangely enough, he hardly touched upon the religious controversies of the Elizabethan Age, which yield a remarkable number of literary parallels to Shakespeare's play. It may be of interest to give a selection here, not as source but as illustrative material for a deeper understanding of *The Merchant of Venice* in its contemporary setting.

Shylock Parallels Elizabethan Puritans

In the first place, Shylock's practice of usury seems to have been followed by many Elizabethan Puritans, who were particularly influential in the city of London—as the dramatists knew only too well. Besides the witness of Thomas Wilson, quoted by Siegel, there is a more contemporary criticism of the Puritans by the Dean of Exeter, Matthew Sutcliffe, in his *Answer to a Certain Libel* (1592). He describes them as

> these counterfeit hypocrites, that shaking off their ministry, and disdaining the base account of it, trace in usury, merchandise, farms and other suchlike occupations, giving over themselves to serve mammon.

and he goes on to accuse the Puritan leader, Thomas Cartwright, by name of practising usury.

Secondly, Shylock's justification of himself by appealing to the Bible may be taken as reflecting a common practice of the Puritans, as well in usury as in other matters. On the other hand, Antonio's comment, "The devil may cite Scripture to his purpose" (i. 3), together with Bassanio's later remark, "In religion, what damned error, but some sober brow will bless it and approve it with a text" (iii. 2), is a commonplace in the controversial writings, first of the Catholics

---

3. Those who are strict and precise in their adherence to religious observances and moral behavior.

against the Protestants, and later of the Anglicans against the Puritans. Thus Thomas Harding, in his celebrated *Answer to M. Jewel's Challenge* (1564), declares that "All heretics draw their venom out of the Bible under pretence of God's word"; and in his bulkier *Confutation* of Jewel's *Apology of the Church of England* (1565), he repeats this accusation in a variety of ways:

> Oftentimes evil meaning is hid under good words. . . . Among all none pretend truth in words so much as heretics. . . . The devil leadeth man to evil by promise of good. . . . So bringeth the heretic his hearer to error in faith by colour and pretence of truth. . . . These men, that speak so much of truth, that boast so much of the gospel, that rattle nothing but scriptures.

The same sentiment is often to be found in the writings of the Jesuit controversialist, Robert Persons. Thus in his *Brief Discourse* (1580) he points out:

> It was always the fashion of heretics to have scripture in their mouth, and to cleave only to scriptures, and to refuse traditions as inventions of men.

And in his *Brief and Clear Confutation* (1603) he returns to the point, that "All heretics, both old and new, do pretend to follow the scriptures, and do cite infinite places out of the scripture". [Anglican spokesman] John Whitgift makes the same point, in turn, in his *Defence of the Answer to the Admonition* (1574), against Thomas Cartwright—quoting Calvin against the Anabaptists: "They have that (the word of God) evermore in their mouth, and always talk of it".

THE PLAY REFLECTS GENERAL PURITAN CONTROVERSIES

Thirdly, a general resemblance between the Puritans and the Jews was commonly noted in the controversies of the age, in view of the emphasis laid by the former on the literal interpretation of Scripture. They went so far as to insist on the exact observance of the judicial and even of many of the ceremonial laws of Moses, in which they professed to discover the precise form of Church discipline required by God. This was a main point in the lengthy controversy between John Whitgift and Thomas Cartwright—the latter insisting on the strict execution of the Mosaic law against idolaters, adulterers, and heretics, and stoutly maintaining that

> idolatry ought to be punished with death. . . Heretics ought to be put to death. . . If this be bloody and extreme, I am content to be so counted with the Holy Ghost.

Whitgift, however, points out that this is "to lay an intolerable yoke and burden upon the necks of men" and to "bring us into the bondage of the law". He says explicitly that it "smelleth of Judaism", and demands indignantly: "What remaineth but to say that Christ is not yet come?" This accusation appears again in the anonymous *Defence of the Ecclesiastical Regiment* (1574), which was also directed against Cartwright's position:

> I see not what can be intended by this new devised discipline, but only restitution of the veil, and clogging men's consciences with such Jewish observation, from the which we are enfranchised by the Gospel.

Fourthly, Shylock's cruelty in enforcing the law, for which he is called a "stony, inhuman wretch" and compared unfavourably with "stubborn Turks and Tartars" (iv. 1), has many parallels in contemporary descriptions of the Puritans. Thus in his *Answer to a Certain Libel* (1592), Matthew Sutcliffe asks:

> What else should we look for at their hands, seeing in racking of rents, extremity of dealing, usury and unlawful practices of gain, and Turkish and inhuman cruelty, divers of these zelators of puritanism pass both Turks and heathen.

He goes on to declare, in words almost identical with those of Antonio:

> I know none more hard-hearted than the Puritans... As for pettifoggers[4] and scribes, they do skin the poor, and help them not.

Fifthly, Shylock's contempt for the "shallow foppery"[5] of the Christians in contrast to his own "sober house", and his commendation of a "thrifty mind" (ii. 5), would have reminded many in Shakespeare's audience of the Puritan emphasis on sobriety and thrift. This is also glanced at by Gratiano in his amusing characterization of Sir Oracle (i. 3), which, though suggested by the sadness of Antonio, tends in fact to support the delineation of Shylock. His outline is interestingly elaborated by the two chief anti-Puritan writers of the day, Whitgift and [assistant to the Archbishop of Canterbury Richard] Bancroft. In his *Answer to an Admonition* (1572), Whitgift compares the Puritans to the Anabaptists of the continent, whom he describes as follows:

> They earnestly cried out against pride, gluttony, &c. They spake much of mortification; they pretended great gravity;

4. those who quibble over trivia 5. foolish qualities or actions

they sighed much; they seldom or never laughed; they were very austere in reprehending; they spake gloriously; to be short, they were hypocrites, thereby to win authority to their heresy, among the simple and ignorant people.

Similarly, in his *Survey of the Pretended Holy Discipline* (1593), which is closer to the date of Shakespeare's play, Bancroft develops this picture of the contemporary Puritans:

It is not unknown ... what the profession of extraordinary zeal, and as it were contempt of the world, doth work with the multitude. When they see men go simply in the streets, looking downward for the most part, wringing their necks awry, shaking their heads, as though they were in some present grief, lifting up the white of their eyes sometimes, at the sight of some vanity, as they walk; when they hear them give great groans, cry out against this sin and that sin (not in them their hearers, but in their superiors), make long prayers, profess a kind of wilful poverty, speaking most earnestly against some men's having too much, and some men too little (which beateth into the people's heads a present cogitation of some division to be made in time); when I say, the multitude doth see and hear such a kind of men, they are by and by carried away with a marvellous great conceit and opinion of them.

Puritans Seen as Hypocrites Who Kept Away from Others

Sixthly, Shylock's hypocrisy, as pointed out by Antonio in terms of "a villain with a smiling cheek" and "a goodly apple rotten at the heart" (i. 3), and further implied in Bassanio's reference to "the seeming truth which cunning times put on to entrap the wisest" (iii, 2), is easily matched by contemporary descriptions of the Puritans. They are castigated for professing piety, like the Pharisees, while lining their pockets with the proceeds of usury—mere "whited sepulchres", as Bancroft calls them in his *Survey*:

Many sepulchres are gorgeous to the eyes, and yet inwardly have nothing in them but bones and corruption... Men may often times be deceived with shews and probabilities, as always heretofore many have been.

This hypocrisy is often pointed out by Henry Smith in his *Sermons*, which belong to the same period (published after his death in 1593). "There is no sin," he says, "but hath some shew of virtue." And again, "under the colour of goodness evil is always lurking." Then, more particularly of the separatist groups of Puritans, he demands: "Hath it not the shew of error to broach a religion which was never heard of before?"

Seventhly, Shylock's famous refusal to eat, drink or pray with Christians, has its exact parallel in the refusal of Puritans to mix with the common church-goers—keeping themselves apart and "pure" like the Pharisees. There is a good description of this tendency in Bancroft's *Survey,* from which Shakespeare may well have taken Shylock's very words:

> Seeing our church, our government, our ministry, our service, our sacraments, are thus and thus... therefore they will not pray with us, they will not communicate with us, they will not submit themselves to our church... they will have nothing to do with us.

Whitgift, too, has a similar passage in his *Answer to an Admonition*:

> These men separate themselves from the congregation, and will not communicate with us neither in prayers, hearing the word nor sacraments; they contemn and despise all those that be not of their sect, as polluted and not worthy to be saluted or kept company with; and therefore some of them, meeting their old acquaintance, being godly preachers, have not only refused to salute them, but spit in their faces, wishing the plague of God to light upon them, and saying that they were damned and that God had taken his spirit from them, and all this because they did wear a cap; wherefore when they talk of Pharisees, they pluck themselves by the noses.

Finally, just as Shylock is repeatedly described as a devil especially by Lancelot (ii. 2) and by his opponents in the trial-scene (iv. 1), so the Puritans were often called "devils" by their adversaries—as in the cant phrase, "The devil is a Puritan" (alluded to by Shakespeare in *Pericles* iv. 6). The very words of Lancelot characterizing Shylock as "the devil incarnal" (ii. 2), might have been taken from the anonymous anti-Martinist tract, *Martin's Month's Mind* (1589), which speaks of the Puritan Martinists as "very devils incarnate, sent out to deceive and disturb the world."

The parallel suggests a further interpretation of *The Merchant of Venice* in the light of the mediaeval Moralities, in which sin was regarded as a bond with the devil, whence man had to be ransomed by Christ. Thus if the devil is here Shylock, then Man (or Everyman) is Antonio, and Christ is Portia.

CHAPTER 3

Characterization

READINGS ON
THE MERCHANT OF VENICE

Characters in *The Merchant of Venice*

William Hazlitt

William Hazlitt gives short sketches of each of the prominent characters in *Merchant*. In the following essay Hazlitt's favorite character is Shylock, whom Hazlitt admires for his individual spirit and his ability to defend himself in the trial scene. Hazlitt also credits Shylock with having more ideas than any other character in the play. Hazlitt is not fond of Portia or her maid Nerissa, but he praises Portia's skill in the trial scene. He finds Lancelot humorous and Gratiano an admirable jester. Nineteenth-century critic William Hazlitt wrote essays on art, drama, and literature. His works include *Lectures on English Poets, English Comic Writers,* and *Table Talk, or Original Essays on Men and Manners.*

This is a play that in spite of the change of manners and prejudices still holds undisputed possession of the stage. Shakespear's malignant [Shylock] has outlived [Richard] Cumberland's benevolent Jew. In proportion as Shylock has ceased to be a popular bugbear, 'baited with the rabble's curse,' he becomes a half-favourite with the philosophical part of the audience, who are disposed to think that Jewish revenge is at least as good as Christian injuries. Shylock is *a good hater;* 'a man no less sinned against than sinning.' If he carries his revenge too far, yet he has strong grounds for 'the lodged hate he bears Anthonio,' which he explains with equal force of eloquence and reason. He seems the depositary of the vengeance of his race; and though the long habit of brooding over daily insults and injuries has crusted over his temper with inveterate misanthropy, and hardened him against the contempt of mankind, this adds but little to the triumphant pretensions of his enemies. There is a strong,

Excerpted from *Round Table Characters of Shakespear's Plays,* by William Hazlitt (London: Taylor and Hessey, 1818).

quick, and deep sense of justice mixed up with the gall and bitterness of his resentment. The constant apprehension of being burnt alive, plundered, banished, reviled, and trampled on, might be supposed to sour the most forbearing nature, and to take something from that 'milk of human kindness,' with which his persecutors contemplated his indignities. The desire of revenge is almost inseparable from the sense of wrong; and we can hardly help sympathising with the proud spirit, hid beneath his 'Jewish gaberdine,' stung to madness by repeated undeserved provocations, and labouring to throw off the load of obloquy[1] and oppression heaped upon him and all his tribe by one desperate act of 'lawful' revenge, till the ferociousness of the means by which he is to execute his purpose, and the pertinacity with which he adheres to it, turn us against him; but even at last, when disappointed of the sanguinary revenge with which he had glutted his hopes, and exposed to beggary and contempt by the letter of the law on which he had insisted with so little remorse, we pity him, and think him hardly dealt with by his judges. In all his answers and retorts upon his adversaries, he has the best not only of the argument but of the question, reasoning on their own principles and practice. They are so far from allowing of any measure of equal dealing, of common justice or humanity between themselves and the Jew, that even when they come to ask a favour of him, and Shylock reminds them that 'on such a day they spit upon him, another spurned him, another called him dog, and for these curtesies request he'll lend them so much monies'—Anthonio, his old enemy, instead of any acknowledgment of the shrewdness and justice of his remonstrance, which would have been preposterous in a respectable Catholic merchant in those times, threatens him with a repetition of the same treatment—

'I am as like to call thee so again,
To spit on thee again, to spurn thee too.'

After this, the appeal to the Jew's mercy, as if there were any common principle of right and wrong between them, is the rankest hypocrisy, or the blindest prejudice; and the Jew's answer to one of Anthonio's friends, who asks him what his pound of forfeit flesh is good for, is irresistible—

'To bait fish withal; if it will feed nothing else, it will feed

1. disgrace suffered as a result of abuse

my revenge. He hath disgrac'd me, and hinder'd me of half a million, laughed at my losses, mock'd at my gains, scorn'd my nation, thwarted my bargains, cool'd my friends, heated mine enemies; and what's his reason? I am a Jew. Hath not a Jew eyes; hath not a Jew hands, organs, dimensions, senses, affections, passions; fed with the same food, hurt with the same weapons, subject to the same diseases, healed by the same means, warmed and cooled by the same winter and summer that a Christian is? If you prick us, do we not bleed? If you tickle us, do we not laugh? If you poison us, do we not die? And if you wrong us, shall we not revenge? If we are like you in the rest, we will resemble you in that. If a Jew wrong a Christian, what is his humility[2]? revenge. If a Christian wrong a Jew, what should his sufferance be by Christian example? why revenge. The villainy you teach me I will execute, and it shall go hard but I will better the instruction.'

SHYLOCK DEFENDS HIMSELF

The whole of the trial-scene, both before and after the entrance of Portia, is a master-piece of dramatic skill. The legal acuteness, the passionate declamations, the sound maxims of jurisprudence, the wit and irony interspersed in it, the fluctuations of hope and fear in the different persons, and the completeness and suddenness of the catastrophe, cannot be surpassed. Shylock, who is his own counsel, defends himself well, and is triumphant on all the general topics that are urged against him, and only fails through a legal flaw. Take the following as an instance:—

> '*Shylock.* What judgment shall I dread, doing no wrong?
> You have among you many a purchas'd slave,
> Which like your asses, and your dogs, and mules,
> You use in abject and in slavish part,
> Because you bought them:—shall I say to you,
> Let them be free, marry them to your heirs?
> Why sweat they under burdens? let their beds
> Be made as soft as yours, and let their palates
> Be season'd with such viands? you will answer,
> The slaves are ours:—so do I answer you:
> The pound of flesh, which I demand of him,
> Is dearly bought, is mine, and I will have it:
> If you deny me, fie upon your law!
> There is no force in the decrees of Venice:
> I stand for judgment: answer; shall I have it?'

2. In what way does he show Christian forbearance?

The keenness of his revenge awakes all his faculties; and he beats back all opposition to his purpose, whether grave or gay, whether of wit or argument, with an equal degree of earnestness and self-possession. His character is displayed as distinctly in other less prominent parts of the play, and we may collect from a few sentences the history of his life—his descent and origin, his thrift and domestic economy, his affection for his daughter, whom he loves next to his wealth, his courtship and his first present to Leah, his wife! 'I would not have parted with it' (the ring which he first gave her) 'for a wilderness of monkies!' What a fine Hebraism is implied in this expression!

PORTIA AND GRATIANO

Portia is not a very great favourite with us; neither are we in love with her maid, Nerissa. Portia has a certain degree of affectation and pedantry about her, which is very unusual in Shakespear's women, but which perhaps was a proper qualification for the office of a 'civil doctor,' which she undertakes and executes so successfully. The speech about Mercy is very well; but there are a thousand finer ones in Shakespear. We do not admire the scene of the caskets: and object entirely to the Black Prince, Morocchius. We should like Jessica better if she had not deceived and robbed her father, and Lorenzo, if he had not married a Jewess, though he thinks he has a right to wrong a Jew. The dialogue between this newly-married couple by moonlight, beginning 'On such a nigh,' etc. is a collection of classical elegancies. Launcelot, the Jew's man, is an honest fellow. The dilemma in which he describes himself placed between his 'conscience and the fiend,' the one of which advises him to run away from his master's service and the other to stay in it, is exquisitely humourous.

Gratiano is a very admirable subordinate character. He is the jester of the piece: yet one speech of his, in his own defence, contains a whole volume of wisdom.

'*Anthonio.* I hold the world but as the world, Gratiano,
A stage, where every one must play his part;
And mine a sad one.
    Gratiano. Let me play the fool:
With mirth and laughter let old wrinkles come;
And let my liver rather heat with wine,
Than my heart cool with mortifying groans.
Why should a man, whose blood is warm within,
Sit like his grandsire cut in alabaster?
Sleep when he wakes? and creep into the jaundice

By being peevish? I tell thee what, Anthonio—
I love thee, and it is my love that speaks;—
There are a sort of men, whose visages
Do cream and mantle like a standing pond:
And do a wilful stillness entertain,
With purpose to be drest in an opinion
Of wisdom, gravity, profound conceit;
As who should say, *I am Sir Oracle,*
And when I ope my lips, let no dog bark!
O, my Anthonio, I do know of these,
That therefore only are reputed wise,
For saying nothing; who, I am very sure,
If they should speak, would almost damn those ears,
Which hearing them, would call their brothers, fools.
I'll tell thee more of this another time:
But fish not with his melancholy bait,
For this fool's gudgeon, this opinion.'

Gratiano's speech on the philosophy of love, and the effect of habit in taking off the force of passion, is as full of spirit and good

ELEGANT LINES SPOKEN IN THE MOONLIGHT

In act 5, scene 1, while Lorenzo and Jessica wait in the moon-lit evening, Lorenzo reflects on silence and music and its harmonious effect on humans. Approaching, Portia and Nerissa notice how the sights and sounds of the evening blend and contrast.

LOR. The reason is, your spirits are attentive.
For do but note a wild and wanton herd,
Or race of youthful and unhandled colts,
Fetching mad bounds, bellowing, and neighing loud,
Which is the hot condition of their blood.
If they but hear perchance a trumpet sound,
Or any air of music touch their ears,
You shall perceive them make a mutual stand,
Their savage eyes turned to a modest gaze
By the sweet power of music. Therefore the poet
Did feign that Orpheus[1] drew trees, stones, and floods,
Since naught so stockish,[2] hard, and full of rage
But music for the time doth change his nature.
The man that hath no music in himself,
Nor is not moved with concord of sweet sounds,
Is fit for treasons, stratagems,[3] and spoils.
The motions of his spirit are dull as night,
And his affections dark as Erebus.[4]
Let no such man be trusted. Mark the music.
         [*Enter* PORTIA *and* NERISSA.]
    POR. That light we see is burning in my hall.
How far that little candle throws his beams!

sense. The graceful winding up of this play in the fifth act, after the tragic business is despatched, is one of the happiest instances of Shakespear's knowledge of the principles of the drama. We do not mean the pretended quarrel between Portia and Nerissa and their husbands about the rings, which is amusing enough, but the conversation just before and after the return of Portia to her own house, beginning 'How sweet the moonlight sleeps upon this bank,' and ending 'Peace! how the moon sleeps with Endymion, and would not be awaked.' There is a number of beautiful thoughts crowded into that short space, and linked together by the most natural transitions.

An Actor's Portrayal of Shylock

When we first went to see [Edmund] Kean in Shylock, we expected to see, what we had been used to see, a decrepid old man, bent with age and ugly with mental deformity, grin-

---

So shines a good deed in a naughty world.
   NER. When the moon shone, we did not see the candle.
   POR. So doth the greater glory dim the less.
A substitute shines brightly as a king
Until a king be by, and then his state
Empties itself, as doth an inland brooks
Into the main of waters. Music! Hark!
   NER. It is your music, madam, of the house.
   POR. Nothing is good, I see, without respect.[5]
Methinks it sounds much sweeter than by day.
   NER. Silence bestows that virtue on it, madam.
   POR. The crow doth sing as sweetly as the lark
When neither is attended,[6] and I think
The nightingale if she should sing by day,
When every goose is cackling, would be thought
No better a musician than the wren.
How many things by season seasoned are[7]
To their right praise and true perfection!
Peace, ho! The moon sleeps with Endymion,[8]
And would not be awaked.

1.Orpheus: The musician of Thrace was so skillful that even the trees bent to listen to him. 2. stockish: like an unfeeling block 3. stratagems: deeds of violence 4. Erebus: Hell 5. without respect: without reference to circumstances; i.e., in itself 6. attended: listened to 7. by . . . are: give a pleasant taste by appearing at the right time 8. Endymion: The goddess Diana is also the moon; she loved a mortal shepherd called Endymion.

The Merchant of Venice, act 5, scene 1, 70–110.

ning with deadly malice, with the venom of his heart congealed in the expression of his countenance, sullen, morose, gloomy, inflexible, brooding over one idea, that of his hatred, and fixed on one unalterable purpose, that of his revenge. We were disappointed, because we had taken our idea from other actors, not from the play. There is no proof there that Shylock is old, but a single line, 'Bassanio and *old* Shylock, both stand forth,'—which does not imply that he is infirm with age—and the circumstance that he has a daughter marriageable, which does not imply that he is old at all. It would be too much to say that his body should be made crooked and deformed to answer to his mind, which is bowed down and warped with prejudices and passion. That he has but one idea, is not true; he has more ideas than any other person in the piece; and if he is intense and inveterate in the pursuit of his purpose, he shews the utmost elasticity, vigour, and presence of mind, in the means of attaining it. But so rooted was our habitual impression of the part from seeing it caricatured in the representation, that it was only from a careful perusal of the play itself that we saw our error. The stage is not in general the best place to study our author's characters in. It is too often filled with traditional common-place conceptions of the part, handed down from sire to son, and suited to the taste of *the great vulgar and the small.*—"Tis an unweeded garden: things rank and gross do merely gender in it!' If a man of genius comes once in an age to clear away the rubbish, to make it fruitful and wholesome, they cry, "Tis a bad school: it may be like nature, it may be like Shakespear, but it is not like us.' Admirable critics!

Shylock and the Venetian Christians

Arthur Quiller-Couch and John Dover Wilson

Arthur Quiller-Couch and John Dover Wilson argue that Shylock is a more sympathetic character than any of Antonio's Christian friends. The authors concede that Shylock is cruel, but argue that this is justified, considering his daughter's betrayal. Bassanio and the other friends, the authors contend, are thoughtless, heartless, and self-absorbed: neither honest with themselves nor compassionate toward others. Arthur Quiller-Couch wrote novels, short stories, poems, and critical essays. He is the author of *Studies in Literature* and editor of *The Oxford Book of English Verse.* John Dover Wilson, who taught English literature at the University of Edinburgh, is the author of *What Happens in* Hamlet and *Shakespeare's Happy Comedies.*

For the individual Shylock, who in our opinion has been over-philosophised and over-sentimentalised, we may start upon the simple, obvious text that Shakespeare (who, in an age when Jews were forbidden this country, had probably never met with one in the flesh) makes him an intelligible if not a pardonable man; a genuine man, at any rate, of like passions with ourselves, so that we respond to every word of his fierce protest:

> Hath not a Jew eyes? hath not a Jew hands, organs, dimensions, senses, affections, passions? fed with the same food, hurt with the same weapons, subject to the same diseases, healed by the same means, warmed and cooled by the same winter and summer, as a Christian is? . . .

How, then, does Shakespeare do it?—how contrive to make Shylock sympathetic to us? . . . His audience, conventionally minded, may accept the proffer of the bond (Act I, Scene 3) as a jesting bargain made with blood-thirsty intent,

Excerpted from the Introduction to Shakespeare's *The Merchant of Venice,* edited by Arthur Quiller-Couch and John Dover Wilson (New York: Cambridge University Press, 1969). Reprinted by permission of Cambridge University Press.

to be blood-thirstily enacted; but a gentle Shakespeare cannot. There must be more incentive to hate, to lust for a literally bloody vengeance, than any past insults, however conventional, put upon him on the Rialto by Antonio, mildest of men, can dramatically supply. Sufferance is the badge of his tribe.

JESSICA BETRAYS HER FATHER

But he is a fierce Israelite and has an adored daughter. In the interim between the signing of the bond and its falling due this daughter, this Jessica, has wickedly and most unfilially betrayed him. . . .

Jessica is bad and disloyal, unfilial, a thief; frivolous, greedy, without any more conscience than a cat and without even a cat's redeeming love of home. Quite without heart, on worse than an animal instinct—pilfering to be carnal—she betrays her father to be a light-of-lucre carefully weighted with her sire's ducats. So Shylock returns from a gay abhorrent banquet to knock on his empty and emptied house. . . .

The racial pride of Shylock has fenced off his daughter fiercely from any intercourse whatever with the infidels: and her elopement with one of the most heartless fribblers on the list of Antonio's friends, which is to say much, and the 'gilding' of herself, as on an afterthought, with more of her father's ducats before she runs downstairs to the street, leaves us with no alternative. Shylock is intolerably wronged.

ANTONIO AND HIS VENETIAN FRIENDS

Let us turn aside for a moment to Antonio, and to consider his friends and associates taken as a lot. It may not be always true that a man is known by the company he keeps: and most of us have known some man or two or three, of probity and high intellectual gifts, who are never at ease save in company with their moral and intellectual inferiors, avoid their peers, and of indolence consort with creatures among whom their eminence cannot be challenged. Such a man is Antonio, presented to us as a high-minded and capable merchant of credit and renown, but presented to us, also as the indolent patron of a circle of wasters, 'born to consume the fruits of this world,' heartless, or at least unheedful, while his life lies in jeopardy through his tender, extravagantly romantic friendship for one of them.

Now it may be that Shakespeare, in the first half of this

play purposely, of his art, hardened down all these friends and clients of the Merchant. . . . And, if intended, this disheartening of Venice does indeed help to throw up Shylock with his passion into high relief. But, if so, surely it is done at great cost. . . .

We are in Venice—with all Vanity Fair, all the *Carnival de Venise*, in full swing on her quays; grave merchants trafficking, porters sweating with bales, water-carriers, flowergirls, gallants; vessels lading, discharging, repairing; and up the narrower waterways black gondolas shooting under high guarded windows, any gondola you please hooding a secret of love, or assassination, or both—as any shutter in the line may open demurely, discreetly, giving just room enough, just time enough, for a hand to drop a rose. Venice again at night—lanterns on the water, masked revellers taking charge of the quays with drums, hautboys, fifes, and general tipsiness; withdrawn from this riot into deep intricacies of shadow, the undertone of lutes complaining their love; and out beyond all this fever, far to southward, the stars swinging, keeping, their circle—as Queen Elizabeth once danced—'high and disposedly' over Belmont, where on a turfed bank

> Peace, ho! the moon sleeps with Endymion,[1]
> And would not be awaked,

though the birds have already begun to twitter in Portia's garden. Have we not here the very atmosphere of romance.

Well, no. . . . We have a perfect *setting* for romance; but setting and atmosphere are two very different things. [Poet Goeffrey] Chaucer will take a tale of [Italian writer Giovanni] Boccaccio's and in the telling alter its atmosphere wholly: the reason being that while setting is external, atmosphere emanates from the author's genius, is breathed out from within.

Now in the *Merchant of Venice*, barring the Merchant himself, a merely static figure, and Shylock, who is meant to be cruel, every one of the Venetian *dramatis personae* is either a 'waster' or a 'rotter' or both, and cold-hearted at that. There is no need to expend ink upon such parasites as surround Antonio—upon Salerio and Solanio. Be it granted that in the hour of his extremity they have no means to save him. Yet

---

1. in Greek mythology a handsome young man who was loved by the moon goddess and whose youth was preserved by eternal sleep

they see it coming; they discuss it sympathetically, but always on the assumption that it is his affair not theirs:

> Let good Antonio look he keep his day,
> Or he shall pay for this,

and they take not so much trouble as to send Bassanio word of his friend's plight, though they know that for Bassanio's sake his deadly peril has been incurred! It is left to Antonio himself to tell the news in that very noble letter of farewell and release:

> Sweet Bassanio, my ships have all miscarried, my creditors grow cruel, my estate is very low, my bond to the Jew is forfeit, and since, in paying it, it is impossible I should live, all debts are cleared between you and I, if I might but see you at my death: notwithstanding, use your pleasure—if your love do not persuade you to come, let not my letter—

a letter which, in good truth, Bassanio does not too extravagantly describe as 'a few of the unpleasant'st words that ever blotted paper.' Let us compare it with Salerio's account of how the friends had parted:

> I saw Bassanio and Antonio part.
> Bassanio told him he would make some speed
> Of his return: he answered, 'Do not so.
> Slubber² not business for my sake, Bassanio,
> But stay the very riping of the time.
> And for the Jew's bond which he hath of me,
> Let it not enter in your mind of love:
> Be merry, and employ your chiefest thoughts
> To courtship, and such fair ostents³ of love
> As shall conveniently become you there.'
> And even there, his eye being big with tears,
> Turning his face, he put his hand behind him,
> And with affection wondrous sensible⁴
> He wrung Bassanio's hand, and so they parted.

THE FLAWED CHARACTER OF BASSANIO

But let us consider this conquering hero, Bassanio. When we first meet him he is in debt, a condition on which—having to confess it because he wants to borrow more money—he expends some very choice diction.

> 'Tis not unknown to you, Antonio,

(No, it certainly was not!)

> How much I have disabled mine estate,
> By something⁵ showing a more swelling port⁶
> Than my faint means would grant continuance.

2. be slovenly with 3. outward shows 4. wonderfully full of feeling 5. somewhat 6. extravagant living; too much a playboy

That may be a mighty fine way of saying that you have chosen to live beyond your income; but, Shakespeare or no
Shakespeare, if Shakespeare means us to hold Bassanio for
an honest fellow, it is mighty poor poetry. For poetry, like
honest men, looks things in the face, and does not ransack
its wardrobe to clothe what is naturally unpoetical. Bassanio, to do him justice, is not trying to wheedle Antonio by
this sort of talk; he knows his friend too deeply for that. But
he is deceiving *himself*, or rather is reproducing some of the
trash with which he has already deceived himself.

He goes on to say that he is not repining; his chief anxiety
is to pay everybody, and

> To you, Antonio,
> I owe the most in money and in love,

and thereupon counts on more love to extract more money,
starting (and upon an experienced man of business, be it observed) with some windy nonsense about shooting a second
arrow after a lost one.

> You know me well, and herein spend but time
> To wind about my love with circumstance[7]

says Antonio; and, indeed, his gentle impatience throughout
this scene is well worth noting. He is friend enough already to
give all; but to be preached at, and on a subject—money—of
which he has forgotten, or chooses to forget, ten times more
than Bassanio will ever learn, is a little beyond bearing. And
what is Bassanio's project? To borrow three thousand ducats to
equip himself to go off and hunt an heiress in Belmont. He has
seen her; she is fair; and

> sometimes from her eyes
> I did receive fair speechless messages. . . .
> Nor is the wide world ignorant of her worth,
> For the four winds blow in from every coast
> Renownéd suitors, and her sunny locks
> Hang on her temples like a golden fleece,
> Which makes her seat of Belmont Colchos' strand,
> And many Jasons come in quest of her[8]. . . .
> O my Antonio, had I but the means
> To hold a rival place with one of them,
> I have a mind presages[9] me such thrift,[10]
> That I should questionless be fortunate.

Now this is bad workmanship and dishonouring to Bassanio. It suggests the obvious question, Why should he build

7. You need not waste time by this indirect approach. 8. Jason sailed to the shore of
Colchos in the *Argo* to fetch away the Golden Fleece. 9. foretells 10. profit

anything on Portia's encouraging glances, as why should he 'questionless be fortunate,' seeing that—as he knows perfectly well, but does not choose to confide to the friend whose money he is borrowing—Portia's glances, encouraging or not, are nothing to the purpose, since all depends on his choosing the right one of three caskets—a two to one chance against him?

But he gets the money, of course, equips himself lavishly, arrives at Belmont; and here comes in worse workmanship. For I suppose that, while character weighs in drama, if one thing be more certain than another it is that a predatory young gentleman such as Bassanio would *not* have chosen the leaden casket. Let us consider his soliloquy while choosing:

> The world is still[11] deceived with ornament.
> In law, what plea so tainted and corrupt,
> But, being seasoned[12] with a gracious voice,
> Obscures the show of evil? In religion,
> What damnéd error, but some sober brow
> Will bless it, and approve[13] it with a text.

One feels moved to interrupt: 'Yes, yes—and what about yourself, my little fellow? What has altered you, that you, of all men, suddenly use this sanctimonious talk?'

THE CHRISTIANS ARE AS HEARTLESS AS SHYLOCK

And this flaw in characterisation goes right down through the workmanship of the play. For the evil opposed against these curious Christians is specific; it is Cruelty; and, yet again specifically, the peculiar cruelty of a Jew. To this cruelty an artist at the top of his art would surely have opposed mansuetude,[14] clemency, charity, and, specifically, Christian charity. Shakespeare misses more than half the point when he makes the intended victims, as a class and by habit, just as heartless as Shylock without any of Shylock's passionate excuse. . . .

As the reader will have seen, we cannot agree with [critic James] Spedding that Shakespeare deprived Shylock 'of all pretence of grievance or excuse.' On the contrary, we hold that in the abduction of Jessica Shakespeare deliberately gives him a real grievance and excuse, and that the offer of money, belatedly made, comes almost as an insult to his passionate resentment. . . .

11. always 12. as bad food is concealed by a strong sauce 13. prove 14. mildness; gentleness of manner

Shakespeare intended to make Shylock such a cruel, crafty, villainous Hebrew as would appeal to an audience of Elizabethan Christians. The very structure of the plot shows this. But even as Don Quixote carried away Cervantes, and Pickwick Dickens, so Shylock takes charge of Shakespeare, no less imperiously than Falstaff took charge of him. The intelligence of his heart and springs of action once admitted, Shakespeare understands him in detail, down (as [essayist William] Hazlitt noted) to his Biblical language, as when he hears that Jessica has given in Genoa a ring to purchase a monkey, he breaks out with: 'Thou torturest me, Tubal—it was my turquoise—I had it of Leah when I was a bachelor: I would not have given it for a wilderness of monkeys.'

Shylock: A Villain with Humanity

John Russell Brown

John Russell Brown identifies Shylock as a villain who hates, but also shows how Shakespeare gives him lines to defend himself and gain sympathy from the audience. John Russell Brown was a fellow at Birmingham University's Shakespeare Institute at Stratford-upon-Avon and professor of English at the University of Sussex in England. He is the author of *Theatre Language*, *Free Shakespeare*, and *Discovering Shakespeare*.

In Shakespeare's play, the Christians are in no doubt that Shylock is a thorough villain; nine times he is called a devil and, as his hatred leads him to kill like an animal, they can find no answer to "excuse the current" of his cruelty (IV. i. 64). Shylock declares his malice openly; he refuses many times the sum which is owed him and insists on taking Antonio's life. This was his settled resolve, for Jessica heard him say so soon after the bond was sealed, and in his first soliloquy, he is already looking for an opportunity to "feed fat the ancient grudge" he bears Antonio (I. iii. 42). Barabas[1] is a villain for his own aggrandisement and pleasure; Shylock is a villain because of the hate he bears Antonio, the Christian.

This was Shakespeare's emphasis in creating his Jew, but it does not follow that his play is anti-Jewish. It has been pointed out that Shylock and Tubal are not considered to be typical; the devil himself would have to "turn Jew" before there was another one like them (III. i. 70–1). There are only two slurs on Jews in general, one by Launcelot the clown, "my master's a very Jew" (II. ii. 100), and one by Antonio in the trial scene, though even here it is "*His* Jewish heart" which is exclaimed against (IV. i. 80). Shylock is motivated by his hate of a Christian, but, in spite of the latent prejudice

1. the Jew in Christopher Marlowe's play *The Jew of Malta*

this must have aroused in Elizabethan minds, he is not condemned out of hand; he is at least given a chance to show
how he counted his own deeds as righteousness.

SHYLOCK'S HUMANITY

[Critic H.B.] Charlton thought that Shakespeare planned *The
Merchant of Venice* as a play "to let the Jew dog have it", but
that when he came to write, he had to "exhibit a Jew who is
a man." Whatever Shakespeare's intentions may have been,
the "humanity" of Shylock has been proved many times in
the theatre. He is not merely a monster to revile and curse;
his viewpoint is fully given and can, on occasion, command
the whole sympathy of an audience. The first full opportunity for this is his sarcastic dialogue with Antonio:

> Shall I bend low, and in a bondman's[2] key
> With bated breath, and whisp'ring humbleness
> Say this:
> "Fair sir, you spet [spit] on me on Wednesday last,
> You spurn'd me such a day, another time
> You call'd me dog: and for these courtesies
> I'll lend you thus much moneys"?
>
> (I. iii. 118–24)

The early contact with Antonio, who is already known as the
generous and good Merchant, does not seem the most suit-
able place for Shakespeare to make Shylock bid for understanding, but Antonio gives a cold answer which reinforces
Shylock's argument:

> I am as like to call thee so again,
> To spet on thee again, to spurn thee too.
>
> (II. 125–6)

The next full opportunity for Shylock to state his case is the
speech "Hath not a Jew eyes? . . ." in Act III, Scene i, and here
he claims a hearing on the grounds that he suffers as other
men, and will take revenge like them.

So powerful has Shylock's justification proved, that it is
sometimes forgotten that a villain is speaking. It has to be
pointed out [by critic John Palmer] that "what is commonly
received as Shylock's plea for tolerance is in reality his justification of an inhuman purpose." Shakespeare has created
in Shylock an outcast who suffers and is driven to extremity
in his suffering, but no matter how harshly the Christians
treat him, he remains the Jew who intends to kill his enemy,

2. slave's

a harsh, cynical, and ruthless villain. Whether his suffering forces him to be a villain, or whether his villainy causes him to suffer, Shakespeare is not concerned to say. But there is a judgement: at the end of the trial scene, Shylock's designs are defeated and he has to accept conversion to Christianity. This was a punishment from Shylock's point of view, . . . but from Antonio's point of view, it also gave to Shylock a chance of eternal joy. The significance of this judgement must be reserved for fuller treatment later.

SHYLOCK: OLD, MISERLY, AND COMIC

In the meantime there are other aspects of Shylock which must be considered. Besides being a Jew, he is also an old man with a young daughter who escapes from him to marry the man she loves. Many critics have believed that Shakespeare intended this part of the play to gain more sympathy for Shylock. In their view, Jessica is a minx who heartlessly runs away from her old father, steals his money and the ring given to him by his beloved wife, and shamelessly joins his detractors and enemies. It is thought that these wrongs cause Shylock to harden his heart against Antonio.

But nowhere in the play does Shylock show any tenderness towards his daughter; in their one scene together, he merely enjoins her to lock up his possessions and not to watch the Christian revelry. It has already been noted that as a Jewess, loved by a Christian, Jessica stood in a fair way for the audience's sympathy; as the daughter of an old man who escapes from duress, she had another claim. . . .

Old Shylock is also a miser; Launcelot says he is "famish'd in his service" (II. ii. 101–2), Jessica that his "house is hell" (II. iii. 2), and Shylock himself says that money is the means whereby he lives. In such a role, he is fair game for the young lovers; even his own child can rob him and retain the sympathy of the audience. They will laugh with Salerio and Solanio at the old man's passionate outcry "My daughter! O my ducats! O my daughter! . . ." (II. viii. 15–22) for it is a comic revelation that he loves money before all else. The same is true of Shylock's:

> I would my daughter were dead at my foot, and the jewels in her ear: would she were hears'd[3] at my foot, and the ducats in her coffin.
>
> (III. i. 80–2)

3. on her bier

SHYLOCK PROCLAIMS HIS COMMONNESS

In act 3, scene 1, Shylock catalogs those qualities he shares
with all human beings and concludes that, like Christians,
he too seeks revenge when he is wronged.

Hath not a Jew hands, organs, dimensions, senses, affections,
passions? Fed with the same food, hurt with the same weapons,
subject to the same diseases, healed by the same means,
warmed and cooled by the same winter and summer as a
Christian is? If you prick us, do we not bleed? If you tickle us,
do we not laugh? If you poison us, do we not die? And if you
wrong us, shall we not revenge? If we are like you in the rest,
we will resemble you in that. If a Jew wrong a Christian, what
is his humility? Revenge. If a Christian wrong a Jew, what
should his sufferance be by Christian example? Why, revenge.
The villainy you teach me I will execute, and it shall go hard
but I will better the instruction.

The Merchant of Venice, act 3, scene 1, 61–76.

Professor [Elmer Edgar] Stoll has called this an example of
the familiar dramatic trick of comical anti-climax, of

> taking the audience in for a moment and ... then clapping
> upon the seemingly pathetic sentiment a cynical, selfish, or
> simply incongruous one.

Another trick is used in making Shylock repeat, with altera-
tion, Tubal's mention of a monkey; "I would not have given
it for a wilderness of monkeys" (III. i. 112–13) is a kind of
comic climax by repetition.

Stoll is among the critics who have seen Shylock as a
wholly comic figure, but there is a duality about Shylock as
an old curmudgeon as there is in his role as a Jew. Many of
his speeches are so phrased that they can be said in the theatre without any humour, simply as cries of anguish. Such
duality is found elsewhere in Shakespeare. For instance, in
2 Henry IV, the audience does not only laugh at Shallow and
Silence, alternating between the death of old Double and the
price of bullocks at Stamford fair. The trick of comical anti-
climax is used in these speeches, but there is also a moving
picture of two old men with wandering minds, trying to
make the good even with the bad, and trying to understand
mortality. There is a somewhat similar alternation when
Shylock hears of Antonio's losses. The tone, of course, is very
different; instead of an old man alternating meditatively between simple good and evil, Shylock is storm-tossed, vi-

ciously plunging from one side to another, from hope to despair. An audience may tend to laugh at the old miserly father foiled in his plans, but it is hard to laugh at the old man with his mind out of control, and his passion raging. The reaction of the audience is more complex still when he is seen to regain control and bend all his energies towards the object of his hate: "I will have the heart of him if he forfeit."

The picture of Shylock is not yet complete. A Jew says, "I will have the heart of him if he forfeit," but a usurer continues: "for were he out of Venice I can make what merchandise I will." In his first soliloquy, he says he hates Antonio because he is a Christian:

> *But more*, for that in low simplicity
> He lends out money gratis, and brings down
> The rate of usance[4] here with us in Venice.
>
> (I. iii. 38–40)

Antonio's active opposition to usury is said to be the chief reason for Shylock's hatred.

ELIZABETHANS DEBATE THE ISSUE OF USURY

In contrast to the "Jewish problem", the rights and wrongs of usury were a living issue to Elizabethans. There was general agreement that usury (the "lending for gaine, by compact, not adventuring the principall") was a great evil, but some said that it should be legalized and controlled. The Scriptures and the Fathers seemed to condemn it outright, but [protestant reformers John] Calvin, [Theodorus] Beza, and some other divines acknowledged that it had to be tolerated in a modern commonwealth. [Philosopher Francis] Bacon's essay "Of Usury" (1625) argued that it was "inevitable", and the laws of England, while calling usury a sin and aiming at its repression, permitted borrowing up to the rate of ten per cent. The evils of usury were widely known, for borrowing had become a necessity to many. Great Elizabethans, like [poet Philip] Sidney, [politicians] Essex, Leicester, and Southampton were each thousands of pounds in debt, and Queen Elizabeth was forced to borrow very large sums from European bankers. Shakespeare's Company, the Chamberlain's Men, built the Theatre and the Globe on money taken up at a rate of interest which was a continual burden to them. In spite of all sermons preached against it, usury became increasingly common; the translator of Philip Caesar's *Discourse against Usurers* (1578)

4. usury

believed that if inquiry were made, "the stocke of many Churches would bee founde out at Vsurie". In 1595 he was "counted a shameless man" who made request "to borrow without offering vsurie." But although usury at a limited rate was sometimes allowed in theory, and more and more people took advantage of it in practice, it seems to have been generally agreed that evil consequences followed its unbridled use. All classes of people would remonstrate with the rapacious and ruthless usurer, and would revile and mock him.

The literature of the time did so frequently. In *Zelauto*, for instance, [playwright Anthony] Munday made a usurer the villain of a flesh-bond story. The ballad of Gernutus [the Jew of Venice] tells a similar story about a Jewish usurer, and the author brought home the moral of his strange tale by pointing out:

> That many a wretch as ill as he
> doth live now at this day,

and wishing them like sentence to the Jew's.

SHYLOCK THE USURER

As a rapacious usurer who drew his victims to their ruin, Shylock would be condemned by every member of an Elizabethan audience. In picturing him as such, and in giving a long argument on the rights and wrongs of usury, Shakespeare added to his source as found in [Italian writer Ser Giovanni's] *Il Pecorone*. Shylock's opening dialogue might have been studied from life: the astute man of business plays his own game, bides his time, and makes Bassanio do the talking. Bassanio is not practised at this, and his impatience soon betrays how much he needs the money; in return he receives a long disquisition on Antonio's hazards. When Antonio enters, Shylock maintains the lead in the conversation, ordering it to his own ends. A usurer was cunning and deceitful by profession, and when Shylock proffers friendship to Antonio and proposes the "merry" bond, an Elizabethan audience might fear the worst: it was said that a "Vsurer lendeth like a friend but he couenanteth[5] like an enemie." Some critics have thought that Shylock's desire for friendship is genuine, but in view of the usurer's reputation, it is more probably a gamble for the monstrous forfeiture. If Antonio's ships *did* come home, at the worst Shylock would only lose the interest his money might have gained at usury

---

5. makes a covenant

elsewhere; at the best, he could use one of the many tricks, familiarized in novels, plays, sermons, and treatises, by which a usurer could delay the payment beyond the named day. Such a trick is alluded to in *Zelauto*, where the usurer is away from home on the expiration of the bond. In [French writer Alexander Silvayn's] *The Orator*, the merchant suspects that the Jew has caused his money to be delayed "by secret meanes." Shylock is risking very little in proposing his "merry" bond, and even Bassanio sees the danger. Antonio's generosity must have been very great when he walked into the usurer's trap.

Even as a usurer, Shylock is given an opportunity to justify himself. It seems as if Shakespeare was determined not to create a "stage villain", who would always evoke a simple, hostile response. Shylock is a most complex and dominating character; he appears in only five scenes and yet for many people he is the centre of the play's interest. As an old miserly father he is comic, as a Jew he is savage and ruthless, as a usurer he seeks to ensnare the needy and Antonio, their protector. Yet in all these roles he is also a man who suffers and triumphs, speaks at times with great nobility, and has a "kind of wild justice" in his cry for revenge.

Portia Fails the Test for Inner Gold

Harold C. Goddard

Harold C. Goddard argues that Shakespeare portrays
Portia as an actress whose glamorous role overshad-
ows her inner sense of mercy and goodness. Besides
his studies of Shakespeare's characters, Goddard has
researched the work and times of American writers
Ralph Waldo Emerson and Henry David Thoreau and
written *Studies in New England Transcendentalism.*

However it may be now, there was a time when anyone who
had been through high school knew that *The Merchant of
Venice* is an interweaving of three strands commonly known
as the casket story, the bond story, and the ring story. The
teacher in those days always pointed out the skill with which
Shakespeare had made three plots into one, but generally
left out the much more important fact that the three stories,
as the poet uses them, become variations on a single theme.

The casket story obviously stresses the contrast between
what is within and what is without. So, however, if less obviously, do the other two. The bond story is built about the
distinction between the letter and the spirit of the law. But
what are letter and spirit if not what is without and what is
within? And the ring story turns on the difference between
the outer form and the inner essence of a promise. When
Bassanio rewards the Young Doctor of Laws with Portia's
ring, he is keeping the spirit of his vow to her as certainly as
he would have been breaking it if he had kept the ring on his
finger. In the circumstances literal fidelity would have been
actual faithlessness.

Yet in spite of this thematic unity (into which the love
story of Lorenzo and Jessica can also be fitted) we find one
of the keenest of recent critics asking: "What in the name of
all dramatic propriety and economy are the casket scenes

doing? They are quite irrelevant to the plot, and . . . for the characterization of Bassanio, a positive nuisance. . . . They are a mere piece of adornment. And the answer to that 'why' is no doubt just that Shakespeare knew that they were effective episodes, and that no audience with the colour of the scenes in their eyes and the beauty of his verse in their ears was going to trouble its heads that they were no more than episodes. Shakespeare was writing for audiences and not for dramatic critics."

Of course Shakespeare the playwright was writing for audiences. But how about Shakespeare the poet?

Drama, as we have said, must make a wide and immediate appeal to a large number of people of ordinary intelligence. The playwright must make his plots plain, his characters easily grasped, his ideas familiar. The public does not want the truth. It wants confirmation of its prejudices. That is why the plays of mere playwrights have immediate success but seldom survive.

What the poet is seeking, on the other hand, is the secret of life, and, even if he would, he cannot share with a crowd in a theater, through the distorting medium of actors who are far from sharing his genius, such gleams of it as may have been revealed to him. He can share it only with the few, and with them mostly in solitude. . . .

The Merchant of Venice leaves an impression of bright costumes, witty conversations, gay or dreamy melody, and romantic love. Gold is the symbol of this world of pleasure. But what is under this careless ease? . . .

The court scene becomes something quite different from what it seems to be. It is still a trial scene, but it is Portia who is on trial. Or, better, it is a casket scene in which she is subjected to the same test to which she has submitted her suitors. Can she detect hidden gold under a leaden exterior?

Concerning Portia's own exterior the poet leaves us in no doubt. To the eye she is nothing if not golden, and she does nothing if she does not shine. The praise showered on her within the play itself has been echoed by thousands of readers and spectators and the continued appeal of her role to actresses is proof of the fascination she never fails to exercise. No one can deny her brilliance or her charm, or could wish to detract from them. (If I do not linger on them here, it is because ample justice has been done to them so often.) Yet Portia, too, like so many of the others in this play, is not precisely all she seems to be. Indeed, what girl of her years, with her wealth, wit, and beauty, could be the object of such universal adulation and come through unscathed? In her uprush of joy when Bassanio chooses the right casket there is, it is true, an accent of the humility that fresh love always bestows, and she speaks of herself as "an unlesson'd girl, unschool'd, unpractis'd." There the child Portia once was is speaking, but it is a note that is sounded scarcely anywhere else in her role. The woman that child has grown into, on the contrary, is the darling of a sophisticated society which has nurtured in her anything but unself-consciousness. Indeed, it seems to be as natural to her as to a queen or princess to take herself unblushingly at the estimate this society places on her.

> *Who chooseth me shall gain what many men desire.*
> Why, that's the lady: all the world desires her;
> From the four corners of the earth they come . . .

says Morocco. And tacitly Portia assents to that interpretation of the inscription on the golden casket. . . .

PORTIA, THE ACTRESS-HEROINE

The casket motif, the court scene, and the ring incident taken together comprise a good share of the story. Each of them is intrinsically spectacular, histrionic, or theatrical—or all three in one. Each is a kind of play within a play, with Portia at the center or at one focus. The casket scenes are little symbolic pageants; the court scene is drama on the surface and tragedy underneath; the ring incident is a one-act comedy complete in itself. What sort of heroine does all this demand? Obviously one with the temperament of an actress, not averse to continual limelight. Portia is exactly that.

When she hears that the man who helped her lover woo and win her is in trouble, her character and the contingency fit each other like hand and glove. Why not impersonate a Young Doctor of Laws and come to Antonio's rescue? It is typical of her that at first she takes the "whole device," as she calls it, as a kind of prank. Her imagination overflows with pictures of the opportunities for acting that her own and Nerissa's disguise as young men will offer, of the innocent lies they will tell, the fun they will have, the fools they will make of their husbands. The tragic situation of Antonio seems at the moment the last thing in her mind, or the responsibility of Bassanio for the plight of his friend. The fact that she is to have the leading role in a play in real life eclipses everything else. There is more than a bit of the stage-struck girl in Portia.

And so when the curtain rises on Act IV, Shakespeare the playwright and his actress-heroine, between them, are equipped to give us one of the tensest and most theatrically effective scenes he had conceived up to this time. What Shakespeare the poet gives us, however, and what it means to Portia the woman, is something rather different. . . .

The introduction and identifications over, Portia, as the Young Doctor of Laws, says to Shylock:

> Of a strange nature is the suit you follow;
> Yet in such rule that the Venetian law
> Cannot impugn[1] you as you do proceed.

This bears the mark of preparation, if not of rehearsal. It seems a strange way of beginning, like a partial prejudgment of the case in Shylock's favor. But his hopes must be raised at the outset to make his ultimate downfall the more dramatic. "Do you confess the bond?" she asks Antonio. "I do," he replies.

> Then must the Jew be merciful.

Portia, as she says this, is apparently still addressing Antonio. It would have been more courteous if, instead of speaking of him in the third person, she had turned directly to Shylock and said, "Then must you be merciful." But she makes a worse slip than that: the word *must*. Instantly Shylock seizes on it, pouring all his sarcasm into the offending verb:

> On what compulsion *"must"* I? Tell me that.

Portia is caught! You can fairly see her wheel about to face not so much the Jew as the unanswerable question the Jew has asked. He is right—she sees it: "must" and "mercy" have nothing to do with each other; no law, moral or judicial, can force a man to be merciful.

For a second, the question must have thrown Portia off balance. This was not an anticipated moment in the role of the Young Doctor. But forgetting the part she is playing, she rises to the occasion superbly. The truth from Shylock elicits the truth from her. Instead of trying to brush the Jew aside or hide behind some casuistry or technicality, she frankly sustains his exception:

1. call in question

The quality of mercy is not strain'd[2]. . . .

"I was wrong, Shylock," she confesses in effect. "You are right"; mercy is a matter of grace, not of constraint:

> It droppeth as the gentle rain from heaven
> Upon the place beneath. . . .

Shylock, then, supplied not only the cue, but, we might almost say, the first line of Portia's most memorable utterance.

WORDS OF MERCY FROM PORTIA THE WOMAN

In all Shakespeare—unless it be Hamlet with "To be or not to be"—there is scarcely another character more identified in the world's mind with a single speech than Portia with her words on mercy. And the world is right. They have a "quality" different from anything else in her role. They are no prepared words of the Young Doctor she is impersonating, but her own, as unexpected as was Shylock's disconcerting question. Something deep down in him draws them from something deep down—or shall we say high up?—in her. They are the spiritual gold hidden not beneath lead but beneath the "gold" of her superficial life, her reward for meeting Shylock's objection with sincerity rather than with evasion.

A hush falls over the courtroom as she speaks them (as it does over the audience when *The Merchant of Venice* is performed). Even the Jew is moved. Who can doubt it? Who can doubt that for a moment at least he is drawn back from the brink of madness and logic on which he stands? Here is the celestial visitant—the Portia God made—sent expressly to exorcise the demonic powers that possess him. Only an insensible clod could fail to feel its presence. And Shylock is no insensible clod. Can even he show mercy? Will a miracle happen? It is the supreme moment. The actor who misses it misses everything.

And then, incredibly, it is Portia who fails Shylock, not Shylock Portia. The same thing happens to her that happened to him at that other supreme moment when he offered Antonio the loan without interest. Her antipodal self emerges. In the twinkling of an eye, the angel reverts to the Doctor of Laws. "So quick bright things come to confusion." Whether the actress in Portia is intoxicated by the sound of her own voice and the effect it is producing, or whether she

2. mercy must be given freely

feels the great triumph she has rehearsed being stolen from her if Shylock relents, or both, at any rate, pushing aside the divine Portia and her divine opportunity, the Young Doctor resumes his role. His "therefore, Jew" gives an inkling of what is coming. You can hear, even in the printed text, the change of voice, as Portia sinks from compassion to legality:

> I have spoke thus much
> To mitigate the justice of thy plea,
> Which if thou follow, this strict court of Venice
> Must needs give sentence 'gainst the merchant there.

It would be unbelievable if the words were not there. "You should show mercy," the Young Doctor says in effect, "but if you don't, this court will be compelled to decide in your favor.". . .

It is like a postscript that undoes the letter. Thus Portia the lover of mercy is deposed by Portia the actress that the latter may have the rest of her play. And the hesitating Shylock, pushed back to the precipice, naturally has nothing to say but

> My deeds upon my head! I crave the law,
> The penalty and forfeit of my bond.

The rest of the scene is an overwhelming confirmation of Portia's willingness to sacrifice the human to the theatrical, a somewhat different kind of sacrifice from that referred to in the inscription on the leaden casket. . . .

PORTIA EXQUISITELY STAGES SUSPENSE

The skill with which from this point she stages and acts her play proves her play proves her a consummate playwright, director, and actress—three in one. She wrings the last drop of possible suspense from every step in the mounting excitement. She stretches every nerve to the breaking point, arranges every contrast, climax, and reversal with the nicest sense for maximum effect, doing nothing too soon or too late, holding back her "Tarry a little" until Shylock is on the very verge of triumph, even whetting his knife perhaps. It is she who says to Antonio, "Therefore lay bare your bosom." It is she who asks if there is a balance ready to weigh the flesh, a surgeon to stay the blood. And she actually allows Antonio to undergo his last agony, to utter, uninterrupted, his final farewell.

It is at this point that the shallow Bassanio reveals an unsuspected depth in his nature by declaring, with a ring of

PORTIA'S WISE WORDS ABOUT MERCY

When Portia says that Shylock "must" be merciful, he asks how he can be compelled. Portia replies, corrected, that mercy can only be given freely, and when it is, it blesses the giver and the receiver.

POR. The quality[1] of mercy is not strained,[2]
It droppeth as the gentle rain from heaven
Upon the place beneath. It is twice blest;
It blesseth him that gives and him that takes.
'Tis mightiest in the mightiest. It becomes
The thronèd monarch better than his crown.
His scepter shows the force of temporal power,
The attribute to awe and majesty
Wherein doth sit the dread and fear of kings.
But mercy is above this sceptered sway,
It is enthronèd in the hearts of kings,
It is an attribute to God himself,
And earthly power doth then show likest God's
When mercy seasons[3] justice. Therefore, Jew,
Though justice be thy plea, consider this,
That in the course of justice none of us
Should see salvation. We do pray for mercy,
And that same prayer doth teach us all to render[4]
The deeds of mercy.

1. quality: nature 2. strained: forced; i.e., mercy must be given freely 3. seasons: is mixed with 4. render: pay back

The Merchant of Venice, act 4, scene 1, 184–202.

sincerity we cannot doubt, that he would sacrifice everything, including his life and his wife, to save his friend.

Who chooseth me must give and hazard all he hath.

It is now, not when he stood before it, that Bassanio proves worthy of the leaden casket. Called on to make good his word, he doubtless would not have had the strength. But that does not prove that he does not mean what he says at the moment. And at that moment all Portia can do to help him is to turn into a jest—which she and Nerissa are alone in a position to understand—the most heart-felt and noble words her lover ever uttered.

POR.: Your wife would give you little thanks for that,
If she were by to hear you make the offer.

This light answer, in the presence of what to Antonio and Bassanio is the very shadow of death, measures her insensibility to anything but the play she is presenting, the role she is enacting.

From this jest, in answer to the Jew's insistence, she turns without a word of transition to grant Shylock his sentence:

> A pound of that same merchant's flesh is thine.
> The court awards it, and the law doth give it . . .
> And you must cut this flesh from off his breast.
> The law allows it, and the court awards it.

It is apparently all over with Antonio. The Jew lifts his knife. But once more appearances are deceitful. With a "tarry a little" this mistress of the psychological moment plays in succession, one, two, three, the cards she has been keeping back for precisely this moment. Now the Jew is caught in his own trap, now he gets a taste of his own logic, a dose of his own medicine. Now there is no more talk of mercy, but justice pure and simple, an eye for an eye:

> Por.: as thou urgest justice, be assur'd
> Thou shalt have justice, more than thou desir'st.

Seeing his prey about to elude him, Shylock is now willing to accept the offer of three times the amount of his bond, and Bassanio actually produces the money. He is willing to settle on those terms. But not Portia:

> The Jew shall have all justice; soft!⁵ no haste:
> He shall have nothing but the penalty.

Shylock reduces his demand: he will be satisfied with just his principal. Again Bassanio has the money ready. But Portia is adamant:

> He shall have merely justice, and his bond.

When the Jew pleads again for his bare principal, she repeats:

> Thou shalt have nothing but the forfeiture,

and as he moves to leave the courtroom, she halts him with a

> Tarry, Jew:
> The law hath yet another hold on you.

PORTIA'S ACTING LEADS TO COLD INDIFFERENCE

. . . What possessed Portia to torture not only Antonio but her own husband with such superfluous suspense? She knew what was coming. Why didn't she let it come at once? Why

3. pause a little

didn't she invoke immediately the law prescribing a penalty for any alien plotting against the life of any citizen of Venice instead of waiting until she had put those she supposedly loved upon the rack? The only possible answer is that she wanted a spectacle, a dramatic triumph with herself at the center. . . .

To all this it is easy to imagine what those will say who hold that Shakespeare was first the playwright and only incidentally poet and psychologist. "Why, but this is just a play!" they will exclaim, half-amused, half-contemptuous, "and a comedy at that! Portia! It isn't Portia who contrives the postponement. It is Shakespeare. Where would his play have been if his heroine had cut things short or failed to act exactly as she did?" Where indeed? Which is precisely why the poet made her the sort of woman who would have acted under the given conditions exactly as she did act. That was his business: not to find or devise situations exciting in the theater (any third-rate playwright can do that) but to discover what sort of men and women would behave in the often extraordinary ways in which they are represented as behaving in such situations in the stories he inherited and selected for dramatization. . . .

And so Portia is given a second chance. She is to be tested again. She has had her legal and judicial triumph. Now it is over will she show to her victim that quality which at her own divine moment she told us "is an attribute to God himself"? The Jew is about to get his deserts. Will Portia forget her doctrine that mercy is mercy precisely because it is not deserved? The Jew is about to receive justice. Will she remember that our prayers for mercy should teach us to do the deeds of mercy and that in the course of justice none of us will see salvation? Alas! she will forget, she will not remember. Like Shylock, but in a subtler sense, she who has appealed to logic "perishes" by it.

Up to this point she has been forward enough in arrogating to herself the function of judge. But now, instead of showing compassion herself or entreating the Duke to, she motions Shylock to his knees:

Down therefore and beg mercy of the Duke.

"Mercy"! This beggar's mercy, though it goes under the same name, has not the remotest resemblance to that quality that drops like the gentle rain from heaven. Ironically it

is the Duke who proves truer to the true Portia than Portia
herself.

> DUKE: That thou shalt see the difference of our spirits,
>   I pardon thee thy life before thou ask it.

And he suggests that the forfeit of half of Shylock's property
to the state may be commuted to a fine.

> Ay, for the state; not for Antonio,

Portia quickly interposes, as if afraid that the Duke is going
to be too merciful, going to let her victim off too leniently.
Here, as always, the aftermath of too much "theatrical" emotion is a coldness of heart that is like lead. The tone in which
Portia has objected is reflected in the hopelessness of Shylock's next words:

> Nay, take my life and all! Pardon not that!
> You take my house when you do take the prop
> That doth sustain my house. You take my life
> When you do take the means whereby I live.

THE IRONY OF THE PLAY'S SPIRITUAL MESSAGE

Shylock's conviction that Christianity and revenge are syn-
onyms is confirmed. "If a Christian wrong a Jew, what
should his sufferance be by Christian example? Why, revenge." The unforgettable speech from which that comes,
together with Portia's on mercy, and Lorenzo's on the harmony of heaven, make up the spiritual argument of the play.
Shylock asserts that a Jew is a man. Portia declares that
man's duty to man is mercy—which comes from heaven.
Lorenzo points to heaven but laments that the materialism
of life insulates man from its harmonies. A celestial syllo-
gism that puts to shame the logic of the courtroom.

That Shakespeare planned his play from the outset to enforce the irony of Portia's failure to be true to her inner self
in the trial scene is susceptible of something as near proof as
such things can ever be. . . .

Portia enters *The Merchant of Venice* with the remark that
she is aweary of the world. Nerissa replies with that wise little speech about the illness of those that surfeit with too
much (an observation that takes on deeper meaning in the
retrospect after we realize that at the core what is the trouble with Portia and her society is boredom). "Good sentences and well pronounced," says Portia, revealing in those
last two words more than she knows. "They would be better
if well followed," Nerissa pertinently retorts. Whereupon

Portia, as if gifted with insight into her own future, takes up Nerissa's theme:

> If to do were as easy as to know what were good to do, chapels had been churches, and poor men's cottages princes' palaces. It is a good divine that follows his own instructions: I can easier teach twenty what were good to be done, than be one of the twenty to follow mine own teaching.

If that is not a specific preparation for the speech on mercy and what follows it, what in the name of coincidence is it? The words on mercy were good sentences, well pronounced. And far more than that. But for Portia they remained just words in the sense that they did not teach her to do the deeds of mercy. So, a few seconds after we see her for the first time, does Shakespeare let her pass judgment in advance on the most critical act of her life. For a moment, at the crisis in the courtroom, she seems about to become the leaden casket with the spiritual gold within. But the temptation to gain what many men desire—admiration and praise—is too strong for her and she reverts to her worldly self. Portia is the golden casket.

Antonio: The Neurotic Gambler

Ralph Berry

Ralph Berry approaches *The Merchant of Venice* linguistically by focusing on key words repeated in the play—"venture," "hazard," "thrift," "usury," "lottery"—to explain character and human relationships. In particular, he explores the character of Antonio using the word "gamble"; he compares Antonio's neurosis to that of a modern gambler with a subconscious desire to lose. Ralph Berry has taught English at the University of Manitoba in Canada. He is the author of a fiction collection entitled *Plane Geometry and Other Affairs of the Heart* and of critical articles published in the *Iowa Review* and *Appalachee Quarterly*.

The most inviting approach to *The Merchant of Venice* lies, I suggest, through its linguistic texture. It is clear that the play's linguistic identity, as it were, is manifest not so much in images as in a small group of associated words of mainly literal status. The key word I take to be "venture"; and it is obviously linked with "hazard," "thrift," "usury," "fortune," "lottery," and "advantage." These terms recur steadily throughout the play. What they have in common is the idea of *gain*, with a varying degree of risk attached. Suppose, then, that we conceive of the play as a conjugation of the verb *to gain*. All the relationships in the play (with, I think, the sole exception of Old Gobbo and Launcelot) dramatize this verb. The nominal activity of the dramatis personae is in considerable part, love. What the play demonstrates is the interconnections of love and money. So the terms I have cited extend from commerce to personal relations. The formal principle of *The Merchant of Venice*, then, I take to be a series of mutations of "venture."

Excerpted from *Shakespeare's Comedies: Explorations in Form*, by Ralph Berry (Princeton, NJ: Princeton University Press, 1972). Reprinted with permission.

"Venture" virtually opens the play. As a noun, it means a commercial enterprise involving some risk; and its specific application is to overseas trading. It is in this sense that "venture" is introduced, forming the staple of the conversation of Antonio and his friends. . . .

So Antonio, who had stressed the element of *safety* while discussing his ventures with Salerio and Solanio, stresses the element of *risk* with Shylock. It is not a position distinguished for intellectual consistency, or conviction. And underlying the literal, or manifest meaning is the metaphoric. This undercurrent of debate is obliquely hinted at by Shylock, and perhaps understood by Antonio.

The prevailing custom, in the Venice of the play as in England, was that money was lent gratis to friends and with interest to strangers. That is a way of putting it. Another is to say that by lending out money gratis, one makes the recipient one's friend. It was, no doubt, a congenial way of cementing amity between the high-born and those, however cultivated, in trade. Shylock does not speculate overtly on Antonio's motives, but he records the fact: "He lends out money gratis and brings down/ The rate of usance here with us in Venice." (I, 3, 40–41) And Antonio's opening words to Shylock confirm this: it is a claim to moral superiority too strident to be called effortless:

> Shylock, albeit I neither lend nor borrow
> By taking nor by giving of excess[1],
> Yet to supply the ripe[2] wants of my friend,
> I'll break a custom.

> > (I, 3, 57–60)

. . . Antonio is an intelligent man. He is compelled, by a freak of circumstances, to argue with a man whom he loathes and despises. He has to find one solid, intellectually valid reason to endorse the propositions: I am better than you, I am different from you. And he can find nothing better than the claim that ventures are "swayed and fashioned by the hand of heaven." Yet some ventures are, overall, virtual certainties; and for that matter difficulties may arise in gathering one's interest on a loan. What, then, is left? Only a weak gibe, "or is your gold and silver ewes and rams?" The short answer is: yes. Shylock fashions his answer more elegantly: "I cannot tell; I make it breed as fast." And that pregnant phrase in effect concludes the debate. For the imper-

1. interest charged beyond the original loan 2. needing immediate help

sonal will of money is to breed; and Antonio has failed to demonstrate the moral superiority of his breeding methods. Moreover, he fails to take up the covert charge that there are more ways than one of accepting interest. The intellectual weakness becomes the psychological weakness, vis-à-vis[3] Shylock. Hence Antonio, called upon to refute the Jew, can only reject him: "The devil can cite Scripture for his purpose." (I, 3, 94) That is abuse, not argument. The fact is that Shylock has refuted Antonio's claims to moral superiority; and Antonio, I think, knows it.

Hence Antonio—disturbed, shaken, somehow aware of the weaknesses in his position—is in no condition to penetrate Shylock's design. Rather, he blunders forward into the trap. The bond is dangerous as well as ludicrous; yet Antonio cannot retreat without loss of face. For Antonio's own arguments and attitudes bind him to that position. He wants the money; he will not borrow at high interest, "giving of excess"; he must accept at face value Shylock's wish for friendship, dramatized in a spectacularly frivolous bond; to reject the Jew's proposal is to show signs of fear, to rate such a creature as capable of danger; he wishes, perhaps, to make an imposing gesture before his friend, Bassanio. It is a complex of motives, and we have not exhausted them.

We can now attack directly the central problem of Antonio's psychology. The melancholy that shrouds him is surely neurotic in origin. . . . What sort of man is Antonio, and why does he do the things he does? More specifically: can we identify the neurosis that appears to grip him? . . .

What, then, is my explanation for the conduct of Antonio? I return to the key word, "venture." That word has several near-synonyms in *The Merchant of Venice*. None of them is the simple word we should use, in modem English, to express the essential psychological quality of the action. That word is *gamble*.

ANTONIO IS LIKE A NEUROTIC GAMBLER

No one, so far as I know, has concentrated on the implications of *gamble* in the context of this play, though critics often use the term in passing to describe Antonio's reckless acceptance of the bond. Yet gambling is a profoundly significant human activity, which today possesses an extensive literature on its

---

3. face to face with; opposite to another

> **ANTONIO'S RECKLESS CONTRACT**
>
> *Herman Sinsheimer finds it puzzling that Antonio would make a risky deal with a man he hates and has insulted. Sinsheimer speculates about a possible flaw in the play's construction and about Shakespeare's meaning.*
>
> It is puzzling that Antonio trustfully accepts the offer of a Jew whom he despises and insults, to make the loan without interest. He ought to have considered as a merchant in what way Shylock would be interested in the bond. Without doubt it is a psychological flaw, in the play as a whole and the law-suit, that he completely forgets how sorely he has provoked his bond-partner and that he, the proud gentleman, was ready to accept favours from a man whose personality, trade, and tribe he so thoroughly scorns. (It is difficult not to suppose that Shakespeare meant to be ironical.)
>
> Herman Sinsheimer, *Shylock: The History of a Character.* New York: Benjamin Blom, 1947.

operations and psychology. The classic work on the subject is Edmund Bergler's *The Psychology of Gambling* [1958], which I now draw upon to substantiate my view of Antonio.

Many people indulge in a mild, occasional gamble. But Bergler's study is concerned with neurotic gambling. His central thesis is that the neurotic gambler plays to lose. "The unconscious wish to lose becomes . . . an integral part of the gambler's inner motivations." The mechanism of this compulsion to lose he analyzes into three stages:

(i) "Unconscious provocation of a situation in which they are rejected and defeated."

(ii) "Attack, full of hatred and seemingly in self-defense, aimed at their self-constructed enemies."

(iii) "Self-pity, and the enjoyment of unconscious psychic masochistic pleasure."

Psychic masochism, "denotes the unconscious craving for defeat, humiliation, rejection, pain." It constitutes the consummation of the process, and the objective of the gambler.

Now this, which is a generalized structure of the gambler's psychology, fits Antonio very well. Indeed, one could argue that the play's opening line, "In sooth I know not why I am so sad" reveals not so much depression as that ennui[4] which, we are told, is the classic state of the gambler before a hazard. But let us consider the three phases of the mechanism.

4. listlessness; lack of interest; boredom

(i) "Unconscious provocation of a situation . . ." Antonio's fortunes are extraordinarily extended, even in Act I. Salerio and Solanio both feel he *ought* to be worrying more about his ventures. Shylock, the auditor of the play's persons and values, states that "his means are in supposition."[5] (I, 3, 16) Indeed they are. Of six ventures, four are outside the Mediterranean—Antonio's normal field of operations—and two, Mexico and India, are manifestly hazardous. There is no safe local trading here, no real insurance. Yet Antonio acts as a bottomless reservoir of funds for his friend; he is as extravagant a backer as Bassanio a spender. Over and above his ambitious trading ventures, Antonio pledges his person. He seems to court risks: perhaps out of a desire to hazard all for Bassanio, and by losing his principal—his body—gain a supremacy in Bassanio's affections. The motivation is not incompatible with my earlier suggestions. We have to read the sudden decision "Content, in faith. I'll seal to such a bond" (I, 3, 148) from our experience of life, in which such critical decisions are made by the mind for causes which the intellect cannot compass. Here I stress the darker side of the mind, the self-destructive urge which impels the gambler to place his all, not a part, at hazard. Certainly Antonio has a responsibility for his difficulties, that does not square with his later adoption of the role of passive tool of fate.

(ii) The "attack, full of hatred . . . aimed at . . . self-constructed enemies" clearly applies to Antonio's relations with Shylock. What is marked about Antonio is the extraordinary virulence of his hatred of Shylock. Of course, all the Christians loathe him. Salerio and Solanio jeer at him, Launcelot leaves his service, Bassanio can scarcely contain his distaste for him. But at least the Venetians (prior to the trial scene) treat Shylock as an intensely unlikeable human being. Antonio treats him like a dog. "You spit on me on Wednesday last,/You spurned me such a day, another time/You called me dog." (I, 3, 122–124) Is there not something pathological in the intensity of hate which Antonio brings to his dealings with Shylock?

ANTONIO HAS EFFEMINATE QUALITIES

(iii) "Self-pity, and the enjoyment of unconscious psychic masochistic pleasure." This, I suggest, is consistent with An-

5. doubt

tonio's behavior following the bond agreement. There are two reported passages. First, Salerio describes the parting with Bassanio:

> I saw Bassanio and Antonio part:
> Bassanio told him he would make some speed
> Of his return; he answered, "Do not so.
> Slubber[6] not business for my sake, Bassanio,
> But stay the very riping of the time;
> And for the Jew's bond which he hath of me,
> Let it not enter in your mind of love.
> Be merry, and employ your chiefest thoughts
> To courtship and such fair ostents[7] of love
> As shall conveniently become you there."
> And even there, his eye being big with tears,
> Turning his face, he put his hand behind him,
> And with affection wondrous sensible[8]
> He wrung Bassanio's hand; and so they parted.
>
> (II, 8, 36–49)

Is there not here a somewhat feminine quality, a quality expressed commonly in the words: "Don't put yourself out on *my* account"? Antonio's is the unmistakable voice of the woman currently eclipsed by the more dashing rival, and determined to extract the utmost moral gratification from the situation. This is even more apparent in the letter Antonio sends Bassanio:

> Sweet Bassanio, my ships have all miscarried, my creditors grow cruel, my estate is very low, my bond to the Jew is forfeit. And since in paying it, it is impossible I should live, all debts are cleared between you and I if I might but see you at my death. Notwithstanding, use your pleasure. If your love do not persuade you to come, let not my letter.
>
> (III, 2, 315–321)

Even the syntax is feminine: the fluctuating "if... notwithstanding... if..." The "if your love do not persuade you to come, let not my letter" is especially revealing. It is almost coquettish. But it is also the voice of one thriving on rejection: really, is there any likelihood that Bassanio would *not* come?

What Antonio wants, in brief, is to suffer and to have Bassanio witness it. He says as much. "Pray God Bassanio come/To see me pay his debt, and then I care not!" (III, 3, 35–36) The trial scene finds Antonio fully resigned to the extremity of his sentence: there is no life force left in the man.

> I do oppose
> My patience to his fury, and am armed

---

6. be slovenly with 7. outward shows 8. wonderfully full of feeling

To suffer with a quietness of spirit
The very tyranny and rage of his.

(IV, 1, 10–13)

Indeed, he positively urges the Court to proceed to judgment, on not less than three occasions (83, 116, 241–242). It all comes down to the extraordinarily interesting and revealing metaphor that Antonio chooses to express his situation: "I am a tainted[9] wether of the flock,/Meetest for death." (IV, 1, 114–115) A wether, though scarcely any critic appears conscious of this simple fact, is a castrated ram. Wethers cannot breed. Hence, with a sad irony, Antonio refers back to his earlier exchange with Shylock:

Antonio: Or is your gold and silver ewes and rams?
Shylock: I cannot tell; I make it breed as fast.

(I, 3, 91–92)

Antonio's financial operations have proven sterile. But surely the human implications of "wether" go beyond the allusion to trading methods. . . .

Antonio's sense of failure, his readiness—even longing—for death, are marked. Both as a man, and as merchant-venturer, Antonio is sterile. The metaphor dominates him.

So far, then, Antonio's conduct fits the generalized structure of the neurotic gambler. But we can do better than this. Bergler distinguishes several subcategories of gambler, one of which seems strikingly applicable to Antonio. It is the passive-feminine male gambler. Bergler describes the type thus: "This type displays the characteristics of the classical gambler, with the addition of a tendency toward unconscious feminine identification. This identification makes it possible for him to enjoy, in defeat, the emotional sensation of being overwhelmed." As I have already suggested, there is a certain feminine quality in Antonio. "Passive-feminine" appears an ideal way of characterizing him. And the "tendency toward unconscious feminine identification" is pronounced in Antonio's final "bid her be judge/Whether Bassanio had not once a love." (IV, 1, 274–275) . . .

What sort of relationships does he tend to form? Here again Bergler has a suggestive answer:

Passive-feminine gamblers consistently seek "stronger" partners. The women they choose to marry are shrews; the men they choose for their friends are "strong," "superior" characters, who exploit or dominate them. Submissive, always on

9. diseased

the lookout for someone to admire, they are the typical fol-
lowers. They are of course unconscious of all this since lack
of initiative and absence of normal activity are easily ratio-
nalized.

This applies exactly to Antonio and Bassanio. Bassanio, of
course, is really a fairly tough character. His suppliant situations in the play should not deceive us. He is extraordinarily good at getting his own way, and reveals a basic shrewdness in the crisis of the casket choice. Bassanio is the type of
aristocrat who exploits his charm to ensure that he is never
on the losing side. What he risks is other people's money.
Bassanio is one of life's winners; no wonder Antonio admires him.

In sum, Antonio exhibits a recognizable (in twentieth century terms) neurosis, that of the passive-feminine gambler;
this is the key to his conduct and personal relations. His
commercial activities are not merely a source of income;
they express the cast of his mind. *Venture*, for him, is a high-
risk activity whose ultimate psychological objective is a personal disaster allied to certain compensatory satisfactions.
The pound of flesh that Shylock demands has its hidden
counterpart in the price Antonio exacts of Bassanio: that he
should come, "To see me pay his debt, and then I care not!"

CHAPTER 4

Structure and Language

READINGS ON
THE MERCHANT OF VENICE

Two Contrasting Worlds in *The Merchant of Venice*

Norman N. Holland

Norman N. Holland claims that there are two worlds in *The Merchant of Venice:* Portia's Belmont and Shylock's Venice. He contends that Belmont is a world of beauty, mythology, music, plenty, and love, a place where lovely things flourish. Venice, he concludes, is a masculine world where money and commerce govern anxious lives stressed by competition, scarcity, and harsh justice, a place of fragmentation and dwindling. Norman Holland has taught English at the Massachusetts Institute of Technology. He has taught a television course for credit on Shakespeare, published articles in the *Atlantic*, the *Nation*, and the *Hudson Review*, and published books on Restoration comedy and psychoanalytic criticism of Shakespeare.

The Merchant of Venice is an unusually complex and intricate work, and Shylock is only part of it. The play has in all five plots. Two are major. We can consider the first as the episodes in which Bassanio, looking for a rich wife, wins the heiress Portia by fulfilling the conditions of her father's will and choosing the correct one of three caskets, gold, silver, and lead. We can consider the second as the episodes in which the title character, the merchant of Venice (*not* Shylock, but Antonio), to finance Bassanio's wooing of Portia, borrows three thousand ducats from Shylock, promising to give a pound of his flesh if he fails to pay on time. We can consider as two lesser plots Lorenzo's eloping with Shylock's daughter, Jessica, and the problem of the rings: Portia gives Bassanio a ring when she marries him, and her maid, Nerissa, gives her suitor, Gratiano, a ring. When Portia dresses up as a young doctor of laws to save Antonio's life at the hands of Shylock, she demands the rings as payment (another money element). Finally, there are the doings of Launcelot Gobbo, Shylock's servant, if we can call them a fifth plot. For the most part all Launcelot does is crack the loutish jokes allotted to the Elizabethan clown, but in the course of the play, he does exchange his job with Shylock for a job with Bassanio.

These five plots in turn take place in two different worlds, one the world of Shylock's Venice, the other the world of Portia's Belmont (or, to translate the name, Beautiful Mountain). These two worlds are divided, ritually divided. To go from the one to the other, you must cross the seas, cross water (always a good, ritual thing to do). One world, Venice, is the harsh world of commerce and reality where fortunes are tempest-tossed upon the seas. The other world, Belmont, is a world of beauty, folktale, legend, and mythology. The whole plot associated with Portia's being courted by Bassanio is a kind of fairy tale. "Once upon a time there was a very rich man who had a beautiful daughter. When he died, he provided that she must marry the man who could guess correctly which one of three caskets held her picture. One casket was gold, one casket was silver, and one casket was lead." It could have come right out of Grimm or Andersen. It does, in fact, come out of that great medieval collection of folktales, the *Gesta Romanorum*. The story of Shylock and his pound of flesh is also a folktale going back to Roman times, but in Shylock's Venice the fairy tale becomes a harsh reality; in Portia's Belmont the fairy tale retains its shimmering, moonlit quality, issuing forth in music and feasting. In Shylock's Venice, people are mostly interested in whose fortunes are rising and whose are falling: "What news on the Rialto?" In Portia's Belmont, people are interested in myths and legends; they talk about them, about the Golden Fleece, for example, or Hercules, Troilus and Cressida, and many others.

Portia's World of Belmont

Bassanio comes into Portia's world like the handsome prince out of a fairy tale to set free the imprisoned beauty. In fact, this fairy tale is much like the myth behind the Birnam Wood episode in *Macbeth*. Bassanio comes like a summer king, like the new spring, as Portia's messenger says of Gratiano when he comes to announce Bassanio:

> I have not seen
> So likely[1] an ambassador of love.
> A day in April never came so sweet
> To show how costly summer was at hand,
> As this fore-spurrer[2] comes before his lord.

(II. ix. 90–94)

Portia herself is a summer queen, still imprisoned by the winter past, or as the play says, "a living daughter curbed by the will of a dead father" (I. ii. 23). The fact that there are associated with Belmont three caskets, three rings and three brides, Portia, Nerissa, and Jessica, also has a mythological sound to it. Goddesses tend to come in threes in mythology: the three Fates, for example, or Paris' choice among Hera, Athena, and Aphrodite.

In Belmont, though, there are many myths besides the summer-king and the "triple goddesses," as they are called. In Belmont we hear of Alcides or, in his more usual name, Hercules, and in the beautiful scene between Lorenzo and Jessica at the opening of Act V, we hear a perfect garland of legendary lovers: Troilus and Cressida, Pyramus and Thisbe, Dido and Aeneas, Jason and Medea, and in talking of these old tales, Lorenzo and Jessica transfigure their own young love through a formalism of poetry into the very stuff of legend.

Lorenzo.
> The moon shines bright. In such a night as this,
> When the sweet wind did gently kiss the trees
> And they did make no noise, in such a night
> Troilus[3] methinks mounted the Troyan walls,
> And sighed his soul toward the Grecian tents
> Where Cressid lay that night.

Jessica.
> In such a night
> Did Thisbe[4] fearfully o'ertrip the dew,
> And saw the lion's shadow ere himself,
> And ran dismayed away.

Lorenzo.
> In such a night
> Stood Dido[5] with a willow in her hand
> Upon the wild sea banks, and waft her love
> To come again to Carthage.

Jessica.
> In such a night
> Medea[6] gathered the enchanted herbs
> That did renew old Aeson.

1. handsome 2. forerunner 3. Troilus the Trojan was deprived of his lover, Cressida, who was taken away to the Greek camp. 4. the young woman of Babylon who killed herself after the suicide of her lover Pyramus, who had committed suicide when he mistakenly thought his lover Thisbe was dead 5. the widowed queen of Carthage whom Aeneas loved and deserted 6. the sorceress who helped Jason to fetch away the golden fleece and afterward refused to leave him; Aeson was Jason's father

Lorenzo.

In such a night

Did Jessica steal from the wealthy Jew,
And with an unthrift love did run from Venice
As far as Belmont.

Jessica.

In such a night

Did young Lorenzo swear he loved her well,
Stealing her soul with many vows of faith,
And ne'er a true one.

Lorenzo.

In such a night

Did pretty Jessica, like a little shrew,
Slander her love, and he forgave it her.

(V. i. 1–22)

Lorenzo and Jessica go on to pay Shakespeare's most exquisite tribute to music, for Portia's Belmont is a world not
only of legend but also of harmony.

How sweet the moonlight sleeps upon this bank!
Here will we sit and let the sounds of music
Creep in our ears; soft stillness and the night
Become the touches of sweet harmony.
Sit, Jessica. Look how the floor of heaven
Is thick inlaid with patens[7] of bright gold.
There's not the smallest orb which thou behold'st
But in his motion like an angel sings,
Still quiring[8] to the young-eyed cherubins;
Such harmony is in immortal souls,
But whilst this muddy vesture of decay[9]
Doth grossly close it in, we cannot hear it.

• • •

For do but note a wild and wanton herd
Or race of youthful and unhandled colts
Fetching mad hounds, bellowing and neighing loud,
Which is the hot condition of their blood:
If they but hear perchance a trumpet sound,
Or any air of music touch their ears,
You shall perceive them make a mutual stand,
Their savage eyes turned to a modest gaze
By the sweet power of music. Therefore the poet
Did feign that Orpheus[10] drew trees, stones, and floods;
Since naught so stockish,[11] hard, and full of rage
But music for the time doth change his nature.
The man that hath no music in himself,
Nor is not moved with concord of sweet sounds,
Is fit for treasons, stratagems,[12] and spoils;
The motions of his spirit are as dull as night,

7. plates 8. singing 9. the mortal earthly body; so long as we are mortal we cannot hear
immortal music 10. the musician of Thrace who was so skilled even trees bent to listen to him 11. like an unfeeling block 12. deeds of violence

And his affections dark as Erebus.[13]
Let no such man be trusted. Mark the music.

(V. i. 54–88)

And who is that man that hath no music in himself nor is not moved with concord of sweet sounds—he is, of course, our old enemy, Shylock, who late in the play makes some nasty remarks about the effects of bagpipes, and earlier says:

> What, are there masques? Hear you me, Jessica:
> Lock up my doors; and when you hear the drum
> And the vile squealing of the wry-necked[14] fife,
> Clamber you not up to the casements[15] then,
> But stop my house's ears—I mean my casements;
> Let not the sound of shallow fopp'ry enter
> My sober house.

(II. v. 27–35)

Neither harmony nor legend has charms for him.

THE HARSH MASCULINE WORLD OF SHYLOCK'S VENICE

Shylock's Venice is a man's world. Virtually all the characters we see in Venice—Antonio, Bassanio, Solanio, Salerio, Gratiano, the Gobbos, both father and son—are men. Indeed, of the three women we see in Venice, all three disguise themselves as men while they are there: Jessica to elope with Lorenzo, Portia and Nerissa to play the young doctors of laws in the courtroom scene. Portia's Belmont, on the other hand, is a world dominated by women. Men come there only as suitors and wooers, worshipers at the shrine of love. The props we find in that moonlit, legendary land are rings and caskets, symbols, as [psychoanalyst Sigmund] Freud so tactfully put it in his essay on this play, of "the essential thing" in woman. The props for Venice, on the other hand, are bags with coins in them and that knife that Shylock so gleefully whets upon the sole of his shoe.

The male world of Shylock and Venice runs on a scarcity economy. Everything has its price; nothing is given away (except by Antonio, who, as we shall see, is a very special case). The world of Shylock's Venice is sad: in the opening line of the play, Antonio wonders, "I know not why I am so sad." His friends suggest it is because "Antonio is sad to think upon his merchandise," but that, he says, is not the reason, nor do we ever learn why Antonio is sad. Portia, too, in her opening line, says she is sad: "My little body is aweary

13. Hell 14. making the player twist his neck 15. windows that open on hinges

of this great world." Her maid, however, points out, "They are as sick that surfeit[16] with too much as they that starve with nothing." In other words, the sadness in Portia's Belmont is a kind of lovesick melancholy, a sadness of surfeit; the sadness in Shylock's Venice is a sadness of scarcity, a taxing worry—we moderns would call it anxiety or insecurity. Solanio and Salerio imagine the merchant's state of mind:

Solanio.

> Believe me, sir, had I such venture forth,
> The better part of my affections would
> Be with my hopes abroad. I should be still[17]
> Plucking the grass to know where sits the wind,
> Peering in maps for ports and piers and roads;[18]
> And every object that might make me fear
> Misfortune to my ventures, out of doubt
> Would make me sad.

Salerio.

> My wind cooling my broth
> Would blow me to an ague[19] when I thought
> What harm a wind too great might do at sea.
> I should not see the sandy hourglass run
> But I should think of shallows and of flats,[20]
> And see my wealthy *Andrew* docked in sand . . .
> . . . Should I go to church
> And see the holy edifice of stone
> And not bethink me straight of dangerous rocks. . . .
>
> (I. i. 15–31)

In that divisive, anxious Venice, we hear Shylock calculate the rate of interest, and even Antonio's friends count off one by one Antonio's ships as they supposedly sink, leaving him to the harsh justice of Shylock.

In Venice, things divide and fragment. In Belmont, however, things multiply and grow. As Portia says, when Bassanio guesses the right casket:

> You see me, Lord Bassanio, where I stand,
> Such as I am. Though for myself alone
> I would not be ambitious in my wish
> To wish myself much better, yet for you
> I would be trebled twenty times myself,
> A thousand times more fair, ten thousand times more rich,
> That only to stand high in your account,[21]
> I might in virtues, beauties, livings,[22] friends,
> Exceed account.
>
> (III. ii. 149–157)

16. gorge themselves 17. always 18. anchorages 19. fever 20. sandbanks 21. estimation 22. possessions

Everything multiplies in Belmont. In fact, Portia's love for Bassanio doubles itself on the spot, when Gratiano, his companion, immediately proposes to Nerissa, Portia's companion. That is the magic of love, that it can somehow multiply, make nothing into everything. Even division in Belmont becomes a kind of multiplication, as when Portia speaking to Bassanio makes a slip of the tongue:

> Beshrow your eyes!
> They have o'erlooked[23] me and divided me;
> One half of me is yours, the other half yours—
> Mine own, I would say; but if mine, then yours,
> And so all yours!

(III. ii. 14–18)

Shylock's Venice is the court of hard justice, the law of the talon, an eye for an eye, a tooth for a tooth. Into that harsh court about to divide Antonio's body, comes Portia, in the guise of a doctor of laws, bringing Belmont's loving, bountiful, multiplying mercy:

> The quality[24] of mercy is not strained;
> It droppeth as the gentle rain from heaven
> Upon the place beneath. It is twice blest;
> It blesseth him that gives and him that takes.
> 'Tis mightiest in the mightiest; it becomes
> The thronèd monarch better than his crown.
> His sceptre shows the force of temporal power,
> The attribute to awe and majesty,
> Wherein doth sit the dread and fear of kings;
> But mercy is above this sceptred sway;
> It is enthronèd in the hearts of kings;
> It is an attribute to God himself,
> And earthly power doth then show likest God's
> When mercy seasons[25] justice.

(IV. i. 182–195)

MULTIPLE IMAGES REINFORCE THE TWO WORLDS

Critics sometimes say that that speech, Portia's speech on mercy, is the heart of the play, that *The Merchant of Venice* is a play about justice and mercy, and so it is. But it is also a play about division and multiplication, about man against woman, about scarcity against plenty, or as Lorenzo says, "Fair ladies, you drop manna in the way of starvèd people." As Lorenzo's image of food suggests, you might sum it all up by saying the two worlds of Venice and Belmont correspond to two ways of using our mouths. Shylock's mouth bites. He

23. bewitched 24. nature 25. is mixed with

snaps out phrases, mouthing them over and over compulsively as:

> I'll have my bond! Speak not against my bond!
> I have sworn an oath that I will have my bond.
> Thou call'dst me a dog before thou hadst a cause,
> But since I am a dog, beware my fangs.
>
>   •   •   •
>
> I'll have my bond. I will not hear thee speak.
> I'll have my bond, and therefore speak no more.
>
>   •   •   •
>
> I'll have no speaking; I will have my bond.
>
>   (III. iii. 4–17)

Shylock bites and gnashes. Repeatedly he is called a cur and a dog with teeth and fangs. He himself brings in the image of a rat gnawing in the bowels of a house. To Antonio he says, "Your worship was the last man in our mouths," and of Antonio's flesh he demands it "to bait fish withal. If it will feed nothing else, it will feed my revenge." Twice in Venice feasts are planned, once for Portia as the young doctor of laws, but she must rush away; once as a way of getting Shylock out of his house so that Jessica and Lorenzo can elope. The feasts of Venice are false or they are broken. In Belmont, by comparison, the play abounds in feasts, a feast for the prince of Morocco, a feast for Bassanio, a feast for Lorenzo and Jessica. In a very real sense, the beautiful mountain of Belmont is the bountiful mother feeding her dependents, while Shylock in Venice is the harsh, threatening, and stingy father.

That harsh father hates and his hate creates hate, and also penury, hunger, and loneliness. The bountiful mother, Portia, as freely as the rain, gives mercy and love and money. Love and money—90 percent of modern anxieties, a psychologist once told me, come from love or money—they are the things of life as well as plays, and perhaps the juxtaposing of love and money is what makes *The Merchant of Venice* so much more intricate, so much more satisfying as a play than *Romeo and Juliet* with its simple black-and-white contrasts of love and fighting. The two worlds in which the comedy's five plots take place, do, of course, contrast, but they contrast in a rich, dynamic way, the harsh man's world of Venice and price and scarcity as against the bountiful woman's world of riches and plenty, Belmont.

Distinguishing the two contrasting worlds of the play, however, does not tell us what binds together its five plots.

The answer to that question depends in turn on the issue of usury. To us, usury means excessive or illegal interest on money borrowed or lent. In Shakespeare's day, usury (or "usance," the word the play uses) referred to any interest at all, excessive or not excessive, on money borrowed or loaned. All through the Middle Ages and well into Shakespeare's time it was both a deadly sin and a crime to charge or give any interest whatsoever. . . .

The question we need to answer, then, is why was it so horrendous to do such an ordinary thing as charge interest? *The Merchant of Venice* tells us the answer in Act I, scene iii, when Antonio signs with Shylock the fateful bond. Shylock says of Antonio, "I hate him for he is a Christian; but more, for that in low simplicity he lends out money gratis and brings down the rate of usance here with us in Venice." In other words, Antonio is unwilling to commit the sin of usury. By refusing to take interest, Antonio drives down the rate of interest that Shylock can charge, so that, in part, Shylock's hatred of Antonio is a commercial hatred, the hatred of a business rival. As Antonio says, "I neither lend nor *borrow* by taking or by *giving* of excess," for giving interest was as sinful as taking it. More to the point, Antonio asks, "When did friendship take a breed for barren metal of his friend?" This is the key to the crime and sin of usury, *a breed of barren metal*. It was [Greek philosopher] Aristotle who decided that interest was unnatural. The Greek word for interest on money was *tokos*, which means offspring. In other words, the man who lends money makes the money breed more money. Thus, [Italian poet] Dante, in *The Divine Comedy*, put usurers in the same circle of hell as sodomites, both being sinners who distort the natural processes of breeding. It is unnatural to make money breed, because money, being metal, is at the bottom of the great chain of being.[26] Breeding belongs only to plants or animals or man.

Thus, in this same scene (I. iii), Shylock tries to justify his charging of interest by quoting the totally inapposite case of Jacob and Laban and the spotted sheep in the Bible, inapposite because breeding animals is not the same thing as breeding money. The story of Jacob and Laban has nothing at all to do with the question of charging interest, as Antonio immediately points out:

26. the idea that all elements in the world are ordered and interconnected in a vertical line with God at the top

> This was a venture, sir, that Jacob served for,
> A thing not in his power to bring to pass,
> But swayed and fashioned by the hand of heaven.
>
> (I. iii. 87–89)

And he asks, "Is your gold and silver ewes and rams?" to which Shylock cynically replies, "I cannot tell; I make it breed as fast."

The essence, then, of the sin of usury is making metal breed metal, money, money. It is no sin, however, as Antonio points out, to make money from money provided some other factor, a factor of risk or "venture," enters in, as when Antonio himself sends cargoes out upon the sea. The word Antonio uses is "venture," that is, taking a chance, taking some kind of risk. To put it in modern terms, it would be ethical to buy common stocks or even preferred stocks, but not bonds. Common stocks involve an element of risk or venture; bonds (in theory, at least) do not.

This contrast between breeding and multiplying money and venturing it underlies the Shylock-Antonio plot. The same idea, however, underlies all the plots.

The Play as a Fairy Tale

Harley Granville-Barker

Harley Granville-Barker analyzes the techniques
Shakespeare employs to blend two very different fairy
tales into a unified play. He credits Shakespeare with
effectively bridging time and distance between the
two settings without referring to hours and miles. He
cites elements of plot and language to show how
Shakespeare gives each story proper emphasis,
rounds the characters of Bassanio and Portia, and
links the stories and themes. Harley Granville-Barker
was a dramatist, actor, and producer. He directed the
British Institute in Paris and delivered a series of lectures at Princeton University in America. He is the
author of the plays *The Voysey Inheritance, Waste,* and
Madras House and, with G.B. Harrison, the critical
work *A Companion to Shakespeare Studies.*

The Merchant of Venice is a fairy tale. There is no more reality in Shylock's bond and the Lord of Belmont's will than in
Jack and the Beanstalk.

Shakespeare, it is true, did not leave the fables as he found
them. This would not have done; things that pass muster on
the printed page may become quite incredible when acted
by human beings, and the unlikelier the story, the likelier
must the mechanism of its acting be made. Besides, when
his own creative impulse was quickened, he could not help
giving life to a character; he could no more help it than the
sun can help shining. So Shylock is real, while his story remains fabulous; and Portia and Bassanio become human,
though, truly, they never quite emerge from the enchanted
thicket of fancy into the common light of day. Aesthetic logic
may demand that a story and its characters should move
consistently upon one plane or another, be it fantastic or

Excerpted from *Prefaces to Shakespeare*, vol. 4, by Harley Granville-Barker (Princeton,
NJ: Princeton University Press, 1946). Reprinted by permission of The Society of Authors, as the literary representative of the Estate of Harley Granville-Barker.

real. But Shakespeare's practical business, once he had chosen these two stories for his play, was simply so to charge them with humanity that they did not betray belief in the human beings presenting them, yet not so uncompromisingly that the stories themselves became ridiculous.

What the producer of the play must first set himself to ascertain is the way in which he did this, the nice course that—by reason or instinct—he steered. Find it and follow it, and there need be no running on the rocks. But logic may land us anywhere. It can turn Bassanio into a heartless adventurer. Test the clock of the action by Greenwich time, it will either be going too fast or too slow. And as to Portia's disguise and Bellario's law, would the village policeman be taken in by either? But the actor will find that he simply cannot play Bassanio as a humbug, for Shakespeare does not mean him to. Portias and Nerissas have been eclipsed by wigs and spectacles. This is senseless tomfoolery; but how make a wiseacre producer see that if he does not already know? And if, while Shylock stands with his knife ready and Antonio with his bared breast, the wise young judge lifting a magical finger between them, we sit questioning Bellario's law—why, no one concerned, actors or audience, is for this fairyland, that is clear.

The Merchant of Venice is the simplest of plays, so long as we do not bedevil it with sophistries.[1] Further, it is—for what it is!—as smoothly and completely successful, its means being as well fitted to its end, as anything Shakespeare wrote. He was happy in his choice of the Portia story; his verse, which has lost glitter to gain a mellower beauty and an easier flow, is now well attuned to such romance. The story of Shylock's bond is good contrast and complement both; and he can now project character upon the stage, uncompromising and complete. Yet this Shylock does not overwhelm the play, as at a later birth he might well have done—it is a near thing, though! Lastly, Shakespeare is now enough of the skilled playwright to be able to adjust and blend the two themes with fruitful economy.

THE PROBLEMS OF TIME AND PLACE WITH TWO UNLIKE STORIES

This blending of the themes would, to a modern playwright, have been the main difficulty. The two stories do not natu-

1. plausible but misleading or fallacious arguments

rally march together. The forfeiture of the bond must be a matter of months; with time not only of the essence of the contract, but of the dramatic effect. But the tale of the caskets cannot be enlarged, its substance is too fragile; and a very moderate charge of emotion would explode its pretty hollowness altogether. Critics have credited Shakespeare with nice calculation and amazing subtlety in his compassing of the time-difficulty. . . .

For him dramatic time was a naturally elastic affair. (It still is, though less so, for the modern playwright, whose half-hour act may commonly suggest the passing of an hour or two; this also is Double Time.) Shakespeare seems to think of it quite simply in terms of effect, as he thought of dramatic space, moving his characters hither and thither without considering the compassing of yards or miles. The one freedom will imply and enhance the other. The dramatist working for the "realistic" stage must settle definitely where his characters are to be and keep them there till he chooses to change the scenery. Shakespeare need not; and, in fact, he never insists upon place at all, unless it suits him to; and then only to the extent that suits him. In this play, for instance, where we find Shylock and Antonio will be Venice, but whereabouts in Venice is usually no matter; when it is—at Shylock's door or in court before the Duke—it will be made clear enough to us. And where Portia is, is Belmont. He treats time—and the more easily—with a like freedom, and a like aim. Three months suits for the bond; but once he has pouched the money Bassanio must be off to Belmont, and his calendar, attuned to his mood, at once starts to run by hours only. The wind serves, and he sails that very night, and there is no delay at Belmont. Portia would detain him some month or two before he ventures; and what could be more convenient for a Shakespeare bent on synchronizing the two stories? For that matter, he could have placed Belmont a few hundred miles off, and let the coming and going eke out the time. Did the problem as a whole ever even occur to him? If it did, he dismissed it as of no consequence. What he does is to set each story going according to its nature; then he punctuates them, so to speak, for effect. By the clock they are not even consistent in themselves, far less with each other. But we should pay just the sort of attention to these months, days or hours that we do, in another connection, to the commas and semicolons elucidating a sentence. They give us, and are meant to, simply a *sense* of time and its exactions. It is the more easily done because our own sense of time in daily life is far from consistent. Time flies when we are happy, and drags in anxiety, as poets never tire of reminding us. Shakespeare's own reflections on the phenomenon run to half a column of the concordance, and he turns it quite naturally to dramatic account.

THE PROBLEM OF BLENDING TWO UNLIKE THEMES

How to blend two such disparate themes into a dramatically organic whole; that was his real problem. The stories, linked in the first scene, will, of themselves, soon part company. Shakespeare has to run them neck and neck till he is ready to join them again in the scene of the trial. But the difficulty is less that they will not match each other by the clock than that their whole gait so differs, their very nature. How is the flimsy theme of the caskets to be kept in countenance beside its grimly powerful rival? You cannot, as we said, elaborate the story, or charge it with emotion; that would invite disaster. Imagine a Portia seriously alarmed by the prospect of an Aragon or a Morocco for husband. What sort of barrier, on the other hand, would the caskets be to a flesh-and-blood hero and heroine fallen in love? Would a Romeo or Rosalind[2] give a snap of the finger for them? As it is, the very sight of Bassanio prompts Portia to rebellion; and Shakespeare can only allow his lovers a few lines of talk together, and that in company, dare only color the fairy tale with a rhetorically passionate phrase or so before the choice is made and the caskets can be forgotten—as they are!—altogether. Nor does anything in the play show the artist's supreme tact in knowing what *not* to do better than this?

But you cannot neglect the Portia story either, or our interest in her may cool. Besides, this antiphony of high romance and rasping hate enhances the effect of both. A contrasting of subjects, scene by scene, is a trick (in no depreciatory sense) of Shakespeare's earliest stagecraft, and he never lost his liking for it. Then if the casket-theme cannot be neglected, but cannot be elaborated, it must somehow be drawn out, its peculiar character sustained, its interest husbanded while its consummation is delayed.

Shakespeare goes straightforwardly enough to work. He puts just as little as may be into Portia's first scene; but for

2. Romeo in *Romeo and Juliet;* Rosalind in *As You Like It*

the one sounding of Bassanio's name there would be only the inevitable tale of the caskets told in tripping prose and the conventional joking upon the suitors. Portia and Nerissa, however, seen for the first time in the flesh, give it sufficient life, and that "Bassanio" one vivid spark more. Later, in due course, come Morocco's choice of the gold casket and Aragon's of the silver. We remark that Morocco is allotted two scenes instead of one. The reason is, probably, that Shakespeare has now enriched himself with the Lorenzo-Jessica story (not to mention the episode of the Gobbos, father and son), and, with this extra weight in the Venetian scale of the action, is put to it to maintain the balance. . . .

He has held his lovers apart, since the air of the Belmont of the caskets is too rarefied for flesh and blood to breathe. And Portia herself has been spellbound; we have only had jaunty little Nerissa to prophesy that love (by the pious prevision of the late lord) would somehow find out the way. But once he brings them together Bassanio must break the spell. It is the story of the sleeping beauty and the prince in another kind; a legitimate and traditional outcome. And once Shakespeare himself has broken free of the fairy tale and brought these two to life (for Bassanio as well has been till now a little bloodless) it is not in him to let them lapse from the scene unproved, and to the full. The long restraint has left him impatient, and he must, here and now, have his dramatic fling. We need not credit—or discredit him, if you like—with much calculation of the problem. It was common prudence both to keep Belmont as constantly in our view as Venice, and the emancipating Bassanio clear of it for as long as possible. And he is now in the middle of his play, rather past it, ready to link his two stories together again. He worked forthrightly; that is written plain over most of his work. Though he might now find that he had here material for two scenes, he would not return in his tracks, telescope Aragon and Morocco —and take, in fact, all the sort of trouble we, who are his critics, must take to explain what a much more compact job he could have made of it! Besides, here is his chance to uplift the two as hero and heroine, and he will not dissipate its effectiveness.

MOVING BASSANIO AND PORTIA BEYOND FAIRY-TALE CHARACTERS

For Bassanio, as we said, has been till now only little less bound than Portia in the fetters of a fairy tale; and later, Shylock and the bond will condemn him to protesting helplessness, and the affair of the rings to be merrily befooled. The wonder indeed is . . . that throughout he measures up so well to the stature of sympathetic hero. Shakespeare contrives it in two ways. He endows him with very noble verse; and, whenever he can, throws into strong relief the Bassanio of his own uncovenanted imagination. He does this here. The fantasy of the caskets brought to its due crisis, charged with an emotion which blows it for a finish into thin air, he shows us Bassanio, his heart's desire won, agonized with grief and remorse at the news of Antonio's danger. Such moments do test a man and show him for what he is; and this one, set in bright light and made the scene's turning point, counts for more in the effect the character makes on us than all the gentlemanly graces of his conventional equipment. Unless the actor is much at fault, we shall hear the keynote to the true Bassanio struck in the quiet simplicity—such contrast to his rhetoric over the caskets, even though this was less mere rhetoric than Morocco's and Aragon's—of the speech which begins

> O sweet Portia,
> Here are a few of the unpleasant'st words
> That ever blotted paper! . . .
> Rating myself at nothing, you shall see
> How much I was a braggart. When I told you
> My state was nothing, I should then have told you
> That I was worse than nothing; for indeed
> I have engaged[3] myself to a dear friend,
> Engaged my friend to his mere[4] enemy,
> To feed my means. . . .

Here speaks Shakespeare's Bassanio; and it is by this, and all that will belong to it, that he is meant to live in our minds.

Producer and actors must look carefully into the way by which in this scene the method that has served for the casket story is resolved into something better fitted to the theme of the bond (dominant from the beginning of the play, and now to absorb and transform the dedicated Portia and her fortunes). It is a change—though we must not insist on the contrast more than Shakespeare does—from dramatic convention to dramatic life. From the beginning the pulse of the scene beats more strongly; and Portia's

> I pray you, tarry: pause a day or two
> Before you hazard; for in choosing wrong,
> I lose your company; therefore forbear awhile. . . .

3. pledged 4. sheer; entire

is not only deeper in feeling (there has been little or nothing to rouse her till now; she has had to be the picture of a Portia, hardly more, with a spice of wit to help her through), but how much simpler in expression! When Bassanio turns to those obsessing caskets she must lapse again for a space into fancies of his swanlike end, her eye the watery deathbed for him, into talk about Hercules and Alcides[5] (borrowed, one fears, from Morocco), about Dardanian[6] wives and the like—even as he will be conventionally sententious over his choice. But note how, within the convention, preparing an escape from it, emotion is roused and sustained. With the rhetoric of Portia's

> Go, Hercules!
> Live thou, I live: with much, much more dismay
> I view the fight, than thou that mak'st the fray.

for a springboard, the song and its music are to stir us,

> *whilst Bassanio comments on the caskets to himself.*

So (let the actor remember) when he does at last speak, the emotional ascent will have been half climbed for him already. And while he pays his tribute of trope and maxim, Portia, Nerissa and the rest watch him in silence, at full strain of attention, and help to keep us, too, intent. The speech itself sweeps unhindered to its height, and the pause while the casket is unlocked is filled and enriched by the intensity of Portia's

> How all the other passions fleet to air.

most cunningly contrived in meaning and melody, with its emphasis on "despair" and "ecstasy" and "excess," to hold us upwrought. The fairy tale is finally incarnate in the fantastic word-painting of the portrait and the reading of the scroll. Then, with a most delicate declension to reality, Bassanio comes to face her as in a more actual world, and the curtains can be drawn upon the caskets for the last time. Observe that not for a moment has Shakespeare played his fabulous story false. He takes his theater too seriously to go spoiling an illusion he has created. He consummates it, and turns the figures of it to fresh purpose, and they seem to suffer no change.

SHAKESPEARE'S USE OF LANGUAGE AND PLOT TO UNIFY THE THEMES

Throughout the scene—throughout the play, and the larger part of all Elizabethan drama for that matter—effects must

---

5. another name for Hercules, who rescued the daughter of the Trojan king from being sacrificed to a sea monster 6. Trojan

be valued very much in terms of music. And, with the far adventuring of his playwriting hardly begun, Shakespeare's
verse is already fairly flawless, and its maneuvering from
mood to mood masterly, if still simple. We have the royal humility of the speech in which Portia yields herself (Bassanio
slips back to his metaphors for a moment after this); then,
for contrast, the little interlude of Gratiano and Nerissa, with
the tripping monosyllables of Gratiano's

> I wish you all the joy that you can wish;
> For I am sure you can wish none from me. . . .

to mark the pace and the tone of it. Then follows the arrival
of Antonio's messenger with Lorenzo and Jessica; done in
plain, easy-moving verse that will not discount the dis-
tressed silence in which he reads the letter, nor the quiet
candor of his confession to Portia. Now comes another
crescendo—two voices added to strengthen it—leading up to
her generous, wide-eyed

> What sum owes he the Jew?
> BASSANIO. For me, three thousand ducats.
> PORTIA.   What, no more!
> Pay him six thousand, and deface[7] the bond;
> Double six thousand, and then treble that. . . .

which itself drops to the gentleness of

> Since you are dear bought I will love you dear.

Then, to strengthen the scene's ending, we have the austere
prose of Antonio's letter, chilling us to misgiving. And since—
in stage practice, and with the prevailing key of the play's
writing to consider—this will not do for an actual finish,
there is a last modulation into the brisk coda of

> Since I have your good leave to go away,
> I will make haste: but till I come again,
> No bed shall e'er be guilty of my stay,
> Nor rest be interposer 'twixt us twain.

Lorenzo and Jessica make another link (though their relation to Belmont is pretty arbitrary) between the two stories. This, however, is but the secondary use of them. There
must be a sense of time passing in Venice while the bond
matures, yet we must have continuous action there, too,
while the ritual at Belmont goes its measured way; so, as
there can be little for Shylock and Antonio to do but wait,
this third, minor theme is interposed. It brings fresh impetus
to the action as well as new matter; and it shows us—very

7. cancel

usefully—another and more human side of Shylock. Shakespeare does not scheme it out overcarefully. The masking and the elopement and the coming and going they involve are rather inconveniently crowded together (the pleasant episode of the Gobbos may have stolen a little necessary space); and one chapter of the story—for were we perhaps to have seen Shylock at supper with Bassanio, Lorenzo and the rest while the disguised Jessica waited on them?—was possibly crowded out altogether.

Once the fugitives, with some disregard of likelihood, have been brought to Belmont, Gobbo in attendance, Shakespeare turns them to account quite shamelessly. They play a mighty poor scene to give Portia and Nerissa time to disguise themselves as doctor and clerk. They will have to play another while doctor and clerk change to Portia and Nerissa again; but for that, as if in compensation, they are to be dowered with the loveliest lines in the play. With the junction of the themes in the trial-scene the constructive problem is, of course, solved. Shylock disappearing, the rest is simple.

The Merchant of Venice
Is a Comedy

Elmer Edgar Stoll

Elmer Edgar Stoll argues that Shylock is a comic villain and that *The Merchant of Venice* is a comedy, not a tragedy. Shakespeare orders the scenes so that Shylock is already identified as a villain by his daughter and his servant before he appears onstage. Shakespeare makes Shylock a miser, a moneylender, and a Jew, three objects of ridicule in Elizabethan times. Elmer Edgar Stoll, who taught English at the University of Minnesota, is the author of *Shakespeare's Young Lovers* and *From Shakespeare to Joyce.*

The puzzle whether the *Merchant of Venice* is not meant for tragedy, for instance, is cleared up when, as [critic George P.] Baker suggests, we forget Sir Henry Irving's acting,[1] and remember that the title—and the hero—is not the 'Jew of Venice' as he would lead us to suppose; that this comedy is only like others, as *Measure for Measure* and *Much Ado*,[2] not clear of the shadow of the fear of death; and that in closing with an act where Shylock and his knife are forgotten in the unravelling of the mystery between the lovers and the crowning of Antonio's happiness in theirs, it does not, from the Elizabethan point of view, perpetrate an anti-climax, but, like many another Elizabethan play, carries to completion what is a story for story's sake. 'Shylock is, and always has been the hero,' says [critic F.E.] Schelling. But why, then, did Shakespeare drop his hero out of the play for good before the fourth act was over? It is a trick which he never repeated—a trick, I am persuaded, of which he was not capable.

Hero or not, Shylock is given a villain's due. His is the heaviest penalty to be found in all the pound of flesh stories,

1. Henry Irving was a nineteenth-century actor who played a large number of parts in Shakespeare's plays. 2. *The Merchant of Venice, Measure for Measure,* and *Much Ado About Nothing* are often called the "problem plays" because their identity as comedies is complex.

Excerpted from *Shakespeare Studies: Historical and Comparative in Method*, by Elmer Edgar Stoll (New York: Ungar, 1960). Reprinted by permission of The Continuum Publishing Company.

including that in *Il Pecorone*, which served as model for the play. Not in the Servian, the Persian, the African version, or even that of the *Cursor Mundi*, does the money-lender suffer like Shylock—impoverishment, sentence of death, and an outrage done to his faith. . . .

In not a single heart do Shylock's griefs excite commiseration; indeed, as they press upon him they are barbed with gibes and jeers. Coriolanus[3] is unfortunate and at fault, but we know that the poet is with him. We know that the poet is not with Shylock, for on that point, in this play as in every other, the impartial, inscrutable poet leaves little or nothing to suggestion or surmise. As is his custom elsewhere, by the comments of the good characters, by the methods pursued in the disposition of scenes, and by the downright avowals of soliloquy, he constantly sets us right.

STRATEGY 1: COMMENTS OF GOOD CHARACTERS

As for the first of these artifices,[4] all the people who come in contact with Shylock except Tubal—among them being those of his own house, his servant and his daughter—have a word or two to say on the subject of his character, and never a good one. And in the same breath they spend on Bassanio and Antonio, his enemies, nothing but words of praise. Praise or blame, moreover, is, after Shakespeare's fashion, usually in the nick of time to guide the hearer's judgment. Lest at his first appearance the Jew should make too favourable an impression by his Scripture quotations, Antonio is led to observe that the devil can cite Scripture for his purpose; lest the Jew's motive in foregoing interest (for once in his life) should seem like the kindness Antonio takes it to be, Bassanio avows that he likes not fair terms and a villain's mind; and once the Jew has caught the Christian on the hip, every one, from Duke to Gaoler, has words of horror or detestation for him and of compassion for his victim.

STRATEGY 2: ORDERING OF THE SCENES

As for the second artifice, the ordering of the scenes is such as to enforce this contrast. First impressions, every playwright knows (and no one better than Shakespeare himself), are momentous, particularly for the purpose of ridicule. Launcelot and Jessica, in separate scenes, are in-

3. an arrogant, outspoken Roman general in Shakespeare's *Coriolanus*   4. artful and skillful strategies

troduced before Shylock reaches home, that, hearing their story, we may side with them, and, when the old curmudgeon appears, may be moved to laughter as he complains of Launcelot's gormandizing, sleeping, and rending apparel out, and as he is made game of by the young conspirators to his face. Here, as [critic William] Poel has noticed, when there might be some danger of our sympathy becoming enlisted on Shylock's side because he is about to lose his daughter and some of his property, Shakespeare forestalls it. He lets Shylock, in his hesitation whether to go to the feast, take warning from a dream, but nevertheless, though he knows that they bid him not for love, decide to go in hate, in order to feed upon the prodigal Christian. And he lets him give up Launcelot, whom he has half a liking for, save that he is a huge feeder, to Bassanio—'to one that I would have him help to waste his borrowed purse.' Small credit these sentiments do him; little do they add to his pathos or dignity. Still more conspicuous is this care when Shylock laments over his daughter and his ducats. Lest then by any chance a stupid or tender-hearted audience should not laugh but grieve, Salanio reports his outcries—in part word for word—two scenes in advance, as matter of mirth to himself and all the boys in Venice. It is exactly the same method as that employed in *Twelfth Night*, Act III, scene ii, where Maria comes and tells not only Sir Toby, Sir Andrew, and Fabian, but, above all, the audience, how ridiculously Malvolio is acting, before they see it for themselves. The art of the theatre, but particularly the art of the comic theatre, is the art of preparations, else it is not securely comic. But the impression first of all imparted to us is of Shylock's villainy—an impression which, however comical he may become, we are not again allowed to lose. In the first scene in which he appears, the third in the play, there is one of the most remarkable instances in dramatic literature of a man saying one thing but thinking another and the audience made to see this. He prolongs the situation, keeps the Christians on tenterhooks,[5] turns the terms of the contract over and over in his mind, as if he were considering the soundness of it and of the borrower, while all the time he is hoping, for once in his life, that his debtor may turn out not sound but bankrupt. He casts up Antonio's hard usage of him in the past, defends the

5. a hooked nail for securing cloth on a frame on which cloth is stretched for drying without shrinkage

practice of interest-taking, is at the point of stipulating what
the rate this time shall be, and then—decides to be friends
and take no interest at all. He seems, and is, loath to part for
a time with three thousand ducats—''tis a good round
sum!'—but at the bottom of his heart he is eager.

STRATEGY 3: SHYLOCK'S SOLILOQUIES

And as for the third artifice, that a sleepy audience may not
make the mistake of the cautious critic and take the villain
for the hero, Shakespeare is at pains to label the villain by an
aside at the moment the hero appears on the boards:

> I hate him for he is a Christian,
> But more for that in low simplicity
> He lends out money gratis, and brings down
> The rate of usance[6] here with us in Venice.

Those are his motives, later confessed repeatedly; and either
one brands him as a villain more unmistakably in that day, as
we shall see, than in ours. Of the indignities which he has endured he speaks also, and of revenge; but of none of these has
he anything to say at the trial. There he pleads his oath, perjury
to his soul should he break it, his 'lodged hate', or his 'humour';
further than that, 'I can give no reason nor I will not,'—for some
reasons a man does not give; but here to himself and later to
Tubal—'were he out of Venice I can make what merchandise I
will'—he tells, in the thick of the action, the unvarnished truth.
As with Shakespeare's villains generally—Aaron, Iago, or
Richard III[7]—only what they say concerning their purposes
aside or to their confidants can be relied upon; and Shylock's
oath and his horror of perjury are, as [critic H.H.] Furness observes, belied by his clutching at thrice the principal when the
pound of flesh escapes him, just as is his money-lender's ruse of
pretending to borrow the cash from 'a friend' . . . by his going
home 'to purse the ducats straight.'

His arguments, moreover, are given a specious, not to say a
grotesque colouring. Similar ones used by the Jew in Silvayn's
Orator (1596), probably known to Shakespeare, are there called
'sophisticall'. But [William] Hazlitt and other critics strangely say
that in argument Shylock has the best of it.

> What if my house be troubled with a rat
> And I be pleas'd to give *ten* thousand ducats
> To have it ban'd ?

6. usury 7. Aaron the Moor in *Titus Andronicus;* Iago in *Othello;* and Richard III in
Richard III

This particular rat is a human being; but the only thing to remark upon, in Shylock's opinion, is his willingness to squander ten thousand ducats on it instead of three. 'Hates any man the thing,' he cries (and there he is ticketed), 'he would not kill!' Even in Hazlitt's time, moreover, a choice of 'carrion flesh' in preference to ducats could not be plausibly compared as a 'humour'—the Jew's gross jesting here grates upon you—with an aversion to pigs or to the sound of the bag-pipe, or defended as a right by the analogy of holding slaves; nor could the practice of interest-taking find a warrant in Jacob's pastoral trickery while in the service of Laban; least of all in the day when Sir John Hawkins, who initiated the slave-trade, with the Earls of Pembroke and Leicester and the Queen herself for partners, bore on the arms which were granted him for his exploits a demi-Moor, proper, in chains, and in the day when the world at large still held interest-taking to be robbery. Very evidently, moreover, Shylock is discomfited by Antonio's question 'Did he take interest?' for he falters and stumbles in his reply—

> No, not take interest, not, as you would say,
> Directly, interest,—

and is worsted, in the eyes of the audience if not in his own, by the repeated use of the old Aristotelian argument of the essential barrenness of money, still gospel in Shakespeare's day, in the second question,

> Or is your gold and silver ewes and rams?

For his answer is meant for nothing better than a piece of complacent shamelessness:

> I cannot tell: I make it breed as fast.

Only twice does Shakespeare seem to follow Shylock's pleadings and reasonings with any sympathy—'Hath a dog money?' in the first scene in which he appears, and 'Hath not a Jew eyes?' in the third act—but a bit too much has been made of this. Either plea ends in such fashion as to alienate the audience. To Shylock's reproaches the admirable Antonio, 'one of the gentlest and humblest of all the men in Shakespeare's theatre', praised and honoured by every one but Shylock, retorts, secure in his virtue, that he is just as like to spit on him and spurn him again. And Shylock's celebrated justification of his race runs headlong into a justification of his villainy: 'The villainy which you teach me I will execute, and it shall go hard but I will better the instruction.'

'Hath not a Jew eyes?' and he proceeds to show that your Jew is no less than a man, and as such has a right, not to respect or compassion, as the critics for a century have had it, but to revenge. Neither large nor lofty are his claims. The speech begins with the answer to Salanio's question about the pound of flesh. 'Why, I am sure, if he forfeit, thou wilt not take his flesh. What's that good for?' 'To bait fish withal,' he retorts in savage jest; 'if it will feed nothing else it will feed my revenge;' and he goes on to complain of insults, and of thwarted bargains to the tune of half a million, and to make a plea for which he has already robbed himself of a hearing. Quite as vigorously and (in that day) with as much reason, the detestable and abominable Aaron defends his race and colour, and Edmund,[8] the dignity of bastards. The worst of his villains Shakespeare allows to plead their cause: their confidences in soliloquy or aside, if not (as here) slight touches in the plea itself, sufficiently counteract any too favourable impression. This, on the face of it, is a plea for indulging in revenge with all its rigours; not a word is put in for the nobler side of Jewish character; and in lending Shylock his eloquence Shakespeare is but giving the devil his due.

A COMIC VILLAIN CAST IN ELIZABETHAN CONVENTIONS

By all the devices, then, of Shakespeare's dramaturgy Shylock is proclaimed, as by the triple repetition of a crier, to be the villain, though a comic villain or butt. Nor does the poet let pass any of the prejudices of that day which might heighten this impression. A miser, a money-lender, a Jew,—all three had from time immemorial been objects of popular detestation and ridicule, whether in life or on the stage. The union of them in one person is in Shakespeare's time the rule, both in plays and in 'character'-writing: to the popular imagination a money-lender was a sordid miser with a hooked nose. So it is in the acknowledged prototype of Shylock, [playwright Christopher] Marlowe's 'bottle-nosed' monster, Barabas, the Jew of Malta. Though far more of a villain, he has the same traits of craft and cruelty, the same unctuous friendliness hiding a thirst for a Christian's blood, the same thirst for blood outreaching his greed for gold, and the same spirit of unrelieved egoism which thrusts aside the

8. the bastard son of Gloucester in *King Lear*

claims of his family, his nation, or even his faith. If Barabas fawns like a spaniel when he pleases, grins when he bites, heaves up his shoulders when they call him dog, Shylock, for his part, 'still bears it with a patient shrug', and 'grows kind', seeking the Christian's 'love' in the hypocritical fashion of Barabas with the suitors and the friars. If Barabas ignores the interests of his brother Jews, poisons his daughter, 'counts religion but a childish toy', and, in various forms, avows the wish that 'so I live perish may all the world', Shylock has no word for the generous soul but 'fool' and 'simpleton', and cries ('fervid patriot' that he is, 'martyr and avenger'): 'A diamond gone, cost me two thousand ducats in Frankfort! The curse never fell upon our nation until now. I never felt it till now.' Such is his love of his race, which, [critic Walter] Raleigh says, is 'deep as life'. And in the next breath he cries, as 'the affectionate father': 'Two thousand ducats in that, and other precious, precious jewels. I would my daughter were dead at my foot, and the jewels in her ear . . . and the ducats in her coffin.'

This alternation of daughter and ducats itself comes from Marlowe's play, as well as other ludicrous touches, such as your Jew's stinginess with food and horror of swine-eating, and the confounding of Jew and devil. This last is an old, wide-spread superstition: on the strength of holy writ the Fathers (with the suffrage in this century of [religious reformer Martin] Luther) held that the Jews were devils and the synagogue the house of Satan. In both plays it affords the standing joke, in the *Merchant of Venice* nine times repeated. 'Let me say Amen betimes,' exclaims Salanio in the midst of his good wishes for Antonio; 'lest the devil cross my prayer, for here he comes in the likeness of a Jew.' And in keeping with these notions Shylock's synagogue is, as Luther piously calls it, *ein Teuffels Nest*,[9] the nest for hatching his plot once he and Tubal and the others of his 'tribe' can get together. "Go, go, Tubal,' he cries in the unction of his guile, 'and meet me at our synagogue; go, good Tubal, at our synagogue, Tubal!' In any one such eagerness for the sanctuary is suspicious; but all the more in those times, when the congregation was of Jews and the business of a Christian's flesh. These sly and insinuating Oriental repetitions would of themselves have given the Saxon audience a shudder.

9. a Devil's Nest

It is highly probable, moreover, that Shylock wore the red hair and beard, mentioned by [critic Thomas] Jordan, from the beginning, as well as the bottle-nose of Barabas. So Judas was made up from of old; and in their immemorial orange-tawny, high-crowned hats and 'Jewish gabardines,' the very looks of the two usurers provoked derision. In both plays the word Jew, itself a badge of opprobrium, is constantly in use instead of the proper name of the character and as a byword for cruelty and cunning.

Poetry and Prose in *The Merchant of Venice*

F.E. Halliday

Though critical of the story and characters in *The Merchant of Venice*, F.E. Halliday praises the poetry, in particular the sound and rhyme of the lines that open act 1 and act five. Halliday also notes that Shylock was the first major character that Shakespeare presented in prose and the court scene the first dramatic scene Shakespeare presented without diversions into poetry, both changes significant in the development of Shakespeare's art. Shakespearean critic and historian F.E. Halliday is the author of *A Shakespeare Companion*, *The Cult of Shakespeare*, and *A Cultural History of England*.

Few plays of Shakespeare are better known, and in this sense more popular, than *The Merchant of Venice*, and it is unfortunate, therefore, that apart from its poetry it is one of the least pleasant. Admittedly the scene and fable have a superficial charm; there are all the elements that go to make a romantic comedy: Venice in the shimmering and disintegrating light of day, the giddy traffic of the Rialto, the argosies with portly sail; Venice flickering in the torchlight of masquers and revellers; the moonlight sleeping upon Belmont; and flitting about the alleys and canals and country houses the brilliantly dressed and gaily chattering figures of Renaissance Italy. And yet it is all so empty, so heartless; the voices ring thinly and the laughter awakes no echo. Apart from Shylock there is no character who feels deeply; Antonio is only a lay figure about whom revolve the action and a crew of adventurers whose main business is to make easy profits out of matrimony, and whose pastime is Jew-baiting. Nor are the ladies much more attractive; there is a touch of priggishness and hypocrisy about Portia, and Jessica, whatever else she may be, is a renegade and a thief.

Excerpted from *The Poetry of Shakespeare's Plays*, by F.E. Halliday. Reprinted by permission of M.S. Halliday.

Yet the play contains some of the loveliest poetry that Shakespeare ever wrote, and is of exceptional interest and importance. It is the last of the great series of lyrical dramas, and at the same time the first of the sequence of comedies in which prose is as important a medium as verse. It is a transitional play, the link between Shakespeare the lyric poet and Shakespeare the dramatic poet, the play in which is heard almost for the last time the pure poetry of the early period, and in which for the first time a major character speaks serious prose.

THE POETIC SOUNDS OF THE PLAY'S OPENING LINES

The scene opens with Antonio's wondering why he is so sad, and in a slow-moving lyrical passage that reads like a duet in music his friends suggest that it is on account of the ventures that he has at sea:

> I should not see the sandy hour-glass run,
> But I should think of shallows and of flats,[1]
> And see my wealthy Andrew[2] dock'd in sand
> Vailing[3] her high top lower than her ribs
> To kiss her burial. Should I go to church
> And see the holy edifice of stone,
> And not bethink me straight of dangerous rocks,
> Which touching but my gentle vessel's side
> Would scatter all her spices on the stream,
> Enrobe the roaring waters with my silks ?

None of the plays has a lovelier opening than this; it is the language of Titania,

> And sat with me on Neptune's yellow sands,
> Marking the embarked traders on the flood,

the blank verse of *A Midsummer Night's Dream*, in which the rhythm is beginning to overlap the lines, and assonance[4] to assume the importance of alliteration.[5] In no other play are assonance, as a purely harmonic device, and internal rhyme (sometimes merely the repetition of the same word) so highly developed as in *The Merchant of Venice*. In Salarino's speech, for example, there is *sandy, and, sand, Andrew, shallow; gentle vessel; roaring waters; dock, rock; kiss, this; sea* and the threefold *see*. Then in his next speech we can clearly detect the beginning of the rhythm in which an imposed reversed beat is emphasized by assonance and extended beyond the line:

---

1. sandbanks 2. the name of the ship 3. lowering 4. repetition of vowel sounds 5. repetition of consonant sounds

> Now, by two-*headed Janus,*
> *Nature* hath *framed strange fellows* in her time . . .
> Though *Nestor* swear the *jest be* laughable.

The true trochee[6] of *nature* is linked by assonance to the 'false' one of *Janus*, to which is attached *headed*, which in turn is related to *fellows*, *Nestor* and *jest be*. The construction is similar to Viola's.[7]

> 'Tis *beauty truly* blent, whose red and white
> *Nature's* own sweet and cunning hand *laid on:*
> *Lady . . .*

NEW DEVELOPMENTS IN SHAKESPEARE'S ART

In I. iii Shylock recounts in prose what Salarino and Salanio have already said in verse, but when Antonio enters the language rises again to the greater dignity of verse. Dramatically, the verse in this and the other Shylock scenes is an advance on anything that Shakespeare had yet written; Shylock *talks* to the other characters, and forces them to talk to him instead of addressing the audience, and the language is more natural, more functional, a medium for the development of character and action; it advances more steadily, with fewer excursions into pure poetry, and more easily, without the encumbrance of a formal rhetoric. Yet this gain in ease and dramatic quality is achieved not without some sacrifice of the poetry. Much of the most memorable poetry of the early plays is in the digressions and elaborations, the personal, lyrical, and scarcely dramatic utterances of Shakespeare himself, when for the moment he abandons the action, and in the person of one of the characters, major or minor, pleasant or unpleasant, pursues a theme that powerfully moves him; when, for example, Biron speaks so eloquently of lovers' eyes, and Proteus[8] of music, the poetry takes control, and the characters are little more than a pretext for the expression of Shakespeare's own feelings. In the Shylock scenes, however, he imposes on himself a severer discipline and rarely intervenes in order to speak himself. As a result the writing, though more dramatic, is less 'poetical', for he had not yet developed the compound metaphor and embracing rhythm which, in the later plays, take the place of simple image and decorative line, and this throws into strong relief the undramatic and rhetorical poetry of which so much of the remainder of the play is 'composed.'

6. a two-syllable sound unit with the accent on the first 7. in *Twelfth Night* 8. Biron in *Loves Labors Lost;* Proteus in *Two Gentlemen from Verona*

There are, however, lines indicative of the compressed poetry that was to come, as when Morocco in II. vii, after a passage of spectacular Marlovian rhetoric, rejects the leaden casket with the words,

> it were too gross
> To rib her cerecloth[9] in the obscure grave.

Then the second casket scene is almost an epitome of Shakespearean characteristics, both of the early and middle styles, and admirably illustrates the transitional nature of the play. Arragon advances to the front of the stage and declaims to the audience in the moralizing and exclamatory rhetoric of the early histories, though with a very different rhythm, then, although he retains the rhetorical structure, the texture of the verse is suddenly tautened, and prolixity[10] becomes a concentration of metaphor more complex than that of Salisbury's:

> How much low peasantry would then be glean'd
> From the true seed of honour! and how much honour
> Pick'd from the chaff and ruin of the times,
> To be new-varnish'd!

Glean, seed, chaff, ruin, varnish; and how the double image of chaff and ruin, the particular and the general, intensifies the brilliance of the illumination. He uses a similar construction when he compares the 'fool multitude' to the martlet, which

> Builds in the weather on the outward wall,
> Even in the force and road of casualty.

Though the martlet simile is Shakespearean of any period, the compound metaphor of the last line, like 'chaff and ruin of the times', is one of the first of those that become a major characteristic of the middle style. A few lines later a servant announces Bassanio's approach in verse that might have come out of a sonnet:

> A day in April never came so sweet,
> To show how costly summer was at hand.

SHAKESPEARE BEGINS TO WRITE
PROSE AND DRAMATIC SCENES

The first scene of the third act is memorable as the first great prose scene in Shakespeare, that is, the first in which a ma-

---

9. enclose her shroud; a cere cloth was a wax covering used to embalm the dead   10. prolonged; excessive length

jor character speaks nothing but serious dramatic prose. It seems probable that Shakespeare originally conceived Shylock merely as a figure of fun to be baited to make a Christian holiday, but if so he had abandoned the conception when he wrote this scene. It opens quietly with Salanio and Salarino talking of, even jesting at, Antonio's losses, but when Shylock comes in they turn quite naturally to the more congenial sport of Jew-baiting. Then Shylock begins to speak—in prose that has the balance and repetition of the Psalms, and like the Psalms a rhythm that still approaches but continually eludes the regularity of verse: 'I would my daughter were dead at my foot, and the jewels in her ear. Would she were hearsed at my foot, and the ducats in her coffin.'

After such grief and hate, the love-making of Portia and Bassanio sounds almost shallow and impertinent, and yet there is exquisite poetry when Portia calls for music—music that must always be associated with *The Merchant of Venice*:

> Let music sound while he doth make his choice;
> Then, if he lose, he makes a swan-like end,
> Fading in music . . .

The variation of *Let music* in *Then, if he lose*, and the elegiac echo and reversal of *music—make his* in *Fading in music*, a much favoured cadence in the poetry of a few years later, are unforgettable. One would have expected Bassanio to make straight for the golden casket, but he rejects it, quibbling and moralizing on meretricious beauty in the manner of Sonnet 68:

> Thus ornament is but the guiled shore
> To a most dangerous sea; the beauteous scarf
> Veiling an Indian beauty,

and it is worth noting how Shakespeare at this period associated certain sounds and images: the sea, India, costly textiles, and the syllable *ar*, as in 'Enrobe the roaring waters with my silks', 'The scarfed bark puts from her native bay', 'spiced Indian air . . . embarked traders on the flood . . . rich with merchandise'.

The court scene is the most consistently dramatic that Shakespeare had yet written; that is, the first big scene in which he applies all his genius to the conduct of the action, never neglecting it to pursue a digression however attractive, never subordinating it to the language, never—or never for more than a moment—allowing the poetry to take control.

But aesthetically it is inferior to the rest of the play, partly for this very reason, partly because the theme is so repugnant and the characters so unlovable. Shakespeare's genius was

---

MUSIC IN *THE MERCHANT OF VENICE*

Caroline F.E. Spurgeon emphasizes the presence of music in the play and illustrates how similes enhance two passages in which music is the central subject.

The constant presence of music in so much of the *Merchant of Venice* must not pass unnoticed here. Although one cannot say it is given by images, yet it is much enhanced by them. The two great moments of emotion and romance are introduced and accompanied by music, and the sweetness of its sound echoes through them, so that in the space of forty-five lines we find it named more often than in the whole of any other play. Although there are actually only two similes drawn from it, it dominates both scenes, and gives rise to a series of pictures in which music is the central thought.

When Bassanio is about to make his choice, Portia orders that music shall sound,

> Then, if he lose, he makes a swan-line end,[1]
> Fading in music.

But if he win—there crowd upon her images of what music then is,

> Even as the flourish[2] when true subjects bow
> To a new-crowned monarch,

or

> those dulcet sounds in break of day
> That creep into the dreaming bridegroom's ear,
> And summon him to marriage.

And in the exquisite scene at the end when Lorenzo and Jessica are awaiting the return of their mistress, 'the sounds of music' again 'creep in our ears', 'to draw her home'; Lorenzo, pointing to the stars, declares,

> There's not the smallest orb which thou behold'st
> But in his motion like an angel sings,

and he goes on to expound to Jessica, in the well-known magical words, that the music of the spheres finds its counterpart in the harmony 'in immortal souls'.

1. Swan . . . end: Swans are supposed to sing only once, just before death. 2. flourish: fanfare of trumpets

Caroline F.E. Spurgeon, *Shakespeare's Imagery and What It Tells Us*. Cambridge, England: Cambridge University Press, 1958.

as yet incompletely articulated: the poet is still in advance of the dramatist, and here Shakespeare is primarily a dramatist. Portia's central speech on Mercy finds its way into most anthologies, for this platitudinous moralizing in inferior verse has long been one of the popularly accepted standards of Shakespeare's poetry. It is, as Hazlitt observes, 'very well—but there are a thousand finer ones in Shakespeare'. Of course there are, and a century of them in *The Merchant of Venice*.

THE POETRY AND MUSIC OF THE FINAL ACT

The play is over; the dramatist has finished, but there still remains a trifling matter of a couple of rings to serve as pretext for another scene, a scene that can be all music and poetry and moonlight in the manner of *A Midsummer Night's Dream*. The place can be the garden of Portia's house at Belmont, the broken Jew can be forgotten and left to hang himself in Venice, and for characters there are three pairs of young lovers. After a scene of pure drama Shakespeare can afford to write a scene of pure poetry—though, as it happens, it is for the last time. And so the stage is set for the beautiful and bawdy nonsense of the rings.

> The moon shines bright: in such a night as this,
> When the sweet wind did gently kiss the trees
> And they did make no noise, in such a night
> Troilus[11] methinks mounted the Troyan walls,
> And sighed his soul toward the Grecian tents,
> Where Cressid lay that night.

The harmony of internal rhyme and assonance throughout this wonderful duet of Lorenzo and Jessica almost makes a formal rhyme-scene appear a clumsy and mechanical contrivance. News is brought that Portia is at hand, but Lorenzo decides to stay and welcome her in the garden. He calls for music, though what he speaks himself is almost music:

> How *sweet* the moon*light sleeps* upon this bank!
> *Here will* we *sit*, and *let* the sounds of *music*
> *Creep* in our *ears:* soft *still*ness and the *night*
> Become the *touches* of *sweet harmony.*
> *Sit, Jessica. Look* how the floor of heaven
> *Is thick inlaid* with patines of *bright gold:*
> There's not the *smallest orb* which thou be*hold'*st
> But in this motion *like* an angel sings,
> *Still* quiring[12] to the young-eyed cherubins;

11. Troilus the Trojan was deprived of his love Cressida, who was taken away to the Greek camp 12. singing

Such harmony is in *immortal souls:*
But whilst this muddy *vesture* of *decay*[13]
Doth grossly close it in, we cannot *hear* it.

Portia enters unobserved, and the poetry shifts to her, though it lacks something of the unalloyed purity of Lorenzo's; there is a slight touch of her affectation and pedantry. She stops the music, and the magic is over.

As a play *The Merchant of Venice* is both made and marred by Shylock; he is himself one of the triumphs of Shakespeare's dramatic genius, and at the same time a main cause of its sudden development; he taught Shakespeare a dramatic language. On the other hand, simply because he is what he is, he lays bare the baser qualities of the other characters, the selfishness, insincerity, brutality, that are only skinned and filmed by their virtues. It is a mercy that Benedick and Beatrice, Rosalind and Viola[14] were not exposed to his influence. But as poetry the play is beyond reproach. Shakespeare rarely surpassed this poetry in which the lyric line of the *Sonnets* is wedded to the more liberal movement of the verse of the next period.

13. the mortal earthly body; so long as we are mortal we cannot hear immortal music
14. Benedick and Beatrice in *Much Ado About Nothing*; Rosalind in *As You Like It;* Viola in *Twelfth Night*

The Language of Argument in *The Merchant of Venice*

G.R. Hibbard

G.R. Hibbard argues that characters in *The Merchant of Venice* speak in the language of argument and persuasion, whether their lines are poetry or prose. In particular, Hibbard contrasts Antonio, who speaks entirely in poetry and whose unguarded expression of his feelings leaves him vulnerable, and Shylock, whose sharp, aggressive, and vivid prose gives him the upper hand. Though Shylock is absent in the final act, the issues he represents are still present. G.R. Hibbard has taught English at the Universities of Southampton, Nottingham, and Waterloo in the United Kingdom. He has published editions of several Shakespearean plays and critical works on sixteenth- and seventeenth-century English literature.

In *The Merchant of Venice* (c 1596) the ratio of prose to verse is somewhat lower than it is in *A Midsummer Night's Dream*, but not substantially or significantly so. The way in which the distinction between the two media operates within the structure of the play is, however, very different. It is true that this distinction does serve, among other things, to separate the characters who are highest in rank—the Prince of Morocco, the Prince of Arragon, and the Duke of Venice, all of whom speak nothing but verse—from the characters who are lowest in rank—Launcelot Gobbo and Old Gobbo, who speak nothing but prose. But this can hardly be its main function, since the social gulf is, in any case, obvious enough, and since none of these figures is of the first importance. Nor does it correspond with the themes and antinomies[1] that many have found in the play. Prose is spoken in

1. contradictions; oppositions; paradoxes

Excerpted from *The Making of Shakespeare's Dramatic Poetry*, by G.R. Hibbard. Copyright © 1981 by University of Toronto Press. Reprinted by permission of the publisher.

Belmont, as well as in Venice; the expression of love is no more confined to verse than the expression of hatred is confined to prose; and the claims of the Old Law, like those of the New, make themselves heard through either medium. This lack of correspondence reinforces the scepticism with which one reacts to these attempts to make the play a matter of direct and rather abstract oppositions, and drives one back to the concrete demonstrable fact that the backbone of its action is one trial after another. Not only are its two great climaxes trials, IV.i a literal trial, and III.ii a test of Bassanio's love of Portia, but also it begins with Bassanio's making a trial of Antonio's love for him in the very first scene, continues, in the second, with a test of Portia's obedience to her father's will, and proceeds in a series of trials, of one sort or another, to reach its conclusion with the business of the rings as a comic test of fidelity.

THE MODE OF LANGUAGE IS ARGUMENTATION AND LOGIC

It is, therefore, fitting that the dominant mode of the play, whether the medium be verse or prose, should be the forensic.[2] The language of *The Merchant of Venice* is the language of argument; the structure of the major speeches in it rhetorical.[3] Its characters argue with themselves, as well as with one another. Morocco finds reasons for his instinctive preference for gold; Arragon for his instinctive preference for silver; and Bassanio for his instinctive preference for lead. Each enlists the aid of logic to justify his choice. But long before any of them makes his choice, which he does in verse, Shakespeare has carefully burlesqued their dialectic[4] in the prose soliloquy of Launcelot Gobbo, at the opening of II.ii, where the conclusion that conscience leads to is deliberately rejected in favour of the conclusion that pleasure and convenience lead to, though conscience has the better of the argument:

> Certainly my conscience will serve me to run from this Jew my master. The fiend is at mine elbow and tempts me, saying to me 'Gobbo, Launcelot Gobbo, good Launcelot' or 'good Gobbo' or 'good Launcelot Gobbo, use your legs, take the start, run away'. My conscience says 'No; take heed, honest Launcelot, take heed, honest Gobbo' or, as aforesaid, 'honest Launcelot Gobbo, do not run; scorn running with thy heels'. Well, the most courageous fiend bids me pack.[5] 'Via!'[6] says the fiend; 'away!' says the fiend. 'For the heavens, rouse up a

---

2. of, relating to, or used in debate or argument 3. used for persuasive effect 4. the art or practice of arriving at the truth by the exchange of logical arguments 5. get going 6. get on

brave mind' says the fiend 'and run.' Well, my conscience, hanging about the neck of my heart, says very wisely to me 'My honest friend Launcelot, being an honest man's son' or rather 'an honest woman's son'; for indeed my father did something smack, something grow to, he had a kind of taste[7] —well, my conscience says 'Launcelot, budge not'. 'Budge' says the fiend. 'Budge not' says my conscience. 'Conscience,' say I 'you counsel well.' 'Fiend,' say I 'you counsel well.' To be rul'd by my conscience, I should stay with the Jew my master, who—God bless the mark!—is a kind of devil; and, to run away from the Jew, I should be ruled by the fiend, who—saving your reverence!—is the devil himself. Certainly the Jew is the very devil incarnation;[8] and, in my conscience, my conscience is but a kind of hard conscience to offer to counsel me to stay with the Jew. The fiend gives the more friendly counsel. I will run, fiend; my heels are at your commandment; I will run. (II.ii.1–27)

This speech, recalling the central issue of the morality plays and of [playwright Christopher] Marlowe's *Dr. Faustus* but also handling that issue in a comic fashion, suggests that there are morality elements in *The Merchant of Venice*, but that these too are being treated comically. It also makes it clear that one of the functions of the prose in the play is to work as a sort of counterpoint to the poetry. . . .

ANTONIO SPEAKS IN POETRY

Now, of the characters who play a major role, the only one who is not an amphibian, equally at home in verse and prose, is Antonio, who is wholly a creature of verse. His total reliance on it is, in itself, sufficient to set him off from the rest; but his isolation from them is still further endorsed by the fact that only once does he make use of the rhetorical dialectical mode which comes so habitually to them, and then for a most unusual purpose. Early in the trial scene, when Bassanio attempts to argue with Shylock and makes no progress whatever, Antonio eventually interrupts their dialogue to tell his friend:

> I pray you, think you question with the Jew.[9]
> You may as well go stand upon the beach
> And bid the main flood[10] bate[11] his usual height;
> You may as well use question with the wolf,
> Why he hath made the ewe bleat for the lamb;
> You may as well forbid the mountain pines
> To wag their high tops and to make no noise
> When they are fretten[12] with the gusts of heaven;

7. My father was not too honest; there was a sort of burnt taste about him 8. for "incarnate" 9. i.e. with one naturally hardhearted 10. ocean 11. abate; lessen 12. fretted; tormented

You may as well do any thing most hard
As seek to soften that—than which what's harder?—
His Jewish heart. Therefore, I do beseech you,
Make no more offers, use no farther means,
But with all brief and plain conveniency
Let me have judgment, and the Jew his will.

(IV.i.70–83)

It is a powerful and moving piece of persuasion. Using emphatic repetition and drawing instance after instance from the world of nature, Antonio builds up his plea, culminating in the final sentence introduced by the word 'Therefore,' for the trial to be brought to a speedy end, for the inevitable, as it seems, to be accepted, and for himself to suffer as he must. Whereas the other characters argue for victory, seeking to justify the taking of revenge, the showing of mercy, or the making of a choice, Antonio argues for defeat and self-extinction. But why, one asks, does he have recourse to this manner and for this purpose at this time? And then, looking back over the action, one begins to see a kind of answer. From the outset he has seen himself as the helpless victim of an unintelligible something that he cannot define, the 'it' that he refers to in the speech that opens the play:

In sooth, I know not why I am so sad.
It wearies me; you say it wearies you;
But how I caught it, found it, or came by it,
What stuff 'tis made of, whereof it is born,
I am to learn;
And such a want-wit sadness makes of me
That I have much ado to know myself.

(I.i.1–7)

It is a strange position for the protagonist of a comedy to find himself in. Nor do the events that follow on this opening do anything to improve it; on the contrary, as fortune turns against him, everything conspires to increase his sense of himself as the predestined victim, until, in the trial scene, he actually describes himself as 'a tainted[13] wether[14] of the flock / Meetest for death' (IV.i.114–15). Moreover, he still remains separate and withdrawn even after the trial is over. In the final scene he speaks a mere six and a half lines, one of them being 'I am th' unhappy subject of these quarrels' (V.i.238), as he takes the blame on himself when Portia and Nerissa are wrangling with Bassanio, and Gratiano over the matter of the rings.

---

13. diseased 14. castrated ram

But Antonio's persuasive plea has yet a further significance. It begins with 'the Jew,' it ends with 'the Jew,' and the summing-up in it that precedes the final deduction concludes with 'His Jewish heart.' His powerful and deep-rooted animosity against Shylock is, in the final analysis, as unintelligible to him as his *taedium vitae*.[15] He may rationalize it as the outcome of their religious differences and of their disagreement over the issue of usury, but at bottom he sees Shylock as a brute fact of nature, one who must act as he does because it is not in him to act otherwise, which also happens to be the way in which Shylock sees him. The Jew's first words, spoken in an aside, after Antonio enters to him and Bassanio in I.iii, are:

> How like a fawning publican[16] he looks!
> I hate him for he is a Christian;
> But more for that in low simplicity
> He lends out money gratis, and brings down
> The rate of usance[17] here with us in Venice.
> If I can catch him once upon the hip,
> I will feed fat the ancient grudge I bear him.
>
> (I.iii.36–42.)

Curiously yet firmly and convincingly linked together by their loathing of each other, Shylock and Antonio stand apart from all the other characters; and their separation from them is underscored by the fact that each of them has his own particular manner of utterance. In addition to relying entirely on verse, Antonio, a man governed by feelings, expresses what he feels, whether it be his indefinable sense of sadness, his love for Bassanio, or his scorn and hatred of Shylock, in a naked direct fashion which leaves him extremely vulnerable. Shylock, on the other hand, though fundamentally as much driven by feeling as Antonio, has a shrewdness and a capacity for calculation that enable him to conceal what he feels until the time comes for him to satisfy his desires. In his early dealings with Antonio he counters the Merchant's bluntness with the indirections of irony, which can be disavowed. Not limited to one medium of expression, he succeeds in putting his individual stamp on prose and verse alike, so that both become indelibly his. . . .

His first exchanges with Bassanio establish some of its characteristic features:

15. weariness or boredom with life 16. collectors of taxes for the Romans; a term of bitter abuse to a strict Jew 17. usury

SHYLOCK Three thousand ducats—well.
BASSANIO Ay, sir, for three months.
SHYLOCK For three months—well.
BASSANIO For the which, as I told you, Antonio shall be bound.
SHYLOCK Antonio shall become bound—well.

(I.iii.1–6)

The habit of itemizing things, so typical of the cautious businessman, together with the fondness for repetition, will remain with Shylock for the rest of the play. Employed in the
service of passion, and built into a firm rhetorical structure,
they inform the most deeply felt speech that he makes,
when, in answer to Salerio's question as to what Antonio's
flesh will be good for, he replies:

> To bait fish withal. If it will feed nothing else, it will feed my
> revenge. He hath disgrac'd me and hind'red[18] me half a mil-
> lion; laugh'd at my losses, mock'd at my gains, scorned my
> nation, thwarted my bargains, cooled my friends, heated
> mine enemies. And what's his reason? I am a Jew. Hath not a
> Jew eyes? Hath not a Jew hands, organs, dimensions, senses,
> affections, passions, fed with the same food, hurt with the
> same weapons, subject to the same diseases, healed by the
> same means, warmed and cooled by the same winter and
> summer as a Christian is? If you prick us, do we not bleed? If
> you tickle us, do we not laugh? If you poison us, do we not
> die? And if you wrong us, shall we not revenge? If we are like
> you in the rest, we will resemble you in that. If a Jew wrong
> a Christian, what is his humility?[19] Revenge. If a Christian
> wrong a Jew, what should his sufferance be by Christian ex-
> ample? Why, revenge. The villainy you teach me I will exe-
> cute; and it shall go hard but I will better the instruction.

(III.i.45–62)

A further feature of Shylock's manner that is already apparent in his dialogue with Bassanio is his distrust of figu-
rative language. Having pointed out that there are 'land-rats
and water-rats, water-thieves and land-thieves,' he goes on
to add, lest there be any mistake about the matter, 'I mean
pirates' (I.iii.21–2). The same prose mind and prose idiom
are evident when he speaks in verse, commanding Jessica to
'stop my house's ears—I mean my casements' (II.v.33). In
fact, it is the infiltration of prose rhythms and colloquial
phrases into his blank verse that serves to hold his prose and
verse together, identifying both as his. Blank verse has become completely responsive to a habit of mind, which is also
a trick of speech, when Shylock remarks, after Antonio has

---

18. prevented me from making 19. In what way does he show Christian forbearance?

reminded him that the loan is to be for three months:

> I had forgot—three months; you told me so.
> Well then, your bond; and let me see—but hear you,
> Methoughts you said you neither lend nor borrow
> Upon advantage.
>
> (I.iii.62–5)

The same 'let me see' turns up again some thirty lines later when Shylock says:

> Three thousand ducats—'tis a good round sum.
> Three months from twelve; then let me see, the rate—
>
> (I.iii.98–9).

Up to this point Shylock's mannerisms of speech have been mainly a source of amusement, serving to establish his age and his occupation, but now the hesitations and the parenthetical phrases fall away and the repetitions acquire a sarcastically upbraiding force, as he goes on to describe Antonio's treatment of him in the past and to emphasize the gross discrepancy between that past behaviour and the present request for a loan. In a speech that runs to some twenty-four lines (101–24) he uses 'dog' three times, 'cur' twice, 'moneys' four times, and 'money' once. . . .

Within the context of the scene Shylock's sarcasm causes Antonio to reveal his feelings in the naked direct manner I have referred to earlier, and with such violence that Shylock can take advantage of it to utter his deflating line, 'Why, look you, how you storm!' (132); but, as the action develops, the menacing qualities of which his repetition is capable become more and more pronounced. By the time Shylock can say 'Let him look to his bond' three times in the course of six lines (III.i.37–42), and 'I'll have my bond' five times in the course of fourteen lines (III.iii.4–17), repetition is at once the instrument and the mark of a mind obsessed by a single purpose. Combined with the habit of cumulative itemizing, it finds its culmination in the question and answer method that Shylock has recourse to when justifying his determination to have his bond in the trial scene:

> You'll ask me why I rather choose to have
> A weight of carrion flesh than to receive
> Three thousand ducats. I'll not answer that,
> But say it is my humour[20]—is it answer'd?
> What if my house be troubled with a rat,
> And I be pleas'd to give ten thousand ducats

20. whim

To have it ban'd?[21] What, are you answer'd yet?
Some men there are love not a gaping pig;[22]
Some that are mad if they behold a cat;
And others, when the bagpipe sings i' th' nose,
Cannot contain their urine; for affection,[23]
Mistress of passion, sways it to the mood
Of what it likes or loathes. Now, for your answer:
As there is no firm reason to be rend'red
Why he cannot abide a gaping pig;
Why he, a harmless necessary cat;
Why he, a woollen bagpipe, but of force
Must yield to such inevitable shame
As to offend himself being offended;
So can I give no reason, nor I will not,
More than a lodg'd[24] hate and a certain loathing
I bear Antonio, that I follow thus
A losing[25] suit against him. Are you answered?

(IV.i.40–62)

Shylock's reduction of his enemy to the animal level supports my earlier contention that he sees Antonio precisely as Antonio sees him; but the most fascinating aspect of the speech is its clear demonstration of how an individual idiom can colour and subdue to its purpose the forensic mode which is so typical of the play as a whole. Admirably sustained through the triumphant crows of delighted satisfaction—'O wise young judge,' 'O noble judge!', etc—with which Shylock greets Portia's seeming acquiescence in the justice of his plea, his manner ultimately leaves him wide open to the jeers of Gratiano when the case goes against him.

SHYLOCK LEAVES, BUT HIS ISSUES REMAIN

Shylock dominates *The Merchant of Venice*, until he is forcibly ejected, as it were, from its action, because he has the best, meaning the most dramatically effective, lines in it. To a greater degree, I think, than any character Shakespeare had created before him, he is what he says and how he says it. The man is the words he speaks, bearing out Ben Jonson's dictum in his *Discoveries*:

> *Language* most shewes a man: speake that I may see thee. It springs out of the most retired, and inmost parts of us, and is the Image of the Parent of it, the mind. No glasse renders a mans forme, or likenesse, so true as his speech.

When Shylock leaves the court of justice, defeated and broken, he takes the essential vitality of the play with him. The

21, poisoned 22. roasted young pig with a lemon in its mouth 23. natural disposition
24. deep-seated 25. unprofitable

absence from its last act of the most arresting and unmistakable voice in it, almost, one is tempted to say, a voice crying in a wilderness of monkeys, is something felt, reducing the bickerings over the rings, especially in the stylized exchanges of Bassanio and Portia (v.i.192–208), to mere chatter.

I have said that I miss the sound of Shylock's voice in act v. It is, perhaps, an oversimplification, for the voice cannot be separated from what it says and is so perfectly adapted to saying. It is essentially the voice of protest and also, as that voice so often tends to be, the voice of condemnation, of contempt, and of revenge. It speaks, as does the voice of Antonio, of racial hatred, of religious intolerance, of economic rivalry, and of deep-rooted, instinctive, personal antipathy. And these are issues to which romantic comedy has no answer. They cannot be swept away by ducal decree, still less made non-existent by the donning or the doffing of a disguise. They persist. In a paradoxical kind of way, the Venice of the play is, despite its ridiculous laws and its even more ridiculous administration of them, curiously like the world we live in. At least it is so until Shylock leaves the court to be seen and heard no more. But, while Shylock goes, the serious issues connected with him remain; they have been shelved, not answered or disposed of. Shakespeare tries to restore the atmosphere proper to romantic comedy by moving the action to Belmont once more and falling back on his genius for lyricism. The formalized blank verse duet that Lorenzo and Jessica share at the opening of act v, and Lorenzo's hymn to music that follows it, go some way towards concealing the legerdemain[26] that has so conveniently done the shelving; but Shakespeare does not leave things at this point. Ultimately the great artist's passion for truth gets the better of the need for a happy ending. The long-drawn-out confusions and explanations, shot through with bawdry, are an admission that nothing has really changed, that the world of this play cannot be metamorphosed into the golden world of romance. It is no accident that the last words in the comedy, like the last words addressed to Shylock, come from the lips of Gratiano, a thoroughly dislikable character and, by far and away, the most vulgar figure in it. As he has already gloated over Shylock's downfall, so he now dwells greasily in anticipation on the night he is about to spend with Nerissa. To regard the ending as happy or as a satisfactory solution is to approve of Gratiano, which is, I find, quite impossible.

26. sleight of hand; show of skill or deceitful cleverness

CHAPTER 5

Evaluation

READINGS ON
THE MERCHANT OF VENICE

The Merchant of Venice: An Imperfect Step Toward Later Comedies

D.A. Traversi

D.A. Traversi acknowledges that the elements in *The Merchant of Venice* are incompletely balanced and blended, but he finds the play an interesting retelling of ancient stories and an important step in Shakespeare's development toward mature comic themes. Traversi's analysis focuses on the romantic significance of the casket symbolism, the realistic dimension that Shylock brings to the play, and the harmony and music of the final act. D.A. Traversi has been director of the British Institute in Bilbao and in Barcelona and British Council representative in South America, Spain, and Italy. He has lectured on Shakespeare at Swathmore College in America, contributed articles to literary journals, and published *Shakespeare: The Roman Plays.*

By comparison with Shakespeare's earlier exercises in the comic form, *The Merchant of Venice,* which may have been written in 1596, seems—together with *A Midsummer Night's Dream*—to announce the transition to a more elaborate conception of comedy. The play is in certain respects a little tentative, not altogether assimilated to a single dominating conception. The contrast between Belmont and the Rialto, romantic love and the pursuit of wealth through merchant endeavor, is perhaps incompletely worked out, and the allegory of the caskets can scarcely bear the burden of moral significance which seems to be thrust a little halfheartedly upon it. Above all, the disturbing presence of Shylock threatens to load the comedy with a somber sense of reality that leaves it by contrast, and in his absence, strangely deprived of solidity and meaning. Originally conceived as an object of repudiation, even of ridicule, Shylock almost ends by shattering the framework of comic artifice by introducing a dark and twisted strain from real life; but, although we may think that his presence in a certain sense unbalances the play, *The Merchant of Venice* excels Shakespeare's earliest comedies in the skillful blending of its various elements and indicates, in its greater complexity and more varied reflection of reality, an approach to some of the more permanent features of his mature comic creations.

The action opens, as will often be the case in later comedies, and notably in *Twelfth Night*, upon characters whose reflections are tinged with melancholy, an indefinable discontent with their present state of life. The wealthy merchant Antonio, who appears to lack nothing that riches can provide, is nonetheless possessed, as his first words indicate, by a kind of boredom, dissatisfied, beneath all the opulent references to the world of merchant adventure which surrounds him, with the kind of existence to which he feels himself obscurely condemned:

> In sooth, I know not why I am so sad:
> It wearies me; you say it wearies you;
> But how I caught it, found it, or came by it,
> What stuff 'tis made of, whereof it is born,
> I am to learn.

(I. i)

Much the same is true, though in a different way, of Portia. Committed as a rich heiress in the golden seclusion of Belmont to her father's choice, which she respects as in natural duty bound but cannot fail to find constraining, she confesses that "my little body is aweary of this great world" (I. ii). Each feels confined to an existence which seems to exclude the decisive act of self-surrender, of free dedication to the claims and opportunities which life offers and which finally justify it. Before the play ends Antonio will have found, and taken, his chance to escape this limitation in the opportunity, which is also the risk, of dedicating his wealth, and with it his life, to the happiness of his friend Bassanio; and Portia, in turn, already senses in the gift of herself in marriage a means of release from the golden cage in which she must otherwise decoratively and uselessly dwell.

THE ROMANTIC SYMBOLISM OF THE CASKET EPISODE

Seen from this point of view, the long-drawn-out symbolism of the casket episodes acquires a new significance. Portia's first two suitors are found, each in his own appropriate way, to be wanting. Morocco chooses gold, "which many men desire" (II. vii), only to find that his choice brings him, not life, but its opposite: in the words of the inscription in his casket, "Gilded tombs do worms infold." Arragon, in turn, chooses silver in the name of self-esteem and receives, not the award he has rashly assumed to be his due, but the "fool's head" that this self-regarding choice brings with it:

> Some there be that shadows kiss,
> Such have but a shadow's bliss.

(II. ix)

Each of these weighty personages in effect chooses self and is subjected to the mockery his choice invites. The attitude of Bassanio, for whom Portia has been instinctively waiting, is different. His first words on the subject of his love reveal him as the typical romantic lover in his most positive aspect.

> her sunny locks
> Hang on her temples like a golden fleece;
> Which makes her seat of Belmont Colchos' strand,
> And many Jasons come in quest of her.[1]

(I. i)

That Bassanio may strike us in realistic terms as a thin character, even as one suspiciously ready to rest his hopes upon the sacrifice of his friend, is not important. He is to be judged in terms of the romantic comedy to which he belongs; and it is as such, as a "Jason" dedicated to love's adventure and disposed—unlike his rivals—to risk for it, that he shows himself ready in the moment of his trial to give in order to receive, to choose inner reality rather than the deception of outward show. Taking the risk which the injunction on his casket conveys, and which is in these comedies a law of life—"who chooseth me must give and hazard all he hath" (II. vii)—he receives his appropriate reward in the graceful simplicity of Portia's answering self-surrender:

> You see me, Lord Bassanio, where I stand,
> Such as I am; though for myself alone
> I would not be ambitious in my wish,
> To wish myself much better; yet for you
> I would be trebled twenty times myself;
> A thousand times more fair, ten thousand times
> More rich;
> That only to stand high in your account,[2]

1. Jason sailed to the shore of Colchos in the *Argo* to fetch away the Golden Fleece. 2. estimation

I might in virtue, beauties, livings,[3] friends,
Exceed account: but the full sum of me
Is sum of something which, to term in gross,
Is an unlesson'd girl, unschool'd, unpractised;
Happy in this, she is not yet so old
But she may learn; happier than this,
She is not bred so dull but she can learn;
Happiest of all in that her gentle spirit
Commits itself to yours to be directed,
As from her lord, her governor, her king.
Myself and what is mine to you and yours
Is now converted:[4] but now I was the lord
Of this fair mansion, master of my servants,
Queen o'er myself; and even now, but now,
This house, these servants, and this same myself
Are yours, my lord: I give them with this ring.

(III. ii)

Once again, as in the case of Bassanio, it is easy to misinterpret this, to find Portia's self-presentation as an "unlesson'd girl" disingenuous, even artful, in view of her own later mastery of the complexities of the trial scene. This, however, is once more to ignore the comic terms on the basis of which she was created. What is in question here is not psychological realism but the familiar accountancy of love, which rests on giving rather than on seeking to take, and which finds its fulfillment in generous and free self-dedication as opposed to the vanity of self-assertion. In Portia's lines we may properly feel that the content of Katherine's final speech on the marriage relationship in *The Taming of the Shrew* has been taken up and given a new depth of personal tenderness and a greater humanity of content.

ANTONIO AND SHYLOCK ADD SERIOUS DIMENSIONS TO THE COMEDY

The ideals and satisfactions of romantic love, however, are not allowed to stand alone in this play. In choosing to help Bassanio, Antonio has accepted the risk which the leaden casket enjoined. By so doing, he has taken upon himself the rule of friendship and opened to himself the possibility of obtaining its true wealth, which is not to be assessed in terms of temporal merchandise; but his choice exposes him to the hazards of the world and through them to the real possibility of tragedy. The real world, which shadows the colorful and self-absorbed society of the Rialto, is represented not merely by the brightly colored talk of argosies and swelling

3. possessions 4. transferred

sails, of merchandise and far-flung affairs—topics in which this society delights—but by the somber reality of Shylock.

The interpretation of Shylock's part in the play calls in any event for considerable firmness in discrimination. It may even be that Shakespeare, when he embarked upon his comedy, was not in every respect fully conscious of what he was in fact bringing into being. It is essential, of course, to avoid the modern temptation to sentimentalize Shylock, or to read his character in terms of our own preoccupation with racial realities. The melodramatic villain, the heartless usurer, and the enemy of Christianity all belong to the conception, and an Elizabethan audience would certainly have found nothing unusual or unseemly in the final downfall of all three. This downfall is amply accomplished before the end of the play and is certainly essential to its intended effect. . . .

When Tubal reports that one of Antonio's creditors has been seen abroad with "a ring that he had of your daughter for a monkey," Shylock's reaction—

> Thou torturest me, Tubal: it was my turquoise; I had it of Leah when I was a bachelor: I would not have given it for a wilderness of monkeys—
>
> (III. i)

is sufficiently steeped in emotion, personal and, as it were, racial, to produce an effect that finally evades the merely comic. Incidents of this kind are common in Shakespeare's presentation of Shylock; they are used, beyond the evident intention of condemning the usurious unbeliever, beyond even that of showing an incompletely human being entrapped in the insufficiency of his own attitudes, to lend depth and dramatic verisimilitude to the Jew's passion, to what is seen at certain culminating moments to be his intense desire to *survive* by clinging to his own separate standards. This is the desire which makes him, on his first appearance, declare himself ready to "buy with you, sell with you, talk with you, walk with you," but not, on the other hand, "to eat with you, drink with you, nor pray with you" (I. iii); to cling, in other words, by every means in his power—including, notably, his command over money—to his separate identity in a world implacably, if reasonably, hostile to everything for which he stands.

It is his understanding of these deeper issues behind Shylock's admitted "villainy," even his rejection of the human law of compassion, that enables Shakespeare to present the Jew's reactions to Christian society with a force that makes it impossible for us simply to pass them by. It is not in any sense that Shylock is to be regarded as being in the right. On the contrary, his attitudes are based on what all the comedies agree in regarding as basic human limitations, blind spots which, when persisted in, make a balanced and fully human life unattainable. Shylock is finally condemned by his persistence in his own perverse choices, by the warped attitudes which prompt him to reject life when it is offered him upon the only terms on which, according to these comedies, it is available. . . .

THE TRIAL BRINGS ROMANCE AND REALITY TOGETHER

It is in the light of these considerations that we may best approach the famous trial scene (IV. i) where the two worlds of romance and reality which divide the play so uneasily between them are finally brought together. . . .

By the opening of this scene we shall certainly have learned not to underestimate Shylock, or to give his outbursts of dark and twisted emotion less than their share of human value; but we must add that his own appeal to justice is seen at the crucial moment to be limited by this same resentment, to remain bound up in self and blind to the higher human reality of compassion. It is for this reason, now seen in its relation to the preceding symbolism of the casket scenes, that Portia, transformed from the object of Bassanio's romantic love into the mouthpiece of a more universal law, intervenes in the proceedings. She does so to a double end. In the first place, and throughout the earlier part of the long scene, she grants the Jew, in the name of justice, all that in justice is his right. By so doing, she underlines the reality of Antonio's "hazard," by which he is finally to be redeemed; but, having done this, she goes on to raise her plea beyond "justice" to invoke a "mercy" which is beyond all covenant of law, and which is the gratuitous gift of "heaven": a "mercy" of which all men, just and unjust, Christian and Jew alike, stand in need. . . .

For Shylock, in the very moment of seeming to obtain the judgment which is recognized to be his due, is condemned by his failure to temper "justice" with "mercy," recognizing thereby his share in the universal human situation. He too needs "mercy," and is called upon to "give" as well as to exact; and because this lesson of the caskets, translated from allegory to a situation tense with human drama, fails to move him, the very "justice" he has invoked finally breaks in his hands and he is judged in the light of the narrow and implacable standards upon which he has chosen to take his stand.

Act Five Unites Romance and Music

With the departure of Shylock we return, a little uneasily, to the world of poetry and artifice which has generally prevailed whenever he has been absent from the stage. As the various pairs of lovers finally come together, in the appropriate comic manner, romance and music are united in a poetic effect which is sometimes principally decorative (as in the famous duet "In such a night" (V. i) between Lorenzo and Jessica, where the beauty of the verse cannot quite lead us to forget the element of deception and heartlessness by which their love has been shadowed), but which occasionally rises, as in Lorenzo's most eloquent utterance, to a more profound "Platonic" statement of spiritual harmonies:

> How sweet the moonlight sleeps upon this bank!
> Here will we sit, and let the sounds of music
> Creep in our ears; soft stillness and the night
> Become the touches of sweet harmony.
> Sit, Jessica. Look how the floor of heaven
> Is thick inlaid with patines[5] of bright gold;
> There's not the smallest orb which thou behold'st
> But in his motion like an angel sings,
> Still quiring[6] to the young-eyed cherubins;
> Such harmony is in immortal souls;
> But whilst this muddy vesture of decay[7]
> Doth grossly close it in, we cannot hear it.
>
> (V. i)

The enchanted harmonies of music become here the reflection of something more profound, a deeper intuition, glimpsed if not retained, of universal fitness. The absorbing beauty of life which everywhere surrounds man and his inability to maintain other than fugitively his hold upon it becomes at such moments the pervasive background of Shakespeare's comic devices.

It only remains to mention in conclusion the episode of the lovers' gift to Portia and her maid of their rings and of their final return to their respective owners. Drawn in all

5. plates 6. singing 7. the mortal earthly body; so long as we are mortal we cannot hear immortal music

probability from a story by [Italian writer Giovanni] Boccaccio, the incident parallels in a broadly comic key the central
moral of love as consisting of accepted risk, of the sponta-
neous and irrevocable gift of self. The rings were originally
conferred as pledges of mutual fidelity. Portia now confis-
cates them in the name of "justice"—to remind us that, in
"justice," "all men are frail"—and returns them, on the plea
precisely of Antonio, who has already shown under sterner
circumstances his readiness to make the life-giving gift of
self for his friend. As he now says:

> I did once lend my body for his wealth;
> Which, but for him that had your husband's ring
> Had quite miscarried: I dare be bound again,
> *My soul upon the forfeit,* that your lord
> Will never more break faith advisedly;[8]

> (V. i)

and Portia makes the return, in answer to Antonio's renewed,
but this time spiritual, guarantee, in a comic reflection of
"mercy," of that capacity for tolerant and compassionate understanding upon which alone any durable human relationship can be founded. Thus expressed, it may seem that the
device can hardly bear the burden of meaning placed upon
it, and this is indeed an impression which a good deal of this
play is likely to give us. The entire action is dominated, possibly even beyond the author's initial intention, by the human and dramatic stature of Shylock; but, for all the imperfect co-ordination—as we may feel it—of the various
elements which compose it, *The Merchant of Venice* not only
lives as the dramatic retelling of more than one ancient and
familiar story, but suggests themes which elsewhere—in the
relation of reality and make-believe which Shakespeare used
so triumphantly in his later, greater comedies—were to be
more profoundly and coherently developed.

---

8. deliberately

The Merchant of Venice Lacks Dramatic Unity

Gareth Lloyd Evans

Gareth Lloyd Evans analyzes the problem of reconciling the romantic and realistic elements of the play. The problem centers on Shylock: Were he merely a simple, vicious man gloating over the possibility of humiliating Antonio, he would remain a one-dimensional, fairy tale villain. But Evans argues that Shakespeare has made Shylock too realistically human to fit into that world. He becomes a multidimensional character when he responds to the loss of his daughter and defends his Jewishness and his common humanity. Evans concludes that the play is theatrically effective but dramatically irreconcilable. Gareth Lloyd Evans teaches dramatic literature at the University of Birmingham in England and is a drama critic for the *Guardian* and other journals. He is the author of a five-volume guide to Shakespeare's plays and *J.B. Priestley, Dramatist.*

This play, written between 1596 and 1598, is one of the most popular in the whole canon. The first quarto records that it was 'divers times' performed by the Lord Chamberlain's company.[1]...

Appraisal of the play [however] is difficult, since the experience of it, either in the study or in the theatre, is likely, more than with most others, to be conditioned by strong personal predispositions. Is the reader, or member of the audience, Christian or Jew? How far does racialism (a pregnant consideration nowadays) affect one's estimate of the play? For the, perhaps rare, reader or viewer of the play who is able, by some process, to submerge such considerations, there still remains a factor which may colour his view of the

1. the company of actors, including Shakespeare, acting first at the Theatre, then the Swan, then the Curtain, and finally the Globe

play. This factor is literary rather than social, religious or racist. It is simply that some find the play inherently cynical because of the disparate elements in it. It is perhaps naive to state that the romantic resolutions of Belmont are hard to swallow after the stern judgments of the trial scene, or, indeed, to suggest that if this is so it may be an implied condemnation of Shakespeare's inability to reconcile what is seemingly dramatically irreconcilable. Looking at it from a different standpoint, one might ask if it is not possible that Shylock is built too large to be destroyed by mere legality, and this at the hands of characters who have not been created with the understanding and richness of human perception which has been expended on the Jew. . . .

There are indications in the structure of the play of a careful design on Shakespeare's part to maintain a strong sense of that kind of narrative plot associated with the intriguing and the unknown. Quite simply, the play frequently puts its audience in the position of asking—what will happen next? Will Shylock demand the fulfillment of the bond? Will Antonio's argosies [fleet] arrive in time? Will Portia's disguise be noticed in court? Who will choose the right casket? Will Shylock cut the flesh from Antonio and, if so, how? Will Shylock become a Christian? Will the business of the giving away of the rings mean a happy ending? Putting ourselves in the position of one seeing the play for the first time, we realize that these questions are very much in the forefront of our experience of the action. One question after another is posed and answered (except what happens to Shylock), mostly with a kind of convenient adherence to the demands of the plot at any given moment. It is meet, for example, that Antonio should not lose out on the general share out of happiness at the end so, conveniently, the news comes that his enterprises have not foundered. Possibly the popularity of the play rests firmly, though not of course exclusively, upon these questions and the answers that are given to them.

SHAKESPEARE'S FAIRYTALE WORLD

Then there is the question of credibility. We are given no reason for Antonio's melancholy; he just is so. (It could be suggested that Shakespeare has created him thus to produce a sense of isolation which in turn will increase the *frisson*[2] of

2. shiver; shudder

sympathy from us in the predicament he calls upon himself). Whatever the reason, there is something unreal about the character. This quality of unreality is increased by the fact that we are continually conscious that many incidents and episodes, in themselves, have a contrived, framed, unreal flavour. The casket episodes may be delightful but are scarcely credible; the bond may inject excitement into the plot, but its terms are in the realm of fantasy; Professor Moelwyn Merchant says, 'The whole legal structure of the play is, of course, fallacious', and certainly the trial may be exciting, but, is, in the last analysis, incredible; the appearance of Portia in a High Court, masquerading as a renowned lawyer, although an occasion for satisfying our romantic sensibilities, is palpably beyond the realms of possibility. And as if to emphasize this fantasy element in the play, the last act in Belmont, where any moral compunctions about what has happened before are wholly ignored, making the Belmont scene an idyllic haven, is immured from the harsh issues which have been enacted near the Rialto.

The creation of this unreal world through a set of incredible circumstances is reinforced by the disposition of certain scenes. The audience is lured into an aura of fantasy by the casket episode, and it is noticeable that Shakespeare extends this aura by separating the casket affair into four distinct parts. Morocco makes his debut in Act II.2 and his choice in Act II.7; Aragon chooses wrongly in Act II.9 and Bassanio, correctly, in Act III.2. On each occasion the fantasy quality is reinforced. Morocco's first speech to Portia, after he had asked her to lead him to the caskets, has all the inconsequential bravado of a pantomime potentate:

'. . . By this scimitar[3]
That slew the Sophy[4] and a Persian prince,
That won three fields[5] of Sultan Solyman,[6]
I would o'er-stare the sternest eyes that look,
Out-brave the heart most daring on the earth,
Pluck the young sucking cubs from the she-bear,
Yea, mock the lion when 'a roars for prey,
To win thee, lady . . .'

[II.1.24–31]

His reactions to the contents of the casket are in the best traditions of rhodomontade[7] melodrama:

---

3. curved sword   4. shah of Persia   5. battles   6. the Turkish emperor   7. pretentious boasting or bragging; bluster

'Cold indeed, and labour lost.
Then farewell, heat, and welcome, frost.'

[II.7.74–5]

Aragon, in his turn, no less reinforces the mode of delightful fable:

'I am enjoin'd by oath to observe three things:
First, never to unfold to anyone
Which casket 'twas I chose; next, if I fail
Of the right casket, never in my life
To woo a maid in way of marriage;
Lastly,
If I do fail in fortune of my choice,
Immediately to leave you and be gone.'

[II.9.9–16]

These three promises take us unequivocally into the realm of fairy story and give us a standpoint from which to take stock of the world which Portia inhabits. A young and beautiful princess attended only by minions[8] waits for the outcome of an edict made by her dead father. She is visited by two exotic potentates but her heart is a'quiver lest one of them should open the right casket and claim her. She need not fear—only Prince Charming will open the right one, for he is true in heart. All might well end very happily, except that this particular Prince Charming has involved himself in an enterprise which endangers a near and dear friend. The happy ending must be postponed until the danger is removed and its wicked progenitor cast away.

FROM THE FAIRYTALE TO THE REAL WORLD

Yet how wicked is Shylock? It is remarkable how easy it is to assume that Shylock's intentions, from the very beginning, are utterly vicious, but this is not so. In order to believe that, we have both to deny completely the emphasis on fable in the play and to overstress the implications of one particular speech of Shylock. When he first encounters Antonio he rails to himself about Antonio as a publican. He hates him for being a Christian, he despises him for his attitude to usury. He says he will not forgive him and hopes that 'if I can catch him upon the hip' he will be happy. To 'catch upon the hip' does not suggest killing. It has the flavour of those threats which melodramatic villains whisper to themselves

---

8. servile self-seekers who attempt to win favor by flattering influential people

about the hero. It is a wrestling term, suggesting Shylock will be happy to give Antonio a fall which will be painful and humiliating.

Indeed the whole of the preliminaries to the signing of the bond are conducted by Shylock with the excited expectation of humiliating his adversary but no more. At first he and Antonio spar with each other, then, the sparring over, Shylock begins the process of real humiliation. Antonio is the challenger, Shylock speaks from his position of advantage. He taunts Antonio whose former jibes at Jewry have now turned to requests for Jewish help:

'Fair sir, you spit on me on Wednesday last,
You spurn-d me such a day; another time
You call'd me dog; and for these courtesies
I'll lend you thus much moneys?'

[I.3.121–4]

Throughout this scene the atmosphere is compounded of Shylock's fierce joy in humiliating Antonio and Antonio's grim determination to swallow the jibes for the sake of Bassanio. Up to Act III.1 the motivations of Shylock are presented, albeit strongly, within the terms of the fabulous world which the casket scenes in particular have created, but suddenly, in this scene, the rules of fairy tale are broken. Jessica's departure from her father's house with his money is, in itself, of a piece with the fairy tale atmosphere. The beleaguered young maiden, tied to a mean and cruel father, escapes romantically by night from his clutches into the waiting arms of her dashing young lover. If Shylock had been allowed by Shakespeare to remain in the mode of the surrounding actions of the play—that of fairy story—the morality of Jessica's taking of her father's money would not arise in our minds; the villain would merely be getting his deserts. In Act III.1, however, Shylock moves from one mode into another. He associates the departure of his daughter with Christian perfidy. It is, very significantly, as if a piece of his own flesh had been torn from him:

'I say my daughter is my flesh and my blood'

[III.1.32]

It is at this point that the bond as an element in the plot acquires a more realistic significance and when, immediately following upon his cry about his daughter, he shouts that Antonio must 'look to his bond', Shylock himself moves from his position as agent in a fantasy into human dimensions. He is no longer confined within the conditioned reflexes of the fairy tale mode and is beginning to generate his own reactions to situations. Yet what surrounds him is still largely cast in that fairy tale mode. Immediately after Shylock's declaration about fulfilling the bond we have a casket scene (when Bassanio makes the right choice) and we are jolted back to a world of fable. This itself is interrupted by the news about Antonio's ships. Yet, even now, the element of happy-ever-after is strong, for Portia's almost merry speech, offering money to pay Shylock, has all the flavour of that confidential optimism by which the pantomime princess assures her audience that, in the end, all will be well:

> 'When it is paid, bring your true friend along.
> My maid Nerissa and myself meantime
> Will live as maids and widows. Come, away;
> For you shall hence upon your wedding day.'
>
> [III.2.310–13]

Portia maintains her relatively merry mood in the delight she displays with Nerissa at the prospect of disguising themselves, a scene which induces that feeling of excitement we feel in a fairy story or pantomime when the fragile heroine leaves to take arms against the cruel monster:

> 'But come, I'll tell thee all my whole device
> When I am in my coach, which stays for us
> At the park gate; and therefore haste away,
> For we must measure twenty miles today.'
>
> [III.4.81–4]

But the villain himself has stepped out of the cage of fairy tale and, by Act III, he is a wounded, dangerous, and strangely pitiable creature. He has gone far beyond the simple function of being a mere melodramatic impediment to the romantic course of true love. . . .

The Jew of Elizabethan imagination was a dark figure, half real, half out of fable, and his characteristics—cupidity, obsessive, self-indulgent thrift, meanness of spirit and a set of religious beliefs at variance with Christianity—are all put before us by Shakespeare in his character, Shylock. But there is much more. Shakespeare allows Shylock free play on our emotions. Antonio's sparse reponse to Shylock's taunts:

> 'I am as like to call thee so again,
> To spit on thee again, to spurn thee too.'
>
> [I.3.125–6]

only serves to make us wonder whether he does not have

some justice in his attitude to Antonio. The defection of Jessica in complicity with a Christian although by itself merely a part of the fable, becomes, when set against Shylock's tortured grief, something to make us pause. His plea to be granted the benefit of the letter of the law may seem, in isolation, irrationally spiteful, but against Portia's legal petit-point, it becomes no more than a demand for the equity of an eye for an eye and a tooth for a tooth. These factors, in themselves, cause us to wonder whether, in fact, Shakespeare, having accepted the semi-mythological conception of the Jew as the basis of his character (after all, he knew his box office), bent a little backwards, not so much to avoid taking sides as to allow his own sense of fair play to manoeuvre. Certainly, to put Shylock legalistically, as he does, on a dramatic par with Christian legality, argues for a disposition on his part to favour Shylock.

There are, however, two other factors which push the figure of Shylock away both from the conventional idea of the Jew and, most certainly, from the fable mode of his context. The first is the man's pride. He has the virtue of total fidelity (expressed without mealy-mouthed compromise) to his heritage as a Jew. He clings to usury, not only because it is profitable but because it is a built-in tenet of his religion. The small details of his pride swell into largeness when he bases that pride upon strictly human grounds, 'Hath not a Jew eyes?' In the speech from which this line comes, Shakespeare opened the doors for an audience response which, in depth and variety, take one's experience of the play far beyond the realms of fable.

The second is in the implied reconciliation between the Christian and the Jewish attitude. The 'punishment' of Shylock is conceived, particularly by Antonio, less as a punishment than an opportunity for Shylock to allow himself the possibility of eternal grace by entering the Christian religion. But is this, for the audience, a fair and acceptable bargain? Having already been taught to admire Shylock's fidelity to his race and religion—we are now asked to welcome his defection from it. We are asked to applaud a man being brought to the true religion when we have been convinced that, for this man, Jewry is the only religion.

Shylock in fact becomes too human to be accommodated within the fable. However much scholarship may point to the processes of reconciliation in this play, it is only if we can continue to regard Shylock as a monster/comic, that we can join in the dance. Portia, and Portia alone, is raised to a level which can be regarded as on a par with what Shakespeare makes of Shylock from the time of the news of his daughter's elopement to his own final shuffling departure. It is not without significance that the truly successful productions of this play have always depicted Shylock and Portia, in the trial scene, as equal adversaries, and, mutually recognizing the other as equal, they both demand, and should receive, an equal amount of sympathy and understanding from the audience. Portia represents Christian law and a spirit of reconciliation, Shylock no less, represents a Jewish law, and a fidelity to his own religious principles. If the tension, strung between two poles of equal strength, is maintained in the theatre, speeches like Portia's on mercy and Shylock's 'What judgment . . .' ennoble the whole action. If the poles are of unequal strength, the sense of the agencies of a fable overcoming, by trickery and sententious moralising, a powerful human figure is, not to exaggerate, sickeningly obvious.

The play can only be made, as a whole, compatible to itself in production by allowing the strength of the fable element *and* the strength of the Shylock element full play. The result is inevitably a powerful demonstration of the singular *theatrical* effectiveness of what is, dramatically, irreconcilable.

The Merchant of Venice Is Clear, Simple, and Successful

E.M.W. Tillyard

E.M.W. Tillyard takes issue with critics who complain that the play's simplicity detracts from its dramatic quality. He acknowledges two minor flaws in the plot, but otherwise praises its interesting characters, who change but remain consistent with the atmosphere and themes of the play. Tillyard suggests that perhaps the simplicity and smoothness of the play disguise its substance and meaning. E.M.W. Tillyard taught at Jesus College, Cambridge University, in England. He is the author of *Shakespeare's History Plays, The English Epic and Its Background,* and *The Elizabethan World Picture.*

There is a discrepancy between what the public and what the critics have made of the *Merchant of Venice*. The public have loved it and found little wrong with it; the critics have given conflicting interpretations or have found much wrong with it. [Critic] W.P. Ker even went so far as to accuse it of fundamental disharmony.

> A story like that of the *Three Caskets* or the *Pound of Flesh* is perfectly consistent with itself in its original popular form. It is inconsistent with the form of elaborate drama, and with the lives of people who have souls of their own, like Portia or Shylock. Hence in the drama which uses the popular story as its ground-plan, the story is never entirely reduced into conformity with the spirit of the chief characters. The caskets and the pound of flesh, in despite of all the author's pains with them, are imperfectly harmonised; the primitive and barbarous imagination in them retains an inconvenient power of asserting its discordance with the principal parts of the drama.

In this dispute I am on the side of the public, thinking some of the critics' interpretations far-fetched and Ker's condem-

Excerpted from *Shakespeare's Early Comedies*, by E.M.W. Tillyard. Copyright © 1965 by Stephen Tillyard. Reprinted by permission of Chatto and Windus, London.

nation the exact opposite of the truth. Not that Shakespeare's task was not even more complex than Ker indicated, for it went beyond that of humanizing fairy-tales and included one of the formulas of classico-Italian comedy: that of the young folk getting the better of a harsh and avaricious father by trickery. As Grumio said in the *Taming of the Shrew*, 'Here's no knavery! See, to beguile the old folks, how the young folks lay their heads together' ([Shakespeare's] *Taming of the Shrew*, I, ii, 135). The episode of the rings, too, is comic not romantic. Thus, Shakespeare was committed to making his play a comedy as well as a fairy romance. Allowing for a couple of queer lapses and a certain predisposition in his audience not shared by ourselves, the play triumphs and, within its well-defined limits, emerges a masterpiece.

Two Flaws in the Play's Plot

The two lapses need not detain us long. The first, indeed, looks like a cut, not an error of judgement. It has to do with Bassanio's speech when he chooses the right casket. In the two corresponding scenes both Morocco and Arragon, in speeches of fifty-five and forty-eight lines respectively, pondered the inscriptions on the caskets; Bassanio, on the other hand, speaks only thirty-three lines and says nothing about the inscriptions. Now this lets us down, for in a fairy-tale we feel cheated if we do not get a strict pattern. If Morocco and Arragon pondered on the inscriptions, Bassanio was bound by the rules of faery to do the same. Moreover, the inscription on the casket he chooses—'Who chooseth me must give and hazard all he hath'—is so perfectly apt to Bassanio himself and to the whole tenor of the play that it is criminal to omit a reference to it at this of all places. The other lapse is the way in which Portia describes how she and Nerissa will disguise themselves as youths. It occurs (III, iv) immediately after she has sent Balthazar to Doctor Bellario: that is when she has the serious matter of Antonio's rescue principally in mind and when she is determined to personate a Doctor of Laws. Nothing here could be more inept than the boast of 'proving the prettier fellow of the two' and speaking 'between the change of man and boy/ With a reed-voice.' Possibly Shakespeare wished by his tone here to make it perfectly clear before the trial scene that the play was a comedy and that we need have no anxiety about the issue of the trial; but, if so, he made it clear at a cost.

CHARACTERS CHANGE WITHIN THE PLAY

As to the predisposition in an audience, we recognize pretty well by now that in Shakespeare we must be ready for a character to cease being his differentiated self, spout a piece of impersonal rhetoric, and revert to that self. . . . But in the *Merchant of Venice* we must be content with more: with seeing a character turning into a different character or into an allegory. We must, in fact, read the play as we have to read [poet Edmund] Spenser: with no fixed expectations of what a character is like or will turn into. The Portia who begins as a witty young woman turns into the princess of the Beautiful Mountain, dangerous and difficult of access, into the perfectly dutiful and affectionate wife, into a tomboy, into an allegory of Mercy, and ends as something not unlike her first self, only maturer and more in command of every situation. Bassanio, beginning as the good-hearted but improvident young man of conventional comedy, gathers dignity and poise to qualify as the fairy prince subjected to his ordeal. And I think there would have been less trouble over Shylock if critics had been less anxious to make him quite self-consistent. Bred on Spenser and other allegory, an Elizabethan audience would have had no difficulty in accepting these transformations; while it is worth recollecting that in *Richard III* Shakespeare had recently created a character who changed from a credible, if eccentric, human being into the monstrous villain of melodrama. . . .

An Elizabethan audience would have no difficulty in accepting the many changes of Portia. Actually, modern audiences have managed pretty well to exercise the kind of adaptability I have been postulating and have insisted on adoring the *Merchant of Venice* as a perfectly viable stage-play.

THE PLAY IS CLEAR AND SIMPLE

One thing that has prevented men from accepting the *Merchant* unequivocally as a masterpiece is the ease of execution. Can anything so pellucid[1] in sense and of so smooth a gliding have really called forth the author's full powers? In retort, I would point to a remark of [French writer Honoré de] Balzac in *La Cousine Bette*. The author is reflecting on the sense of ease in some of Raphael's paintings and of strain in others, and he goes on:

1. transparent; clear in meaning

> In the begetting of works of art there is as much chance in the
> character of the offspring as there is in a family of children;
> that some will be happily graced, born beautiful, and costing
> their mother little suffering, creatures on whom everything
> smiles and with whom everything succeeds.

The *Merchant* is like one of these fortunate children. Or consider this common experience in learning to speak a foreign
language. There are times when all goes wrong, when the
knowledge you think you command simply refuses to make itself available and you stutter as you may not have done a week
ago; and there are times when all goes right, when all your re-
sources await your pleasure and you find yourself a better lin-
guist than you ever thought you could be. Some such happy facility appears to mark the *Merchant of Venice*, whatever in
actual fact were the pains that it cost its maker. To have
achieved this happy facility in compassing a varied, even apparently incongruous, array of themes was one of Shakespeare's major triumphs; and I rejoice to be able to quote [critic
Harley] Granville-Barker to the effect that the play 'is—for what
it is—as smoothly and completely successful, its means being
as well fitted to its end, as anything Shakespeare wrote'.

ANTONIO'S FRIENDS ARE DECENT PEOPLE

I have accused the critics of advancing far-fetched interpretations and would like to point one out, pleading at the same
time for a renewed simplicity of vision and a renewed heed
to what the text tells us. As long as I can remember and until very recently, I have taken it for granted that the young
men encompassing Antonio were a light-hearted and prodigal set; in fact the sort of young men you would expect in
Venice on the evidence of the [Robert Browning's] *Toccata of
Galuppi.* I cannot say whence I derived that impression; but
this very ignorance suggests its prevalence, its being generally taken for granted. [Critic Arthur] Quiller-Couch gives
the doctrine in its extreme form in his introduction to the
New Cambridge Shakespeare edition, where he called Antonio not only the careful merchant but

> the indolent patron of a circle of wasters, 'born to consume
> the fruits of this world', heartless, or at least unheedful, while
> his life lies in jeopardy through his tender, extravagantly ro-
> mantic friendship for one of them.

Turn to the text, and you find the very opposite of heed-
lessness among Antonio's friends. In II, viii, after Salerio has
described the parting of Bassanio from Antonio, Solanio says

I pray thee, let us go and find him out,
And quicken his embraced heaviness
With some delight or other.

(II. viii, 51)

And when in III, iii, Shylock meets Antonio before the trial
seeking exercise outside the prison in charge of the gaoler,
Solanio is there to keep Antonio company. In the first scene
Antonio's friends are sincerely worried about his state of
mind, though they may seem to joke about it. Even the irrepressible Gratiano, the buffoon of the circle, is sincere and
well-intentioned in his remonstrance with Antonio (as he
says, 'I love thee, and 'tis my love that speaks' (I, i, 87)) even
if he is far from understanding his trouble. He seriously
warns Antonio not to be melancholy for the sake of 'opinion',
which means here 'reputation' or even 'publicity'.... Gratiano's speech is, in essence, a warning against such behaviour and a hint that the sufferer had better pull himself together. He is in fact the well-meaning eupeptic[2] who cannot
believe in the plight of those less happily extroverted than
himself. Lorenzo in his honeymoon excitement makes free
with the money his Jessica has lifted from her father but, arrived in Belmont, he shows the most impeccable approval of
Portia's generosity in allowing Bassanio to hurry to Venice
on Antonio's account and pays this tribute to Antonio's high
worth:

> But if you knew to whom you show this honour,
> How true a gentleman you send relief,
> How dear a lover of my lord your husband,
> I know you would be prouder of the work
> Than customary bounty can enforce you.

(III, iv, 5)

In fact Antonio's friends are a perfectly decent lot, of the kind
you might find in the Inns of Court in Shakespeare's London,
gay but not vicious and with at least an underlying sense of
responsibility. That is, if you do not sentimentalize Shylock
and damn the whole pack of them in disgust at Gratiano's
jeers at him when he sees his game has been lost. . . .

FAIRY TALES INFUSED WITH HUMANITY AND FEELINGS

Granville-Barker, like [critics] W. W. Lawrence and Middleton Murry (who derives from Lawrence without directly
saying so), makes the fairy-tale substance of the *Merchant of*

---

2. cheerful, happy person

Venice the centre of the meaning. Shakespeare had chosen two traditional, utterly familiar stories, and his

> practical business was simply so to charge them with humanity that they did not betray belief in the human beings presenting them, yet not so uncompromisingly that the stories themselves become ridiculous.

This is true as far as it goes but it also puts things too simply. Shakespeare's main source, *Il Pecorone*, is not a pure fairy-tale, for it includes the comic theme of the lost ring. Nor does he keep the Shylock story uncontaminated, for he includes in it the current comic motive, classico-Italian in origin, of a child for the sake of love deceiving a harsh and miserly parent and the Morality theme of Justice against Mercy. Shakespeare's business was to extract from all ingredients, romantic, comic, and Morality, the greatest possible meaning.

Whatever the complexity or even seeming incongruity of the matter of the *Merchant of Venice*, its effect is one of harmony and serenity. The cause is the run of the verse and prose, which is easy, unimpeded, reassuring. The spirit that animates the rhetoric is that of sheer goodwill. That spirit animates the *Midsummer Night's Dream* also, but with such great differences that we never suspect the least tautology.[3] The *Dream* ranges over a larger section of the cosmos and is seen from a greater distance. The *Merchant*, though a fairy tale, is occupied with a smaller part of society and is seen from near at hand. In the *Dream* the narrative counts for little, and we have rather a series of juxtaposed human relations. In the *Merchant*, the narrative counts for much and with it the romance or fairy-tale substance. In fact, the *Merchant* is the play of Shakespeare where the mental feelings proper to the romance ... figure largest. There are three tasks or ordeals to be performed or endured. Bassanio must survive the ordeal of the caskets; Portia must achieve the rescue of Antonio; Antonio must endure and survive imprisonment and danger to his life. Possibly Lorenzo and Jessica provide a fourth example. Once the ordeals have been survived, happiness, of indefinite duration, ensues; except for Antonio, who is deliberately made an exception to the general rule. I pointed out that this process, recurrent in the fairy tale, represented a universal trend of human feeling. In spite of the immense counter-attraction of luck, of the de-

3. redundancy; needless repetition

light of getting something for nothing, mankind believes that it is better to earn your happiness and approves the rhythms of the successful voyage, not without danger, or of the man setting out to work in the morning, achieving something difficult or at least solid, and then, appropriately tired, returning home to relax. It is because Shakespeare constructed the *Merchant* on these excessively simple but universal feelings that his play has enjoyed so immense a popularity.

CHRONOLOGY

1557

Shakespeare's parents, John Shakespeare and Mary Arden, marry.

1558

Elizabeth I becomes queen of England.

1561

Philosopher and statesman Francis Bacon is born; he is later advanced as the actual writer of Shakespeare's plays by skeptics in the modern age.

1562

The English begin participating in the New World slave trade from Africa.

1564

William Shakespeare is born; English dramatist Christopher Marlowe is born; Italian painter, sculptor, and architect Michelangelo dies at eighty-eight.

1569

John Shakespeare becomes bailiff of Stratford.

CA. 1570

Emilia Bassano, daughter of a court musician and suggested real-life dark lady of the sonnets, is born.

1572

Ben Jonson, English playwright and poet, is born.

1576

The Theatre, England's first playhouse, is built in London.

1577–1580

Sir Francis Drake's first English voyage around the world.

1578

Historian and printer Raphael Holinshed publishes *Chronicles of English History to 1575*, the source material for Shakespeare's histories.

1582

Shakespeare marries Anne Hathaway.

1583

Daughter Susanna is born.

1584

Sir Walter Raleigh founds Virginia Colony on Roanoke Island.

1585

Twins Hamnet and Judith are born.

1587

Execution of Mary, queen of Scots, by order of Elizabeth I; Marlowe's *Tamburlaine* is performed in London.

1587–1590

Shakespeare acts and tours.

1588

Spanish Armada is defeated by British navy, making way for England's ascendancy in world trade and colonization.

1591

Henry VI, Part 1

1591–1592

Henry VI, Part 2 and *Part 3*.

1592

Plague in London causes closure of theaters; Robert Greene attacks Shakespeare in print, the first known reference to Shakespeare's reputation or work; Galileo proves objects fall at the same rate regardless of their weight.

1592–1593

The Comedy of Errors; sonnets; *Richard III.*

1593

Plague in London continues; Marlowe dies in tavern brawl; *Titus Andronicus; The Taming of the Shrew; The Two Gentlemen of Verona; Love's Labour's Lost; Venus and Adonis* is published.

1594

Lord Chamberlain's Men, Shakespeare's acting company, is formed; *The Rape of Lucrece* is published.

1594–1595

A Midsummer Night's Dream; Romeo and Juliet; Richard II.

1595–1596

The Merchant of Venice.

1596

Shakespeare applies for and receives coat of arms in his father's name, achieving gentleman status; Hamnet Shakespeare dies; *King John.*

1597

Shakespeare buys New Place, property in Stratford that becomes his family's home; *Henry IV, Part 1.*

1598

The Theatre is torn down and the timbers are used for the Globe; *Henry IV, Part 2; Much Ado About Nothing.*

1599

Globe theater opens; *Henry V; As You Like It; Julius Caesar; The Merry Wives of Windsor;* "The Passionate Pilgrim" is published.

1600–1601

Twelfth Night; Hamlet; Troilus and Cressida.

1601

John Shakespeare dies; "The Phoenix and the Turtle" is published.

1602

Shakespeare buys land at Stratford; *Othello.*

1603

Bubonic plague strikes London; Elizabeth I dies; James I becomes king of England; English conquest of Ireland; Lord Chamberlain's Men become King's Men; *All's Well That Ends Well.*

1604

Measure for Measure.

1605

Repression of Catholics and Puritans; Gunpowder Plot to kill James I and members of Parliament; Shakespeare invests in Stratford tithes; world's first newspaper begins publication in Antwerp.

1606

State visit by the king of Denmark; Ben Jonson's *Volpone; King Lear; Macbeth.*

1607

Jamestown, Virginia, is founded; daughter Susanna marries Dr. John Hall.

1607–1609

Antony and Cleopatra; Coriolanus; Timon of Athens (unfinished); *Pericles.*

1608

Plague in London; King's Men acquire Blackfriars theater; granddaughter Elizabeth Hall is born; Mary Arden Shakespeare dies.

1609

Sonnets and "A Lover's Complaint" are published by Thomas Thorpe, an edition believed unauthorized; Johannes Kepler proves planetary orbits are elliptical.

1610

Cymbeline.

1610–1611

The Maydenhead of the first musicke that evere was printed for the Virginalls, first book of keyboard music in England; King James Bible is published; Shakespeare contributes to highway bill, repairing roads between Stratford and London; *The Tempest.*

1612

Shakespeare's brother Gilbert dies.

1612–1613

Henry VIII.

1613

The Globe burns down; Shakespeare's brother Richard dies; Shakespeare buys house in Blackfriars area; Galileo says Copernicus was right.

1615

Miguel de Cervantes completes *Don Quixote* in Spain.

1616

Daughter Judith marries Thomas Quiney; Shakespeare dies; Vatican arrests Galileo.

1623

Anne Hathaway Shakespeare dies; actors Condell and Heminge publish Shakespeare's collected plays in a single volume known as the First Folio.

FOR FURTHER RESEARCH

ABOUT SHAKESPEARE AND *THE MERCHANT OF VENICE*

Peter Alexander, *Shakespeare's Life and Art.* London: James Nisbet, 1959.

Harold Bloom, *Shakespeare: The Invention of the Human.* New York: Riverhead Books, 1998.

Ivor Brown, *How Shakespeare Spent the Day.* New York: Hill and Wang, 1963.

E.K. Chambers, *The Elizabethan Stage.* Vol. 1. Oxford, England: Clarendon, 1951.

——, *Shakespeare: A Survey.* New York: Hill and Wang, 1958.

S.T. Coleridge, *Shakespearean Criticism (1811–1834).* Ed. T.M. Raysor. Cambridge, MA: Harvard University Press, 1930.

Victor L. Cuhn, *Shakespeare the Playwright: A Companion to the Complete Tragedies, Histories, Comedies, and Romances.* Westport, CT: Praeger, 1996.

Levi Fox, *The Shakespeare Handbook.* Boston: G.K. Hall, 1987.

Victor Kiernan, *Shakespeare: Poet and Citizen.* New York: Verso, 1993.

Sidney Lee, *A Life of William Shakespeare.* New York: Dover, 1968.

E.F.C. Ludowyk, *Understanding Shakespeare.* Cambridge, England: Cambridge University Press, 1962.

Richard G. Moulton, *Shakespeare as a Dramatic Artist: A Popular Illustration of the Principles of Scientific Criticism.* New York: Dover, 1966.

John Middleton Murry, *Shakespeare.* New York: Harcourt, Brace, 1936.

A.L. Rowse, *Shakespeare the Man.* New York: Harper & Row, 1975.

S. Schoenbaum, *William Shakespeare: A Documentary Life.* New York: Oxford University Press, 1975.

Caroline F.D. Spurgeon, *Shakespeare's Imagery and What It*

Tells Us, 1935. Reprint, New York: Cambridge University Press, 1987.

Stanley Wells, ed., *The Cambridge Companion to Shakespeare Studies.* Cambridge, England: Cambridge University Press, 1986.

———, *Shakespeare: A Life in Drama.* New York: W.W. Norton, 1995.

ABOUT ELIZABETHAN THEATERS AND TIMES

Joseph Quincy Adams, *Shakespearean Playhouses.* New York: Houghton Mifflin, 1917.

Maurice Ashley, *Great Britain to 1688.* Ann Arbor: University of Michigan Press, 1961.

Arthur Bryant, *Spirit of England.* London: William Collins, 1982.

Elizabeth Burton, *The Pageant of Elizabethan England.* New York: Charles Scribner's Sons, 1958.

John Cannon and Ralph Griffiths, *The Oxford Illustrated History of the British Monarchy.* New York: Oxford University Press, 1988.

Alfred Harbage, *Shakespeare's Audience.* New York: Columbia University Press, 1941.

G.B. Harrison, *Elizabethan Plays and Players.* Ann Arbor: University of Michigan Press, 1956.

A.V. Judges, *The Elizabethan Underworld.* New York: Octagon Books, 1965.

Walter Raleigh, ed., *Shakespeare's England.* 2 vols. Oxford, England: Clarendon, 1916.

Shakespeare and the Theatre. London: Members of the Shakespeare Association of London, 1927.

E.M.W. Tillyard, *The Elizabethan World Picture.* New York: Macmillan, 1943.

George Macaulay Trevelyan, *The Age of Shakespeare and the Stuart Period.* Vol. 2. *Illustrated English Social History.* London: Longmans, Green, 1950.

WORKS BY THE AUTHOR

William Shakespeare, *The Merchant of Venice.* Ed. Roma Gill. Rev. ed. Oxford, England: Oxford University Press, 1992.

———, *The Merchant of Venice.* Ed. M.M. Mahood. Cambridge, England: Cambridge University Press, 1987.

ORGANIZATIONS TO CONTACT

The following Shakespeare societies have information or publications available to interested readers. Descriptions of the organizations are derived from materials provided by the societies themselves. This list was compiled upon the date of publication. Names and phone numbers are subject to change.

International Shakespeare Association
The Shakespeare Centre
Henley St., Stratford-upon-Avon, Warwickshire
CV 37 6 QW, ENGLAND
44-1789-204016 • fax: 44-1789-296083

The association gathers and disseminates information on Shakespearean research, publications, translations, and performances. It maintains and circulates a diary of future performances, conferences, opportunities for graduate work, and educational experiments relating to Shakespeare's works. Its publications include *Congress Proceedings,* a record of the quinquennial World Shakespeare Congress, next held in 2001.

Shakespeare Association of America
Nancy Elizabeth Hodge, Executive Director
Southern Methodist University
Department of English
Dallas, TX 75275

The association provides members with an opportunity to discuss Shakespeare's life, plays, poems, and influence. Through development or continuation of appropriate projects, the association seeks to advance research, criticism, teaching, and production of Shakespearean and other Renaissance drama. It conducts seminars, workshops, and lectures; maintains a mailing list; publishes a semiannual bulletin; and sponsors the annual World Shakespeare Congress.

Shakespeare Data Bank
Louis Marder, Editor and CEO
1217 Ashland Ave.
Evanston, IL 60202
(708) 475-7550 • fax: (708) 475-2415

The data bank compiles past scholarship and updated materials on the biographical, bibliographical, pedagogical, educational, glossarial, textual, scholarly, critical, interpretative, literary, theatrical, authorship, artistic, illustrative, thematic, statistical, historical, and related aspects of Shakespeare and his works. Members maintain the Shakespeare Hall of Fame and museum.

Shakespeare Oxford Society
Leonard Deming, Membership Chairman
Greenridge Park
7D Taggart Dr.
Nashua, NH 03060-5591
(603) 888-1453 or (508) 349-2087
e-mail: business@shakespeare.oxford.im.com

The society provides research material, including books, periodicals, artwork, and archival text, on the history of the Elizabethan period of English literature. It explores and attempts to verify evidence bearing on the authorship of works attributed to Shakespeare, particularly evidence indicating that Edward de Vere, the seventeenth earl of Oxford, was the true author, and searches for original manuscripts in England to support its theories. It conducts research and educational programs and maintains a speakers' bureau. It publishes the quarterly *Shakespeare Oxford Society Newsletter* and sponsors an annual fall conference.

INDEX

All's Well That Ends Well, 25
Andrew (ship), 40
Answer to a Certain Libel
  (Sutcliffe), 72, 74
Answer to Admonition
  (Whitgift), 73–74, 76
Answer to M. Jewel's Challenge
  (Harding), 73
Arcadia, The (Sidney), 18, 42
archetypes, 47–48
Aristotle, 127
As You Like It, 24
Auden, W.H., 49, 50
audience
  on character changes, 182
  vs. dramatic critics, 100,
    181–82
  predispositions of, 172–73

Bacon, Francis, 28, 96
Baker, George P., 138
Bancroft, Richard, 74–75, 76
Bassano, Emilia, 19
Belmont
  feasts in, 126
  folktale/legend in, 120–23
  multiplying in, 124–25
  prose spoken in, 154–55
  sadness in, 124
Bergler, Edmund, 113
Berry, Ralph, 110
Beza, Theodorus, 96
Bible
  Puritans and, 72–73
  references to, 50–51, 69–70

  in Shakespeare's writings, 14
Blackfriars, 26–27
Boccaccio, Giovanni, 171
Book of Common Prayer, 14
Brief and Clear Confutation
  (Persons), 73
Brief Discourse (Persons), 73
Brown, John Russell, 48–49, 92
Burbage, James, 17, 23
Burbage, Richard, 19, 26

Caesar, Philip, 96–97
Calvin, John, 96
Cartwright, Thomas, 72, 73
casket story, 31, 32–33, 49, 101
  blending of stories, 132–33
  fairy tale in, 134–35, 174–75
  function in plot, 99–100
  poetry used in, 149
  romantic symbolism in,
    165–67
characters, 30
  Antonio
    arrest of, 33–34
    criticism of, 183
    effeminate qualities of,
      114–17
    friends' disregard for, 87–88
    friends' inferiority to, 86–87
    hatred for Shylock, 158
    lending Bassanio money,
      30–31, 89
    loss of ships, 32, 33
    love for Bassanio, 48–49,
      62–63

money venture by, 111, 128
as neurotic gambler, 112–14
poetry spoken by, 156–57
on Portia, 63
praise/compassion for, 139
on the rings, 35
sadness in, 62, 123, 165
sarcasm/coldness of, 93
Shylock humiliating, 176
Shylock's dialogue with, 159–61
slur on Jew by, 92
treatment of Shylock, 79
unreality in, 173–74
usury and, 97–98, 127
as victim, 157
Aragon, prince of, 133, 154, 166, 174, 175, 181
poetry and, 149
argue with themselves, 155–56
Bassanio, 32, 187
Antonio's love for, 48–49, 62–63
changes in, 182
choosing of casket by, 32–33, 166, 174
as fairy-tale character, 120–21, 133–35
flawed character of, 88–90
flaws in plot through, 181
gives ring away, 34–35
language of, 150
Portia's wealth and, 45–47, 61
sacrifice for Antonio, 104–105
toughness in, 117
Doctor Bellario, 33
Gratiano, 31, 33, 74, 120–21
speaking last word, 162
as well-intentioned, 184
wisdom in, 83
Jessica, 31–32, 33
criticism of, 82
disguised as man, 123
as disloyal, 86
fairy tale in, 176
going from old to new, 71
introduced before Shylock, 139–40
legend in, 121–22
music and, 64, 151
relationship with Shylock, 94
lack of depth in, 146
Launcelot Gobbo, 31–32, 33, 59, 120
argument with himself, 155–56
going from old to new, 71
humor in, 82
introduced before Shylock, 139–40
language of, 154
Shylock as devil to, 76
slur on Jews, 92
Lorenzo, 32, 33
decency in, 184
legend in, 121–22
music and, 64, 80, 151, 152–53
Morocco, prince of, 31, 133, 166, 181
choice of, 31, 166
language by, 149, 154
speech by, 174–75
Nerissa, 31, 33, 34, 81, 101, 105
disguise of, 123
sadness in, 61–62
speech by, 108
Portia
on Antonio, 63
biblical references through, 42, 70
changes in, 183
criticism of, 81–82
disguise of, 34–35, 40, 41, 123
exterior of, 100–101
fairy-tale world in, 120–21, 134–35
flaws in plot through, 181
as heroine, 101–102
in love with Bassanio, 32–33
on mercy, 102–104, 125
music and, 150, 151, 153
as object/commodity, 38
as professional, 42–43
on the rings, 35

romance and reality in, 169
romantic comedy in, 166–67
sadness in, 61–62, 123–24,
    165
Shylock as equal adversary
    of, 181
stage suspense of, 104–107
suitors of, 31, 32
symbolizing Christ, 76
symbolizing sacrifice, 70
wealth of, 45–47, 61
on words vs. deeds, 108–109
as real vs. fantastic, 129–30
Salanio, 30, 32, 114, 140
    on Antonio's love for
        Bassanio, 48–49
    anxiety in, 124
    disregard for Antonio, 87–88
    on Shylock's voice, 66
    as well-intentioned, 183–84
Salarino, 30, 32
Salerio, 30, 33, 114
    anxiety in, 124
    disregard for Antonio, 87–88
    poetry in, 147–48
    as well-intentioned, 183–84
Stephano, 35
Tubal, 32, 92, 95, 139, 144, 168
Venice, Duke of, 154
    see also Shylock
Charlton, H.B., 93
Chettle, Henry, 18
Christians
    economic interdependence
        with, 49–50
    as heartless, 90
    mercy by, 51
    moving from Jew to, 71, 179
    prejudice against Jews, 79–80
    Puritans separating from, 76
    revenge and, 108
    Shylock as villain to, 92
    Shylock moving from Jew to,
        178
    stereotyped, 47, 48
Chronicles, 18
comedy, 164–65, 171, 181
    in Shylock, 57, 95

vs. real world, 167–68
Comedy of Errors, The, 18
Condell, Henry, 19, 28
*Confutation of Jewel's Apology
    of the Church of England*
    (Harding), 73
Cursor Mundi, 139
Curtain (theater), 17, 19
Cymbeline, 27

Dante, 127
*Defence of the Answer to the
    Admonition* (Whitgift), 73
*Defence of the Ecclesiastical
    Regiment*, 74
Dethick, William, 23
de Vere, Edward, 28
Discourse Against Usurers
    (Caesar), 96–97
Discourse upon Usury (Wilson),
    54, 72
Discoveries (Jonson), 161
Divine Comedy, The (Dante),
    127

Elizabethan era
    Lopez affair during, 38–39
    mercantilism during, 40
    misers/money-lenders to, 143
    usury in, 41, 96–97
    women as professionals
        during, 42–43
    see also Puritans
Elizabeth I, Queen of England,
    15, 39
    death of, 25
    money borrowed by, 96
    Shakespeare writing for, 21
Empson, William, 51
Essex, earl of, 38–39, 40
Evans, Gareth Lloyd, 172

Faerie Queene, The (Spenser),
    17–18, 42
fairy tale, 182
    in Belmont setting, 120–21
    through casket story, 134–35,
        174–75

through incredibility, 173–74
vs. reality of characters,
129–30
Shylock's move to reality from,
175–79
through universal human
feelings, 184–86
feasts, 126
Field, Richard, 19
First Folio, 28
Fortune (theater), 17
Freud, Sigmund, 123
Frye, Roland Mushat, 20
Furness, H.H., 141

gambling, 112–14
Globe (theater), 23, 24
burning of, 27
and usury, 96
Goddard, Harold C., 99
Granville-Barker, Harley, 129,
184
Greene, Robert, 18
Groatsworth of Wit (Greene),
18

Hall, John, 26
Halle, Edward, 18
Halliday, F.E., 146
Hamlet, 24, 43
Harding, Thomas, 73
Harrison, G.B., 24, 27
Hazlitt, William, 78, 141, 152
Heminge, John, 19, 28
Henry IV, 21
Henry V, 23
Henry VI, 18, 21
Henry VIII, 27
Hibbard, G.R., 154
Holinshed, Raphael, 18
Holland, Norman N., 119
Hunsdon, Lord Henry, 19

Il Pecorone (Giovanni), 97,
138–39, 186
imagery
Shylock's biting, 125–26
see also symbolism

James I, King of England, 26
Jew of Malta, The (Marlowe),
17, 37–38, 39
Jews
as devils, 144
Elizabethan idea of, 177–78
Lopez affair and, 38–39
parallels with Puritans, 54,
55–56, 73
Shylock as stereotype of, 58
Shylock's vengeance of, 78–80
slurs on, 92–93
stereotyped, 37–38, 47
in Venice, 50
see also Shylock
Jonson, Ben, 14, 22, 24
anti-Puritan writings, 72
on Shylock's language, 161
Jordan, Thomas, 145

Kay, Dennis, 14, 17, 37
Kean, Edmund, 83–84
Kempe, William, 19, 24
Ker, W.P., 180
King John, 21, 22
King's Men, 25
see also Lord Chamberlain's
Men
Kyd, Thomas, 17

La Cousine Bette (Balzac),
182–83
Langer, Susanne, 59
language, 185
of Antonio vs. Shylock, 158
Antonio's feminine, 115
of argument, 155–56
biblical, 42
of love and money, 46, 62–63
poetry, 147–53, 156–57
prose/verse distinction,
154–55, 170
scriptural, 69–70
of Shylock, 65–67, 158–61
after Shylock's absence,
161–62
unifying themes through, 135,
137

"venture" words, 110–11
Lawrence, W.W., 184–85
Lee, Sidney, 21
legend, 121–22
Levin, Harry, 13
Lives (Plutarch), 24, 26
London, 15, 16–17, 20
Looney, Thomas, 28–29
Lopez affair, 38–39
Lord Chamberlain's Men, 19,
    21, 23, 25, 37
    see also King's Men
love
    and money, 45–47, 48–49, 126
    for/by Shylock, 68
Love's Labour's Lost, 21, 38
Lyly, John, 21

MacBeth, 18, 120, 26
Mahood, M.M., 25
Marlowe, Christopher, 17, 37
Marston, John, 72
Martin's Month's Mind, 76
Measure for Measure, 25, 138
Merchant, Moelwyn, 175
Merchant of Venice, The, 22
    anti-Semitism in, 37–38
    blending of time/place in,
        130–32
    comedy in, 64–65, 164–65, 171
    contrasting worlds in, 120,
        125–27
        Portia's Belmont, 120–23
        Shylock's Venice, 123–25
    critics vs. audience on, 180–81
    incredibility in, 173–74
    as least pleasant play, 146
    as "problem play," 41–42
    references to Elizabethan era,
        38–43
    as religious play, 69
    sadness in, 61–62
    as smooth and simple, 182–83
    as tragedy vs. comedy, 138
    unknown in, 173
    see also characters; language;
        plot; symbolism; themes
mercy

vs. law, 70–71, 102–104
    and revenge, 50–51
    Shylock needing, 169–70
Meres, Francis, 22
Merry Wives of Windsor, The,
    21–22, 24
Metamorphoses (Ovid), 14
Middleton, Thomas, 72
Midsummer Night's Dream, A,
    15, 21, 38
    anti-Semitism in, 38
    comedy in, 164
    harmony in, 185
    language in, 147, 154
Milward, Peter, 69
money, 38
    Antonio's love for Bassanio
        and, 48–49
    Antonio's venture and, 128
    compatibility with love, 60–61
    as component of
        attractiveness, 45–47
    Shylock's love of, 94
Much Ado About Nothing, 22,
    42, 138
Munday, Anthony, 97
Murry, Middleton, 184–85
music, 63–64, 151
    Lorenzo/Jessica on, 80,
        122–23
    Portia/Nerissa on, 80, 81, 150
    and romance, 170
    vs. Shylock's voice/language,
        65–67
mythology, 121–22

narrative. *See* language
Nashe, Thomas, 54–55
New Place, 23
Noble, Richard, 69
Nuttall, A.D., 44

Orator, The (Silvayn), 98, 141
Othello, 24

Palmer, John, 93
Pericles, 27
Persons, Robert, 73

plot, 30–35, 119–20, 136–37
  blending of time/place in,
    130–32
  flaws in, 181
  three stories in, 99–100, 101
Plutarch, 26
Poel, William, 140
poetry, 147–51
  Antonio speaking in, 156–57
  and music, 152–53, 170
  by Shakespeare, 18–19
  Shakespeare's influences
    from, 17–18
Price, George R., 15, 17, 24
Psychology of Gambling, The
  (Bergler), 113
Pullan, Brian, 50
Puritans, 53–54
  as devils, 76
  hypocrisy of, 54–55, 75
  Shylock as stereotype of,
    55–56
  Shylock parallels, 71–73, 74
  and usury, 54

Quiller-Couch, Arthur, 85, 183
Quiney, Richard, 28
Quiney, Thomas, 28

Raleigh, Walter, 144
Rape of Lucrece, The, 19
Reading Shakespeare's Plays
  (Price), 15
religion. *See* Bible; Christians;
  Jews
revenge
  Christianity and, 108
  Jewish, by Shylock, 78–80, 95
Richard III, 18, 21
rings, story of, 35, 99, 170–71
  as comic, 181
Rose (theater), 17, 39
Rowe, Nicholas, 16, 64
Rowse, A.L., 15, 19

sadness, 61–62, 123–24, 165
San Andres (ship), 40
Sanuto, Marino, 50

scenery. *See* setting
Schelling, F.E., 138
Schoenbaum, Samuel, 20
Sermons (Smith), 75
setting
  blending of time/place in, 133
  charm in, 146
  see also Belmont; Venice
Shakespeare, Anne (sister), 14
Shakespeare, Anne Hathaway
  (wife), 15–16, 27–28
Shakespeare, Edmund
  (brother), 13–14
Shakespeare, Gilbert (brother),
  13–14, 27
Shakespeare, Hamnet (son),
  15–16, 22
Shakespeare, Joan (sister), 13
Shakespeare, John (father), 13,
  15, 25
Shakespeare, Judith (daughter),
  15–16
Shakespeare, Margaret (sister),
  13
Shakespeare, Mary Arden
  (mother), 13, 26
Shakespeare, Richard (brother),
  13–14, 27
Shakespeare, Susanna
  (daughter), 15–16, 26, 28
Shakespeare, William
  birth/family of, 13–14
  coat of arms of, 22–23
  education of, 14–15
  involvement with the Globe,
    23
  marriage/children of, 15–16
  playwriting by
    comedies/tragedies, 24–26
    doubt on authorship of,
      28–29
    first, 19, 21–22
    published, 28
    late, 26–27
  poetry of, 18–19
  references to, in *Merchant of
    Venice,* 42–43
  retirement/death of, 27–28

on Shylock, 91
on time, 131
Shakespeare: A Compact Documentary Life, 20
Shakespeare: His Life, Work, and Era, 14
Shakespeare's Biblical Knowledge, 69
Shylock
  age of, 83–84
  as alien to world in the play, 60–61, 64–65, 68
  arrest of Antonio through, 32, 33–34
  betrayal of, 31–32, 86
  biblical references in, 42, 70
  comic in, 57, 95
    vs. reality, 164–65
  compared with Christians, 90
  at court, 34, 40, 41, 106
  defends himself well, 80–81
  depth of, 146
  as devil, 76
  duality in, 95–96
  to the Elizabethans, 53–54
  fairy tale to reality in, 175–79
  as friend vs. lender, 111–12
  hatred for, 114
  humanity in, 93–94
  hypocrisy of, 54–55, 75
  Jewish revenge in, 78–80, 95
  language of, 65–67, 148, 150, 158–61
  lending of money by, 30–31
  many ideas in, 84
  mercy and, 102, 169–70
  as miser, 56–57, 94
  play after departure of, 161–62
  poetry and, 153
  Portia defeating, 59
  Puritans and, 55–56, 71–76
  relationship with Jessica, 94
  Shakespeare on, 91
  as stereotype of Jews, 58
  symbolizing devil, 76
  symbolizing law, 70–71
  symbolizing racism, 57–58
  sympathy for, 85–86

  as taking life vs. taking living, 50–51
  usury by, 97–98, 127–28
  as villain, 92, 138–45, 168–69
  world of Venice in, 120, 123–25
Sidney, Sir Philip, 17, 42, 96
Siegel, Paul N., 53, 72
Silvayn, Alexander, 98, 141
similes, 151
Sinsheimer, Herman, 113
Sly, William, 19
Smith, Henry, 75
soliloquies, 141–43
Spanish Tragedy (Kyd), 17
Spedding, James, 28, 90
Spenser, Edmund, 17–18, 42
Spurgeon, Caroline F.E., 151
Stoll, Elmer Edgar, 71–72, 95, 138
Survey of the Pretended Holy Discipline (Bancroft), 75
Sutcliffe, Matthew, 72, 74
Swan (theater), 17, 19
symbolism
  casket scene, 165–67
  gold, 100
  Portia, 70, 76
  Shylock, 57–58, 70, 76

Tamburlaine (Marlowe), 17
Taming of the Shrew, The, 21, 25, 167, 181
Tempest, The, 27
theaters, 16–17, 20
Theatre, the, 17, 19, 96
themes, 125
  blending of time/place in, 132–33
  blending together, 135–37
  humanity in, 185
  Jew vs. Christian, 47–48
  law vs. mercy, 70–71
  love and generosity, 62–63
  love and money, 45–47, 48–49, 126
  mercy and revenge, 50–51
  spirituality, 108

Tillyard, E.M.W., 180
time, 130–32
Timon of Athens, 26
*Tragedy of Antony and
   Cleopatra, The,* 26
Tragedy of Coriolanus, The, 26
Tragedy of Julius Caesar, The,
   24
Tragedy of King Lear, The, 25
*Tragedy of Romeo and Juliet,
   The,* 21
*Tragedy of Titus Andronicus,
   The,* 18, 39
Traversi, D.A., 164
Twelfth Night, 15, 24, 140, 165
Two Gentlemen from Verona, 21

usury
   during Elizabethan era, 41,
      96–97
   Jew/Christian
      interdependence on, 50

Puritans and, 54, 72
reasons for disliking, 127–28
by Shylock, 97–98

Van Doren, Mark, 60
Venice, 44–45
   economy of, 49–50, 51
   feasts in, 126
   as harsh/masculine, 120,
      123–25
   prose spoken in, 154–55
   as setting for romance, 87
Venus and Adonis, 19

Walker, Henry, 26
Whitgift, John, 73–75, 76
Wilson, John Dover, 85
Wilson, Thomas, 54, 72
Winter's Tale, The, 27
women, 42–43, 123

Zelauto (Munday), 97, 98